PRAISE FOR
Minimize Injury, Maximize Performance

"There's never been a more important time for this book, and no better book to address the needs of parents wanting to help their kids enjoy all that sports have to offer while minimizing the risk of long-term health issues. Dr. Tommy John makes the information easy to understand and the tips are so practical and so doable."

    —Ashley Koff RD, CFSEO, The Better Nutrition Program

"I owe my career—as so many successful professional athletes do—to playing as many sports as possible as a kid. The fact that specializing in just one sport has become the norm today shows how young athletes are taking the wrong path. If their goal is to excel and stay injury-free, this book will put them on the path every kid should be on—the right one!"

    —Vida Blue, six-time MLB All-Star, three-time World Series champion

"This book is one that parents, athletes, and educators should pay attention to regarding the effect of athletics on the lives of their children."

    —Annie Meyers Drysdale, Olympian, Hall of Famer, four-time All American
      at UCLA in Basketball

"If ever there was a time when we need to step back and look at how youth sports are damaging our children, it is now. And not just now, but we need how: we need some solutions. And that's what Dr. Tommy John has delivered. It's not just a must-read, it's how we save the games we love so much long-term."

    —John Smoltz, eight-time All-Star, World Series Champion and Hall of Fame Pitcher

"I didn't take up golf until l was 16, choosing instead to play cricket, soccer, Aussie rules, tennis and basketball. I never knew how fortunate I was to avoid being a single sport athlete until watching all of my friends—all of which started at a young age and were far better than me at the time—all burn out by the time they were 18. I lucked out, but worry about kids today that aren't making the right choices that are presented in *Minimize Injury, Maximize Performance.*"

    —Cameron Percy, seven-year PGA Tour veteran

"Being in the NFL for 13 straight years was no easy task emotionally, intellectually and physically, and working with Dr. Tommy John for most of my time in the sport helped me achieve a longer career. His approach from a healing and performance standpoint is oftentimes outside of the box, and some of the principles require consistency and grit, but he knows that's what it takes to become the highest performing human athlete possible."

    —Charles Tillman, NFL veteran of the Chicago Bears and Carolina Panthers

"*Minimize Injury, Maximize Performance* is the eye opener every sports parent needs to read, and I'm excited that Dr. Tommy John is finally sharing what he knows—with those that need to know."

—Patrick Mannelly, long snapper and longest tenured player in Chicago Bears history

"Science, technology, and the 'business of youth sports' are taking away from what baseball, and every sport for that matter, was built on. Now more than ever, we are overworking our kids and protecting the pros—all in the name of money. *Minimize Injury, Maximize Performance* finally reveals what all sports parents absolutely need to know—but may not be ready to hear—in order to be the best sports parent possible. But for those ready to listen, the sky is the limit for their son or daughter."

—Goose Gossage, nine-time All-Star and World Series Champion

"Tommy John is the doctor that may care more about your kids than their coach. This book isn't just about sparing young athletes from unnecessary surgeries caused by specialized sports. It's about saving time, saving money, and most importantly, saving kids from an industry that's taking advantage of both parents and players alike."

—Jason Kennedy, host of E! News

"A book able to improve the health and well-being of every single young athlete that reads it."

—John Schaech, actor

"Dr. John lays out a comprehensive path that supports players through a balanced strategy of training and recovery techniques as well as nutrition. This information is invaluable for the future of all our young athletes!"

—Elizabeth Walling, www.livingthenourishedlife.com

"Finally, someone who gets it. As a certified Nutritional Therapy Practitioner (NTP), it is so refreshing and long overdue to read about the role of traditional foods in preventing Tommy John surgery and other sports-related injuries. Very few doctors, specialists and coaches understand this. This book will enlighten the reader as to why proper diet is as much a part of the solution as more commonly understood reasons, such as poor mechanics and overtraining."

—Craig Fear, Certified Nutritional Therapist (www.fearlesseating.net)

MINIMIZE INJURY, MAXIMIZE PERFORMANCE

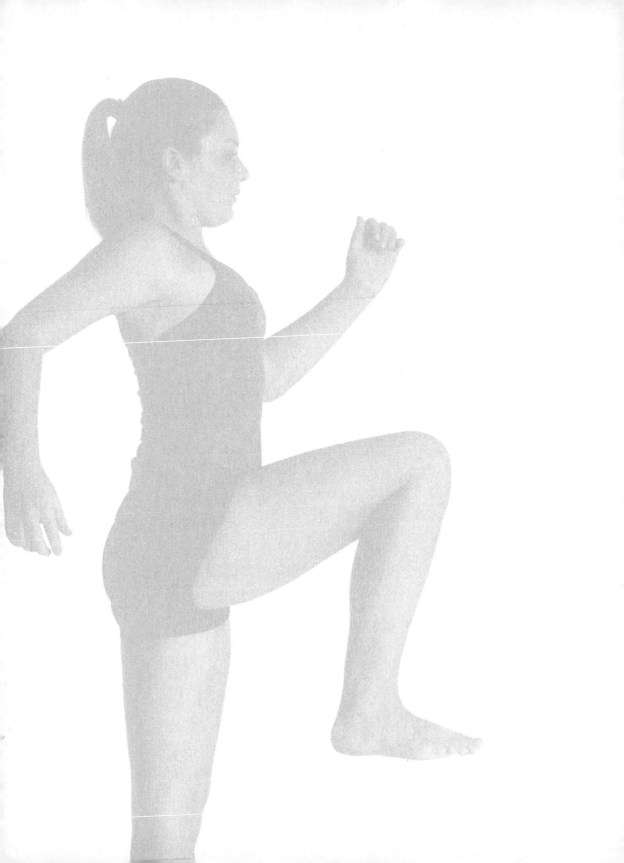

MINIMIZE INJURY, MAXIMIZE PERFORMANCE

A Sports Parent's Survival Guide

DR. TOMMY JOHN

with Myatt Murphy

Da Capo

LIFE
LONG

Copyright © 2018 by Tommy John

Hachette Book Group supports the right to free expression and the value of copyright. The purpose of copyright is to encourage writers and artists to produce the creative works that enrich our culture.

The scanning, uploading, and distribution of this book without permission is a theft of the author's intellectual property. If you would like permission to use material from the book (other than for review purposes), please contact permissions@hbgusa.com. Thank you for your support of the author's rights.

Da Capo Press
Hachette Book Group
1290 Avenue of the Americas, New York, NY 10104
www.dacapopress.com
@DaCapoPress

Printed in the United States of America

First Edition: June 2018

Published by Da Capo Press, an imprint of Perseus Books, LLC, a subsidiary of Hachette Book Group, Inc. The Da Capo Press name and logo is a trademark of the Hachette Book Group.

The Hachette Speakers Bureau provides a wide range of authors for speaking events. To find out more, go to www.hachettespeakersbureau.com or call (866) 376-6591.

The publisher is not responsible for websites (or their content) that are not owned by the publisher.

Print book interior design by Trish Wilkinson

Library of Congress Cataloging-in-Publication Data has been applied for.

LSC-C

ISBNs: 978-0-7382-3380-2 (paperback); 978-0-7382-3528-8 (ebook)

10 9 8 7 6 5 4 3 2 1

This book is for you Taylor.
You always believed in me.
You single-handedly taught me about what was
most important in this life—happiness.
I love you.
"I'll see you in another life, brotha."

Contents

Foreword

You know, over the decades, I've been asked a lot of questions about my twenty-six-year career as a professional athlete. Questions ranging from "Who did you like playing for the most—the Dodgers or the Yankees?" to "What's the one pitch you wish you could take back?" I've been interviewed about every team I've either played against or been a part of, and every ball player I've ever competed or partnered with along the way.

But what's always surprised me is that no one has ever bothered to ask about what baseball was like for me as a kid growing up in Terre Haute, Indiana.

Maybe it's because most fans would rather hear about the glory days instead of when I was just starting out playing ball with my friends. Then again, I now wonder whether it's because sports parents today that I meet just assume that all pro athletes—me included—had the same type of childhood that their kids are going through. A life of around-the-clock practice with access to top talent coaching and state-of-the-art training tools. All of which made me the best possible athlete I could be—a young athlete able to earn his shot in the big leagues.

But in reality, my childhood wasn't like that at all.

In fact, it was pretty much the exact opposite of what's being pushed on many kids today.

Growing up in Terre Haute, I never had a professional baseball lesson—not one lesson—and the only coach I ever had from the time I was eight years old until I got into American Legion ball at sixteen was my dad. The only coaching I ever had (if you want to call it that) was when I saved all my money one year to buy a book called *How to Pitch,* by Bob Feller. I read it, picked up a few tips—and that was about it.

Sure, we had indoor facilities, but they weren't the massive multipurpose sports complexes that parents today spend big bucks on to have their kid play tournaments and practice year-round in to hone their skills. If someone said they were going to an "indoor facility," it just meant they were going to use the bathroom. Because indoor sports facilities didn't exist!

And when it was time to quench your thirst, there weren't any fancy sports drinks to be pushed on us. When we practiced bunting, my dad would put shin guards down on first base and third base. If you hit the shin guard three times, you got an A&W root beer float as a reward. If you didn't, then you knew where the water fountain was.

Don't get me wrong. My friends and I were active all year, but we never played a single sport year-round. Indiana was (and still is) a basketball state, so baseball was just something you did between basketball seasons. We practiced basketball from September through March until the state tournament was over and then we were done—a total of seven months, tops. But from April through part of August, we played baseball before starting the cycle all over again.

Even during baseball season, we didn't have the complicated schedules and multilayered practices most kids suffer through today. The way we did it in Terre Haute, we had games on Tuesday and Thursday nights for the first half of the season, then played on Monday, Wednesday, and Friday evenings the second half of the season. And on the days we didn't have ball games, we practiced, but all we ever worked on was bunting, fielding, running the bases, and playing the infield—you know, just throwing the ball around and getting batters out.

And that was it.

There were no travel teams to contend with. None of us ever felt the anxiety that a lot of kids feel today about falling behind in the sport because we weren't doing all the "right" things. I never felt that I had to be good at baseball or felt any pressure from my parents whatsoever. In fact, if my dad had applied any pressure to me, my mom would've coldcocked him.

I just went out and played baseball. That's all I ever did—and all of my friends ever did. Every last one of us were all the same in Terre Haute. None of us had anything that gave us an edge. We were just a bunch of kids playing baseball, and more important, having fun.

And guess what?

Throughout my entire career, playing among the legends of the sport throughout the '60s, '70s, and '80s, I came to find out that pretty much all pro athletes—no matter what position we played, or for that matter, what sport we played—had a similar type of childhood.

We all played multiple sports growing up. We all took time off and never overdid it. We all grew up feeling no pressure and played sports simply because we loved playing them—not because we ever felt we had to. No one among the teams that I played on came from wealth or had access to extra coaching and top-of-the-line equipment when they were kids. But—most of all—none of them were having unnecessary surgeries, I can tell you that.

We all lived the same kind of life—when youth sports were merely a pastime. And not the business they've become today.

When I became the first person to have ulnar collateral ligament reconstruction surgery in September 1974, I was happy that the procedure saved my arm. But I never would have guessed my name would be attached to an operation now more common with kids than pro athletes, thanks to what youth sports have become.

It was a decade later—around 1984—when I first heard the term "Tommy John surgery." When I asked Dr. Frank Jobe (the surgeon who pioneered the method and had operated on me) where he came up with the name, he admitted it started because he got tired of saying what the real name was! As he began sharing his knowledge with other orthopedic surgeons about the procedure, it was easier for him to refer to it as "you know, the surgery that I did on Tommy John." A little further down the road, all he needed to do was say, "You know, Tommy John surgery." And from that point forward, it just stuck.

But it wasn't until around 2000 when I first heard of the surgery attached to kids.

Back then, the first few times, the news reported how young athletes were wearing out their elbows from specializing in one sport and having the procedure done, and it surprised me. Now, truthfully—I pay no attention to it. That's because it's happening so often that I've become used to it. And if I'm used to it—the guy whose name is attached to it—just imagine how "normal" the procedure (and all the surgeries now being routinely performed on kids) must seem to parents with sons or daughters playing sports today.

When did injury and overuse become the norm? It shouldn't be—because it never was in the first place. And with this book, I know it will stop being the norm—because I firmly believe that things happen in our lives for a reason.

I truly believe that what ended my son Tommy's baseball career—a botched arthrogram that infected his shoulder—was because there were better things meant for him out in the world other than playing ball. Tommy was a very accomplished baseball player who had great potential before that incident, and it ended his baseball career—and ultimately changed his life. But because of it, he became Dr. Tommy John and helped so many young athletes that have come through his practice and listened to his lectures.

The truth is, any dad would be proud to see his son follow in his footsteps, especially if he's spent a lifetime doing something that he loves. But this book was written by my son in the hopes that your child never follows in his dad's footsteps. So that they never undergo surgery—or even just end up benched—for an injury they should never have suffered from in the first place.

And if Tommy saves one kid—just one—from having to go under the knife, then the book you're holding in your hands is a success. The only question really left is this: Will that kid be yours?

Tommy John Jr.

Introduction

The call came into my office in the dead of winter, at a time of year when baseball should only be looked forward to—not forced upon.

It had been the mom of a high school junior named Jared, a kid who not only loved playing as a catcher but stood a shot at having a future in baseball, something very few do. The only thing standing in his way? A torn ulnar collateral ligament in his elbow he was told required surgery—a surgery that also meant the inevitable possibility of ending Jared's future before it began.

"Please . . . can you save my son's arm?"

It wasn't the first time a parent asked me that question, desperate to avoid what every doctor spoken to previously had claimed was unavoidable. But after looking at Jared's arm to find the ligament partially torn but intact, I told him he had nothing to worry about and that his body could mend this. I described the process and what needed to happen—and how the road ahead wouldn't be easy. I told him that what I would ask him to do would seem unconventional at times, but it's what his body needed to heal itself from within.

Jared committed himself to doing exactly what was asked of him. (In fact, he remains to this very day one of the most compliant patients I've ever turned around.) And in one month, about the time he would have been scheduled for surgery, Jared was back throwing again, making the playoffs at his high school just a few months later.

I attended his first game back and could hear the whispers behind me.

"That's the guy. That's the one who worked with Jared."

But to be honest, I was too busy watching a young athlete who was one of the best high school catchers I had ever seen. A young athlete who went on to be signed by the University of South Carolina and had a healthy college career. A young athlete whose body had been pushed to the point of needing surgery, but who had avoided it by listening to what his body was trying to tell him.

Jared wasn't the first kid I saved from going under the knife—and he won't be the last. But he was the one that reminded me that I couldn't save all of them and that the best way to try the impossible was to educate parents about what is possible. Something needed to be written—that contained everything necessary in one easy-to-understand package. That a solution was needed to share with all young athletes in America—no matter what their age, sport, or gender—and not just the one I was lucky enough to repair and root for from the stands.

Being the son of a Major League Baseball (MLB) pitcher, I grew up as you may have expected, immersed in the sport and playing it for as long as I can remember. But as a training and rehabilitation expert specializing in soft tissue injuries for over fifteen years, I've also witnessed firsthand the outcomes of injury, innovation, and principled healing. So, imagine my surprise when I discovered how the young athletes playing sports today had become a major portion of the rising tide of the injured we're now seeing flood into doctor's offices nationwide.

Like my dad, I am also a former ball player, even though I never reached his heights in the sport. After playing college ball and receiving my bachelor's and master's degrees in health and exercise science from Furman University, I played two seasons of pro ball as a pitcher with the Schaumburg Flyers, the Tyler Roughnecks, then went on to sign a free agent contract with the Los Angeles Dodgers and was invited to their spring training.

Only to have my MLB dream stripped away before it began—due to injury.

Upon retiring, I created (along with the help of others) a training and rehabilitation system and began working with adult and geriatric clients dealing with a multitude of injuries and chronic conditions, such as torn ACLs, UCLs, plantar fasciitis, and herniated disks. But because of my love of sport, I simultaneously opened up a baseball performance company where I logged more than eleven thousand baseball lessons to players ranging from six to thirty years of age. But with each passing year, I began to see an uncanny connection between my older injured patients and the kids that were coming to see me for baseball tips.

The young athletes I was teaching were suffering from the same ligament and tendon damage as the older adults I was treating.

Every season, more and more young athletes began to step through my door with injuries and imbalances—issues I had only previously seen in older patients in their fifties or sixties that had decades of mileage on their bodies. I also began to notice how these young athletes were missing key performance traits that should be present in kids today, including nervous system development, fundamental movement patterns, and even the simple act of being able to breathe properly.

More often than not, I found myself offering rehab advice instead of instruction about the game, explaining to parents that although they paid for a lesson, their children had wear-and-tear throughout the body that shouldn't be there. I showed them how despite being great athletes, children were not even capable of balancing on one leg or closing their eyes without falling over. I even explained to a few parents how their children didn't have ADD just because they always squirmed when seated—it's that the children had never lost the Galant's reflex, a primitive reaction that causes the abdominal muscles to contract when the skin over a child's spine is touched.

I helped many open their eyes to what sport and society were doing to the development of their child—and how they could reverse it. But I soon came to realize I could only help the kids that came through my door and the parents willing to listen. That's when I decided to close the doors of my baseball school for good to spend four years earning my doctorate in chiropractic—a decision made, ironically, when I was the same age my dad was when he had his famous groundbreaking surgery.

For him, that day had been a moment where he looked at his injury not as an end, but an obstacle.

For me, it was the day I knew I had to push away the obstacles preventing parents from recognizing what was behind the injuries plaguing our youth—to put an end to them once and for all.

Dr. Tommy John

CHAPTER 1
The Unspoken Epidemic

*No matter how much we love the game ... we're
just human beings who choose to play a sport for
a short period of time.*

Right now, more than 36 million kids[1] play organized sports each
year in the United States. It's a number that comes out to roughly
two out of every three boys and more than half of girls between
the ages of five and eighteen years old. As a parent, it should be inspir-
ing to see how those numbers break down, since that must mean kids
today are more active and healthy than ever before.

But it's because of how kids are more active than ever—and what's
not being done in tandem—that's causing their bodies to fall apart.

As a lifelong athlete and former baseball coach, in addition to being
a training/rehab specialist and doctor of chiropractic care, I'm aware
of the positive impact a structured, well-organized youth sports program
can have on a young athlete's life. I've both personally experienced and
witnessed in the thousands of young athletes that I've worked with over
the years how sports builds self-esteem and self-discipline,[2] develops social skills and leadership qualities, and can improve their overall health
and well-being.

New data continue to prove how extracurricular sports help young
athletes evolve into better human beings off the field, from reducing

their risk of preadolescent smoking and drinking[3] to improving their cognitive skills,[4] making them more able to follow instruction and focus. There's even plenty of evidence that being a young athlete increases your odds of landing a better job[5] as an adult to having healthier muscles at a cellular level decades after you retire.[6]

But that's when it's done the right way.

When it's done the wrong way—the way in which many coaches and sports parents innocently believe is the right approach—current research is revealing that being involved in youth sports may be doing more harm than good.

According to the National Safe Kids Campaign,[7] more than 2.6 million children aged nineteen and under are treated in emergency rooms for sports and recreation each year. Furthermore, Nationwide Children's Hospital, one of America's largest pediatric health care and research centers, reports that in addition to ER care, another 5 million kids[8] are seen by their primary care physician (or a sports medicine clinic) for injuries.

So, why do I care about your child? After all, as a training/rehab specialist and doctor of chiropractic care, shouldn't every doctor be happy when business is booming?

Not this doctor—and it's because of a little thing called legacy.

You see, there was a time when my dad's name (Tommy John) meant something different than it does today. As a former Major League Baseball (MLB) pitcher, whose 288 career victories rank as the seventh-highest total among left-handers in major league history, he was not only an accomplished baseball player but the very first to both have (and fully recover from) a procedure where a damaged ulnar collateral ligament in the elbow is surgically reconstructed, using a tendon from another part of the body.

Not only did he come back midway through his twenty-six-year career in the pros after going under the knife, but my dad went on to play professional baseball better than he had ever played before. But while it's true he was the first to have Tommy John surgery—a procedure now named after him—my dad was far from the last, and the number of athletes having it done now is growing exponentially.

The number of pitchers that had Tommy John surgery in 2014 alone surpassed those operated on from 1990 to 2000 combined. In fact, many doctors have noticed a *ten times* average increase in athletes needing the surgery since 2000. And although my dad fully recovered, only 20 percent of those who have it ever make it back to their previous level of performance. Worse yet, between 25 and 30 percent of athletes that undergo Tommy John surgery find themselves no longer able to play baseball two years afterward.

Why should these statistics be so alarming? Because even though a staggering 25 percent of all active MLB players (and 15% of current minor leaguers) have had Tommy John surgery, the statistics I just shared with you aren't attached to professional ball players.

It's what's happening to our young athletes.

In 2010 alone, 31 percent of all Tommy John procedures were on young athletes, but by 2016, that number had nearly doubled. The truth is, Tommy John surgery is a procedure that shouldn't be happening in anybody under nineteen years of age. Yet as it stands, 57 percent[9] of all Tommy John surgeries are being performed on young athletes between fifteen and nineteen years old. But the injuries occurring today aren't just related to baseball and damaged elbows—what we're seeing now is an across-the-board injury epidemic.

Every week, my practice handles a surge of young athletes injured from every sport imaginable, especially football, basketball, softball, volleyball, baseball, and soccer. In fact, a new study[10] from the Center for Research and Policy at Nationwide Children's Hospital in Ohio found that between 1990 and 2014, the number of soccer-related injuries treated in emergency rooms in the United States annually increased by 78 percent—and the yearly rate of injuries increased by 111 percent—among kids seven to seventeen years of age.

The injuries range from the common to the severe, from rotator cuff tendinitis, muscle strain, stress fractures, growth plate injuries, and sprained or torn ligaments, particularly ACLs (anterior cruciate ligaments). One 2017 study[11] discovered that the number of injuries to the ACL—one of the major ligaments that provide stability to the knee joint—has risen dramatically among six- to eighteen-year-old patients over the past twenty years. Researchers found the overall incidence of ACL tears increased by 2.3 percent per year, and the rate of ACL tears surgically reconstructed has risen steadily by 3 percent per year as well.

So, what's changed since we were kids, why are our children suffering as a result, and—most important—is it even possible to put a stop to it? The truth is this:

What has changed over the past twenty years is plenty. Why our kids are suffering more today than ever before isn't due to one thing—*it's because of three.* And can you put a stop to it? Can you prevent your son or daughter from becoming a statistic, so his or her future isn't met with an invasive surgery or much worse? In other words, *can you not only injury-proof your young athlete but help him or her perform at their highest level?*

You can now, and it starts by understanding how the odds turned against kids in the first place.

CHAPTER 2
The Causes That Compound

No matter what their injury may be, and regardless of what sport they might play, almost every single time I begin my evaluation of young athletes to figure out how to help them, their parents typically blame their injury on the same cause: "I guess they just didn't warm up correctly."

If only it were as simple as that.

When it comes to youth sports, we've placed so much emphasis on warming up that most parents never allow themselves to step back and see the big picture. No warm-up in existence will ever prevent injury. It's what their child does within a sport—and away from that sport—that decides whether he or she falls on the injured list or the A-list.

It may all boil down to three specific causes behind this injury epidemic: the business of youth sports (from the coaches to the corporations), the American Dream, and regrettably, the choices parents truly believe are helping their children—but actually harming them instead.

IT'S MORE OFTEN LESS ABOUT THE KIDS—AND MORE ABOUT THE CASH

But that shouldn't surprise you, right? After all, youth sports is estimated to be a 9 to 15 billion-dollar industry (depending on who you ask) that continues to skyrocket. But how it's reached those heights isn't due to more kids participating in youth sports. In fact, according to Project Play,[1] participation in team sports among children aged six to twelve is lower now than it was a decade ago. It's because the business of youth sports has made a year-long training schedule the new norm.

Behind the scenes—and in most cases, right in front of our very eyes—our children are being put through a gauntlet of coaches, camps, and countless lessons unnecessarily. What was once meant to be played for a season is now pushed 24/7, 365 days a year. All courtesy of new "select teams" that extend a child's time playing the game, coaches and parents who believe "more is better" when it comes to practice, as well as indoor facilities and elite showcases that encourage kids to train during the off-season and even year-round.

Today, there is no off-season for our youth athletes. Because if their uniform ever found its way back into their closet, the money would stop rolling in.

This situation is developing young athletes in desperate need of medical intervention at younger and younger ages when *inflammation, surgery,* and *rehabilitation* shouldn't even be words in their vocabulary. These surgical and rehabilitation procedures go beyond jumper's knee, Little League elbow, or any of the common aches and pains active kids sometimes experience. It's about significant damage to ligaments, tendons, and joints that require serious care—injuries from which many never come back.

Even worse, at a critical phase of developmental growth when children should be naturally developing balance, coordination, agility, and spatial awareness (among other important functional skills), they are being forced instead to overtrain and perform specialized movements that are creating muscular imbalances and deficiencies within their body. Because the human body is so adaptive, many kids can keep up and persist for a period of time. The problem is, their body eventually can't maintain the pace and demands it is being put under.

It's why the bodies of many of today's young athletes aren't keeping up—they're giving up.

WELCOME TO THE AMERICAN DE-EVOLUTION

America may be the land of the brave and home of the free, but when it comes to being fit, our kids are failing miserably compared to other countries. In a recent landmark study[2] of the fittest children and youth that collected data from 1.14 million children between nine and seventeen years old in fifty countries around the world, America came in close to dead last (47th place) despite the US passion for youth sports. The highest-ranking countries were in Africa and central-northern

Europe, whereas the United States and countries in South America were consistently on the bottom regarding performance.

Youth sports may be leaving our kids overtrained and less developed, but the culture of America also plays a role in contributing to the health issues persistent among young athletes. The American diet is leaving kids malnourished, overfed, and improperly hydrated. In addition, the American lifestyle is not only affecting its youth's activity level and posture, but causing kids to be less aware, overstimulated, and disconnected from certain vital physiological and neurological responses that promote healing.

THE TOUGHEST SPORT OF ALL—RACING TO KEEP UP WITH THE JONESES

Finally, both the business of youth sports and the American dream have caused parents to believe that any child can become a superstar athlete. That all it takes to make their sons' or daughters' athletic dreams come true is to push hard enough—and the youngsters will succeed.

Today's parents are left to feel shame by not loading up their kids' schedule with sports so as to reach their fullest potential. It's made the adults either too distracted or afraid to listen when their kids need to slow down. It's made them blind to the fact that they're being sold a bill of goods by whatever coach wants to train their kids next. It's made every sports parent think that if their sons or daughters aren't playing the game early, often, and always—then those children will simply get left behind.

When all they're really getting is injured.

One of the biggest concerns I have is the fear I see in the eyes of most parents who come to me when their sons or daughters are injured. Even though they realize the best thing for their kids at that moment is having them slow down or stop playing their sport for a while, their greater worry is about where their children will rank if they take the time to heal.

It's now the norm to think you're a "bad" parent by not signing up for—and paying for—as many things as possible, which in its way has made many of us (whether we want to admit it or not) equally blameworthy for the issues afflicting our youth. The good news is, even if that's you—even if you've become part of the problem, you can now be part of the solution to reverse the damage caused by all three causes I have cited of sports-related injuries.

So, let's get started!

CHAPTER 3

From Injury to Evolution—the Tommy John Solution

Before my dad retired from baseball in 1989, the Oakland A's decided to test the shoulder strength of all their pitchers. And to everyone's surprise, he had the strongest pitching shoulder among all of them—and was the oldest player by far on the team. It wasn't that he was the hardest thrower—it was just his body's ability to endure.

When it comes to working with athletes, it's my job to look at all the components that make up each athlete's life, asking every detail from the moment they wake up until they fall asleep—before, during, and after each season. Then, I step back from it all to create a system that will help those young athletes function at a higher level—not just as athletes, but as human beings.

But I can't witness firsthand what's going on with your child.

That's why I developed the Tommy John Solution.

FOUR STEPS—ONE SOLUTION

The Tommy John Solution is a fusion of thousands of hours of research, clinical experience, and personal experimentation I've used successfully for years with athletes of all ages—from amateur through pro—merged with the same simple healing philosophies my dad relied on throughout his career.

The four principles that make up the Tommy John Solution—**Rethink**, **Replenish**, **Rebuild**, and **Recover**—address the four crucial areas that decide how your son's or daughter's body grows, how it heals, and how far it can evolve toward becoming the best version of itself. It's a game-changing four-step process that gives parents the power to both avoid and repair the damage accrued by youth sports.

But the Tommy John Solution isn't just about injury avoidance—and it's more than just about sports. It simultaneously corrects the developmental deficiencies happening right now in your son or daughter. It's a return to traditional methods and techniques that restore what was once natural in all human beings—and removes the barriers preventing your child from experiencing his or her unlimited potential.

ONE SOLUTION—UNLIMITED POTENTIAL

The fact is this: When I speak with other doctors and professionals, they all agree that all athletes—male or female, regardless of their age or sport—would be better prepared for whatever they wanted to excel at in life by following many of the principles within the Tommy John Solution.

In other words: *It's not a book that's only for a son or daughter engaged in sports. It's a book for anyone—and that includes you.*

The Tommy John Solution may have been born from what I've seen in my practice, as well as from watching how my father recovered from a surgery that almost took him out of the game. But at its very essence, this is not a youth sports program; it's a human performance program. It's an instruction manual on how you can better prepare the members of your family for whatever they wish to accomplish, attack, or take on in life.

It's not particular to any sport.

It's not particular to any age.

Wherever you are in the developmental process—whether that's an eighty-four-year-old man with an injury or an eight-year-old boy with interest in being the world's greatest soccer player; whether that's a pro athlete or a tomboy looking to show her stuff on the field—it's about functioning as high as you would like to function. It's essentially a program for life, a philosophy that the entire family can take in and see improvement from the inside out, top to bottom.

It's not just about sports—it's about sustainability and what happens to your son or daughter when the sport is over.

The name Tommy John always used to be associated with a baseball player before it became connected to a painful surgery. Now, it's finally attached to a solution. A solution that's not just about saving elbows—it's about saving lives—and attributing the name Tommy John to a method that puts the power back in parents' hands to protect their children from injury and watching them evolve into the exceptional athletes they were destined to become.

UNLIMITED POTENTIAL—BUT IT'S ALL OR NOTHING

I've had parents who were entirely on board with certain portions of the Tommy John Solution, but not fully invested in all four. The excuses have ranged from not having enough time or not wanting to put in the effort, to simply being afraid to set limits on their son's or daughter's habits.

But the Tommy John Solution isn't a four-step process just to be creative—it's a tailored prescription. What's important to note is that the human body is dynamic, meaning it's always changing, and everything that comes into it—everything that is observed and experienced—inevitably affects everything.

That being said, it's not a linear relationship. Everything affects everything. It's like one big continuous circle where everything flows into everything. Each of the four sections builds upon the others. So, as you begin to positively change the habits in each section, not only will you be making the other sections easier to do, but you'll see more results from each as well.

In short, there is nothing you can effectively leave out or streamline. The Cliff Notes version of the Tommy John Solution is this. This is as streamlined as it gets if you're truly serious about your young athlete.

CHAPTER 4

TJ's Tryout Test

Before you move any further in the book, the first thing you need to do with your son or daughter is take the following test—a test that will ultimately play a huge role in how far your young athlete will go using the Tommy John Solution.

THE NINE THAT DEFINE

To get parents to recognize the dysfunction that may exist in their son or daughter—to get them to fully understand what could be affecting their child's overall performance from head to toe, so they take the advice I offer seriously—one of the very first things I do with every young athlete (ranging from 8 years old and up) is put him or her through my Tryout Test.

Simply put: By running their son or daughter through a few simple exercises, I could easily "pop the hood" of that child's engine, so to speak, and see what was truly running underneath.

I designed the Tryout Test to open the eyes of parents who may believe their child is an incredible athlete (and very well may be an amazing athlete—for now), revealing some of the huge gaps that may exist when it comes to basic functional movements their child should be capable of doing. I designed it to instantly expose potential issues that could be raising their young athlete's risk of injury and preventing him or her from playing at his or her best.

This Tryout Test is a modified version of what I use in my office. The nine-move routine measures a variety of things simultaneously, including stability, balance, coordination, agility, endurance, mobility, posture, the ability to endure discomfort, kinesthetic awareness (sensing the body's position in space), strength, and power.

Final note: This Tryout Test has never let me down, no matter the athlete's age, sex, or sport. It's something that has woken up so many parents I've worked with over the years to what's truly going on with their kids. And frankly, it's something that I hope eventually becomes a standard for all coaches to use—to gauge their young athletes' abilities before sending them into their sport to either possibly fail or get injured.

But for now, it's just for you and your son or daughter. Take it knowing its importance. Take it before moving any further in this book. But most important, take it seriously—for your child's sake.

BEFORE YOU BEGIN

When to take the test: Because this is a test to be respected and not something to be taken lightly, I typically prefer this test to be given on a day when the young athletes have not had any prior practice, competition, or exercise in place. Also, their muscles shouldn't be fatigued from any activity a day or two before. In other words, there shouldn't be any excuses for why they may not perform as well on certain movements within the test.

What to wear: When athletes perform my Tryout Test, I keep it simple by telling them to wear loose clothing and their most comfortable shoes. Any outfit that doesn't restrict their movement is ideal. But because your son or daughter may break a sweat with certain movements, sticking with a T-shirt, a pair of shorts, and a decent pair of sneakers is a no-miss combination.

What you'll need:
- Stopwatch
- Mat
- Chin-up bar (If you don't want to invest in one, using a straight supportive tree branch to both hang from and do pull-ups on, is fine. Or head to a local playground, where it's common to find an easy substitute to hang from.)

- Tape measure
- Lightweight pole (a broom handle or a piece of PVC tubing will do)
- Something to use as a starting line (a piece of tape, chalk, a stick, etc.)

HEY TJ! ISN'T THIS AN FMS?

Being a sports parent, if your child attends any legitimate indoor or outdoor training center, you may have had someone ask whether he or she has ever had a functional movement screen (FMS). It's a similar method used by practitioners to look at movement patterns (such as mobility at the hips, or mobility at the shoulders) while an athlete performs specific tasks. That way, the practitioner can identify functional problems early and prescribe certain exercises.

Are they reliable? I support them, and so does science,[1] but they're not free. The Tryout Test is a modified version of an FMS, but instead of setting up an appointment and paying for it afterward, this is a do-it-yourself assessment that costs nothing to measure your young athlete.

THE MOVES

The Rules

- Have your son or daughter do each of the nine movements in the order given.

- For the Shoulder Lift-off and the Standing Broad Jump, he or she can do each movement up to three times, taking the lowest score of the three.

- He or she can do the entire nine-movement test in one shot if desired. (The order of moves is arranged in a way that gives certain muscles a break. However, if you want to break it up, it's entirely okay to perform the test over two or three days.)

- If your child's score is on the fence between two different scores, always go to the lower number.

- Finally, with each movement, you'll find a range of either seconds, centimeters, or repetitions that are age specific. If your child scores lower than the range shown for his or her age group, it's an indicator of a major functional issue that could be severely impacting your child's athletic performance in regard to that movement and what it measures.

1. PUSH-UP TOP

Examines the ability of the core stabilizers to efficiently transfer force from strong feet to strong hands—and vice versa.

SETUP: Get into a push-up position with your hands spaced shoulder-width apart, and your legs extended straight behind you, feet together. Your hands should be directly below your shoulders, so your arms are perpendicular to the floor. Your body should form a straight line from your head down to your heels.

EXECUTE: Keeping your core muscles tight and neck in line with your spine, hold this position for as long as possible.

7 TO 9 YEARS OLD: 20 to 40 seconds

10 TO 12 YEARS OLD: 40 to 60 seconds

13+: 60 to 90 seconds

2. STANDING LEG RAISE

Gauges the strength endurance and communication of glutes and hip flexors opposite to the hip through efficient foot-to-ground force transfer.

SETUP: Stand straight with your arms crossed over your chest, hands touching the opposite shoulder.

EXECUTE: Balancing on one leg, raise your opposite leg up in front of you as high as you can. Hold this position for as long as possible without shifting your position or hopping around to adjust—the goal is to stand firm. Afterward, rest three to five minutes, switch positions and perform the test again with the opposite leg.

7 TO 9 YEARS OLD: 40 to 60 seconds each leg

10 TO 12 YEARS OLD: 90 to 120 seconds each leg

13+: 150 to 180 seconds each leg

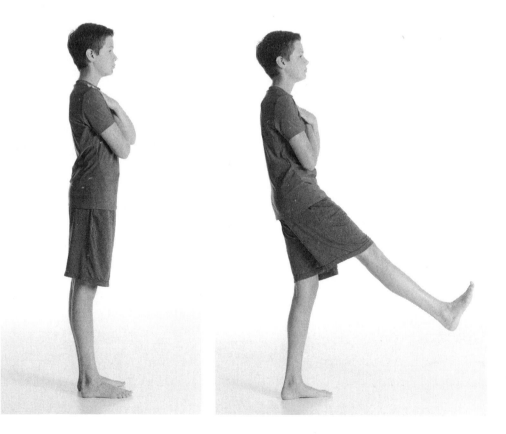

3. SHOULDER LIFT-OFF

Tests shoulder girdle mobility and strength in relation to cervical and thoracic spine alignment.

SETUP: Lie flat on your stomach with your arms extended in front of you and your legs straight and together. Grab a light pole, such as a broom handle or a piece of PVC tubing, with both hands, using an overhand grip, hands spaced slightly wider than shoulder-width apart.

EXECUTE: Keeping everything else stationary, raise your arms up as high as you can and measure the distance between your wrist and the floor.

7 TO 9 YEARS OLD: 11 to 15 cm

10 TO 12 YEARS OLD: 16 to 20 cm

13+: >20 cm (around 7 inches or greater)

4. CROSS-CRAWL SUPERMAN

Looks at the patterning and strength endurance of total body flexors and extensors in an opposing cross-crawl "walking" pattern while maintaining an optimal four-curved spine alignment.

SETUP: Lie flat on your stomach with your arms extended in front of you and your legs straight and together.

EXECUTE: Keeping your head on the floor, raise your left arm and right leg up at the same time, then lower your arm and leg back down into Setup Position, then repeat—this time raising only your right arm and left leg up, then lowering them back down. It should take them about one second to raise and one second to lower—and no longer. Perform the exercise for as long as possible with no pauses.

7 TO 9 YEARS OLD: 60 to 90 seconds

10 TO 12 YEARS OLD: 90 to 120 seconds

13+: 150 to 180 seconds

5. DEAD HANG

Measures the strength endurance of grip flexors in relation to the strength endurance of the shoulder capsule musculature.

SETUP: Hang from a chin-up bar with either an overhand or underhand grip (whichever feels more comfortable on your wrists) with your fingers and thumbs wrapped completely around the bar. Keep a firm—but not too tight—grip on the bar.

EXECUTE: Hold this position for as long as possible.

7 TO 9 YEARS OLD: 30 to 60 seconds

10 TO 12 YEARS OLD: 60 to 90 seconds

13+: 90 to 120+ seconds

6. STANDING BROAD JUMP

Measures the ability to connect the kinetic chain that exists from the feet through the hands. It also gauges the power the athlete is able to generate from the ground and through the legs, core, and arms.

SETUP: Create a line as a starting point. Put a piece of tape on the floor, draw one with chalk, or place a yardstick in front of your feet—whatever works best and won't move when performing the drill. Stand straight with your toes directly behind the line, arms bent with your fists pointing up.

EXECUTE: Swing your arms back as you squat down, then use your arms to drive yourself forward as you jump as far as possible. As you leave the ground, pull your knees up into your body. When you land, you should land heels first. Wherever your heels hit, that's your mark. Measure the distance between the starting line and your mark. (For this movement, I recommend performing three jumps, then taking the average distance of the three.)

TIP: Find a surface where there is less chance of slippage. For example, if you're wearing sneakers and perform this jump on grass, you might slip. Ideally, performing the jump on a turf surface with tennis shoes, or jumping in athletic shoes on a hardwood court would be great.

7 TO 9 YEARS OLD: Because this is an exercise that requires explosive leg power that's not yet developed in most under 10 years of age, I generally don't use this measuring tool until an athlete is at least 10 years old.

10 TO 12 YEARS OLD: **65–85** inches male/**62–80** inches female

13+: **80–110** inches male/**73–83** inches female

7. GYMNAST BRIDGE

Measures the athlete's ability to react with the ground through strong extensors of the body, such as the erectors of the spine, glutes, hamstrings, and calves.

SETUP: Lie on your back, bend your knees, and bring your feet as close to your butt as possible, hip-width apart. Bend your elbows and bring your hands up alongside your ears, placing your palms flat on the ground, fingers pointing toward your feet.

EXECUTE: Keeping your feet and hands flat, raise your body off the ground by pushing up with your legs and arms. At the top, try to round your back as much as possible, letting your head hang between your upper arms. Hold this position for as long as possible.

7 AND UP: With the gymnast bridge, all kids should be capable of performing this exercise, yet a vast majority of young athletes today struggle with this simple movement. Many kids today lack the shoulder strength and stability to simply press themselves upward and hold themselves in that position. In addition, they also suffer from having underdeveloped extensor muscles of the spine and glutes, which prevent extension of the thoracic region of the spine and the hips.

8. TRADITIONAL PULL-UP

The pull-up is used to measure upper body strength endurance. Primarily targeting the major back muscles (the latissimus dorsi, scapular stabilizers, rotator cuff, and biceps), pull-ups also test grip strength in relation to how it's related to back, shoulder, and arm strength. Most orthopedic surgeons only test grip strength by isolating it (simply squeezing a gripping device, for example), which isn't accurate to how grip is typically applied in real life.

SETUP: Reach up and grab the pull-up bar with an overhand grip (palms facing away from you) with your hands slightly wider than shoulder-width apart, thumbs wrapped around the bar. Pull your shoulder blades down toward your spine.

EXECUTE: Pull your elbows down as you bring your chest and shoulders up to meet the bar. Your chin must reach the bar to count as one repetition. Lower yourself back down until your arms are straight. That's one repetition. Try to do as many repetitions as possible until you can no longer get your chin to reach the bar.

7 TO 9 YEARS OLD: 3–9 male/**1–3** female

10 TO 12 YEARS OLD: 6–15 male/**1–5** female

13+: 9–23 male/**2–9** female

9. TRADITIONAL PUSH-UP

The push-up test measures the strength endurance of the upper body. Challenging both the chest and triceps, it also measures the rotator cuff's ability to stabilize the shoulder joint and control the elbow through a full range of motion. It also tests shoulder capsule integrity and mobility, as well as helps identify any weaknesses in the ability of the glutes and abdominals to stabilize and transfer energy efficiently from the hands to the feet and vice versa.

SETUP: Place your hands flat on the floor (shoulder-width apart), keeping your arms straight, elbows locked. Straighten your legs behind you and rise up on your toes, so the top of the balls of your feet are touching the floor. Your body should be one straight line from your head to your feet, head facing down at the floor.

EXECUTE: Bend your elbows, slowly lower yourself until your upper arms are parallel to the floor, then push yourself back up. That's one repetition.

Set a timer for two minutes. Do as many push-ups as you can within that period of time. As you go, if you need to take a break, stop for one or two breaths, then continue.

7 TO 9 YEARS OLD: 10–30 male/10–30 female

10 TO 12 YEARS OLD: 20–40 male/15–30 female

13+: 30–50 male/20–40 female

THE POST-TEST WRAP-UP!

Once your son or daughter has taken the test and you have your results, I want you to ask yourself three very important questions:

Did your child do each of the exercises to the best of his or her ability?

Did he or she follow all the rules?

Did you allow yourself to see something that wasn't there?

That third question may be the most important of the lot because sometimes, parents may only see what they want to see—and I get that. No matter how far your child ends up succeeding in any sport, there will never be a greater fan than you.

But because I'm not there to fully assess your child and offer a fair perspective, it's up to you to see what I can't see—so don't fudge the numbers. By not following the rules, you'll only be proving that you may be part of the problem. The important thing is to assess your son or daughter at the level he or she is truly at.

AFTER YOU'RE FINISHED

At this point, you're ready to proceed with the Tommy John Solution, armed with an exact idea of where your son or daughter ranks in regard to overall movement and human performance.

From here, you now have a blueprint of your young athlete's body and what it's capable of accomplishing. As your child goes through the program, I want you to return to this test each month, and have him or her take it again and again, so that you can see the effect that sticking with the Tommy John Solution is making in your young athlete's life.

Although trust me, you won't necessarily need to take this test every month to figure that out. The program's impact will make itself present 24/7 in how your child performs in his or her sport, schoolwork, and every other aspect of his or her life.

My Kid Passed a Few and Failed a Few—Now What?!

What parents love about the Tommy John Solution is that no matter what degree of dysfunction their son or daughter might have in certain areas of his or her body, the strategies and routines in this book are designed to correct all of them at once. It doesn't matter what age they are, or how many areas of dysfunction they suffer from.

Many practitioners love to design "specialized routines" for young athletes because, to be honest, that's how they make money. But if your young athlete trains in the way he or she is supposed to be training his or her body, a specialized routine is unnecessary. Your child just needs to commit to the right program that corrects every area of dysfunction at once.

That said, no matter which portions of the test your child failed versus completely crushed, I want you to have peace of mind, knowing that those numbers will change soon enough.

My Kid Passed Every Test—Now What?!

Congratulations! If that's truly the case, and if you're honest with yourself (see the sidebar "The Post-test Wrap-up!"), then hearing that your son or daughter completely passed my Tryout Test excites me. Why? Because he or she is at a level that all young athletes should be at for that age.

It also means that you may already be familiar with and doing some of the procedures you're about to discover throughout the rest of the book. But that doesn't mean you have nothing to gain from the Tommy John Solution. In fact, I would argue that you may have the most to gain.

Unlike some parents who may find some of the methods in this book to be unorthodox and harder to adjust to, you're most likely in line with my methodology already. This means that learning some of the other techniques that make up the Tommy John Solution—the ones you haven't discovered yet—may come even easier to you and your young athlete. And where these new techniques take your son or daughter will be as exciting for me to hear about, as it will be for you to watch your child grow even further.

My Kid Failed Every Test—Now What?!

If your son or daughter scored below average in every movement, I don't want you (or your young athlete) to be discouraged. The great news is that you're noticing the dysfunction early, instead of letting it continue. It reveals what we can pinpoint now before it becomes a problem. I want you to be excited that you found it now, because if left unattended, the damage it could potentially cause would only compound.

Even though that means there's a lot of dysfunction to work on, it also means there's a lot of room for growth—and that you're due to benefit even more from using the Tommy John Solution.

Know that these scores are only going to get better if you adhere to the program faithfully. Know that starting today, following the directions in this book are going to change those numbers significantly in the short term. Finally, know that if you think you have an exceptional athlete on your hands now, then prepare for the outstanding athlete he or she is about to become.

PART I
Rethink

The way kids are being taught today, it's as if they're coming into a training center needing to learn how to spell their name correctly. They end up leaving able to press the pen harder to the paper—but their name is still spelled wrong. American training has only been accentuating our errors.

CHAPTER 5
Make the Right Turn Together

When young athletes first come to see me with their mom or dad, there's a distance of about 20 yards from the parking lot to my office door—and I make a point whenever possible to observe them before we ever meet. Why? Because in that short moment of time, there's a lot of information about them that I can instantly glean before I even know what sport they play or why they're coming to see me. As they walk, I'll ask myself:

- Are they walking with their parent slightly distant from them?
- Are they even talking to each other?
- Do they seem excited to walk through my door, or are they cowering with their shoulders pitched forward, staring at the ground?
- Could they make that brief journey of 20 yards without the need to stare down at their phone?

Once we meet, I'm still reading their every action before we bother discussing their training habits, sports involvement, diet, or any pains or concerns they may have. I'll assess such things as:

- Did they exchange eye contact when we shook hands, and were they squared up to meet me?
- When they sat down, did they immediately adjust their posture to sit straight, or did they fold forward like a cocoon?

- Are their hands folded on their lap, or are they moving in different directions?
- When I ask them questions about themselves only they can answer, do they do so—or instinctively look at their parent to speak for them?

All of these little details carry so much weight with what we're about to do. They reveal how seriously those athletes (and their parents) will most likely listen to what I'm about to share with them. These indicators tell me whether technology or too much focus on their sport may be interfering with how the children function physically, as well as how they relate with another human being. They let me know whether those young athletes are truly there to see me because they *want* to—or because they *have* to be there.

These are all important things for me as a professional to know, going in. Because before I can start the process and add anything new into young athletes' life to improve their performance and make them injury-proof, I have to feel confident that they're ready to take a hard look at what may need to be removed from their life.

That's because more often than not, it's not what they *aren't* doing that concerns me—it's what they *are* doing that's a far more pressing issue.

Maybe you're like some parents I've worked with, those who have approached me bluntly asking, "Okay, TJ, just show me what exercises my child needs to do and foods I need to buy to make my kid a star player." If so, then know that's the reason the Rethink section is the very first portion in the Tommy John Solution.

There are several reasons that Rethink comes before any performance-based instruction in the book. One, to make any training and dietary change to your young athlete's regimen stick, it requires rethinking some of the decisions both of you have been making in regard to his or her personal life and intended sport. Decisions that could make anything I could show you how to do (or what to eat) less effective and an absolute waste of time.

Some lifestyle choices could be affecting young athletes in ways that suppress their immune system, destroy their posture, reduce their concentration, promote muscular imbalances within their body, and encourage overtraining. And if that's the case for your child, then there's no degree of training and nutrition I can show you that will reverse that.

Two, Rethink is first because, once in place, after you and your son or daughter start making the right choices in certain areas, it lays the groundwork for the other three steps: Replenish, Rebuild, and Recover. You will suddenly have the time, means, and energy to give the other three areas your absolute all.

Finally, look at Rethink as the first—and I feel most decisive—fork in the road when it comes to getting your young athlete to operate at his or her full potential. It's the portion that requires the honesty and deepest reflection on your part because it's the one that inevitably decides who moves forward and who stays back.

I've had (on more occasions than I would like to admit) parents who didn't abide by my Rethink method, yet performed the other three components of the Tommy John Solution to the last detail. They thought that being strict with the other three would somehow balance out the effect of ignoring the things they weren't willing to either address or give up. And with each and every one, I witnessed their young athlete either completely stall or regress in regard to overall healing and performance.

The Tommy John Solution is an all-or-none effort, and Rethink is the first of the four necessary steps. Welcome to the fork in the road—now it's time to make the right turn together.

THE LOSING LINEUP THAT ALWAYS FAILS

When it comes to certain lifestyle choices proven to be detrimental for young athletes, sometimes the reasons parents do (or allow) them are not always black or white. I've watched a lot of well-intended moms or dads permit certain habits because they seemed harmless to their kids, and watched just as many push other things because they thought they were helpful to their youngsters.

As I tell parents all the time, this section isn't a shame fest—it is an acknowledgment. This is about considering every component that goes into what makes up your young athlete. It's an opening to what's going on with your son or daughter—and a handshake with a problem that could be a lot worse than you realize.

That said, no matter what your intentions were before buying this book, there are a few things I already know about you with absolute certainty:

- You want your young athlete to be less susceptible to injury.
- You want your son or daughter to perform better in a sport.
- And most important, you want your child to grow up to be the best possible version of him- or herself.

If that's you—and let's face it, I know that's you—you're proud of your son or daughter and want the best for him or her. Know that this is the best for your child, and believe it or not, it will be the best for you as well. So, let's start with the obvious:

RELYING ON AS MUCH TECH AS POSSIBLE

Almost everything transpiring today, each and every technological breakthrough, has been at the expense of human movement. It's about bringing your son or daughter from Point A to Point B, while spending the least amount of effort possible.

Decades ago, a rainy day to any kid—let alone an active young athlete—spelled death because it kept them from going outside to play. Today, technology has given young athletes an array of opportunities to keep them entertained, along with plenty of excuses to remain disengaged.

But my concern isn't about preventing childhood obesity, which is a valid concern many parents have in regard to being too involved with tech. It's the impact it can have on their overall development during the most formative years of their life.

It Suppresses Their Immune System

Each time people answer a text, surf social media, use the latest app, or battle online against others, their brain is being bombarded by stimuli. Every bright color, high-definition pixel, pop-up ad, or unexpected sound is a trigger their brain has to react to, yet they can only process so much. The result is an overstimulated brain that throws their sympathetic nervous system—what many call the fight-or-flight response—into hyperdrive.

That "sympathetic" response is their body's natural survival mechanism. It's designed to prepare their body to react quickly to impending danger by releasing hormones that widen the airways in their lungs, make their heart beat faster, and cause the release of stored glucose and fats—all in an effort to tap into instant energy. Unfortunately, those same hormones also cause the suppression of other processes that the body assumes are on the bottom of the priority list when threatened, including the reproductive drive, digestion functioning, and most important, the immune system.

These are inverse proportions that are meant to save people's life. For example, if they were battling a cold and a lion showed up, their body would immediately stop trying to fight the virus so it could use all its energy, such as shuttling blood to muscles and increasing the release of adrenaline, to help them flee from danger or fight that lion off. Then, once they were safe again, their immune system would kick back in and continue to fight off sickness.

Because of too much tech, kids have become more sympathetically driven than ever before. Most are now what is commonly referred to as sympathetic dominant (SD) due to constant stimulation that's keeping that sympathetic response activated all day long (even though no danger is actually present). When that occurs, their immune system stays compromised all day long, making it more difficult for their body to repair the wear and tear that occurs naturally while playing sports, defend itself against viruses, or protect itself from other forms of injury or illness.

It Makes Them Less Aware

When I first start seeing kids who have been training for years but haven't learned as much as they should have, I'll sometimes experiment by putting random strange objects and signs with crazy messages throughout my facility—things out of the ordinary placed both directly in their way or within their line of sight; things that if you were even just slightly aware, your reaction would immediately be, "What is that—and why is it there?"

But young athletes today come in like little zombies, with most getting their instruction, doing their exercises, resting, then moving on—without ever noticing or acknowledging what's unusual about their surroundings.

Overstimulation is creating kids that no longer question, rarely make eye contact, and are oblivious to their environment. It's creating a shorter attention span, poorer personal communication skills, and a marked reduction in the ability to think abstractly. It's building young athletes who are less likely to absorb all the conscious and unconscious nuances necessary to play a sport efficiently.

The way I best describe it to parents is to imagine that your child's brain is a fish tank. When it's always being stimulated by everything going on around them, that tank fills up quickly, and eventually, there's no more room for information to come in. As adults, we have certain ways to empty that tank, whether it's a vacation, personal day, getting a massage, meditation, having a girl's night, or watching the game at the bar with friends. No matter how adults choose to unwind, it removes some of the stimuli that fill our tank, leaving us feeling refreshed, less burdened, and more focused.

But kids today lack the means to decompress. Technology and how often kids use it keeps a constant stream of stimuli flowing into their tank that keeps it filled at all times. It's the reason that even when asked to focus, many young athletes lack the ability to do so. It's why they are less likely to notice certain aches and pains that may be warning signs of an overuse injury. It's what may be keeping them from absorbing all the skills that their coaches are trying to impart on them.

It's Destroying Their Biomechanics

When the human body is in optimal alignment, it operates the way it was intended to work, placing the appropriate amount of responsibility and displacing stress on certain portions of the body to perform specific actions. But even if everything is aligned flawlessly, there is always a risk of injury. That said, just imagine how high that risk becomes when the human body isn't in optimal alignment, which is, unfortunately, the situation we're seeing in so many young athletes today.

The effect of technology on kids' posture today has become, in a word, devastating, due to spending hours upon hours in positions that are unhealthy. But even though many parents today are aware of such terms as *text neck* or *tech neck* (the pain associated with staring down at a cell phone or wireless device too long), they aren't always aware of how it's impacting their young athlete's overall performance.

Forward head carriage: First, what's happening to most kids today is that overuse of tech is reshaping the cervical curve (the first seven vertebrae of their spine located in their neck) in a way that's only supposed to be present in both the very young and very old. When properly aligned, the hole of their ears should be directly above where their collarbone meets their shoulder blade when viewed from the side. But on average, their head is shifting forward an average of 4 to 5 inches.

From a neurological perspective alone, it's an irregular angle that keeps their spinal cord—part of their central nervous system, responsible for controlling every task throughout their body—in a perpetually impaired position. But the other danger is that for every inch, it adds roughly an extra 10 pounds of force on that area of the spine already responsible for supporting their head (which can weigh between 10 and 12 pounds). That's a 50- to 60-pound load being placed on their upper back and neck that causes pain and problems simply by walking around.

Imagine the devastating effect that can have when young athletes are practicing skills and motions that aren't (in many cases) movements natural to their body. Even if they slouch all day but somehow manage to have perfect form when practicing or performing their sport, they are being impaired behind the scenes. That's because after spending a full day bearing that 50- to 60-pound load on their spine, shoulders, torso, and back, they now depend on those same overworked, tired muscles to perform at their best, which they simply cannot do.

Even if their muscles are miraculously fresh, purely from a biomechanical standpoint, it's easier for their muscles to create action at the shoulder when their head is in proper alignment. So many sports rely on action at the shoulder to perform specific movements, whether it's to throw a ball, block a spike, push off a defender, or simply support the body when doing something as simple as a cartwheel, let alone a forward somersault or anything more technical. Having their head forward minimizes their body's ability to perform those movements as efficiently or as explosively.

Pelvic roll: Just because their sport such as soccer, isn't shoulder dominant, here's the thing: The brain is a lot smarter than many give it credit for. What it likes to do is pick the path of least resistance. What that means is, when your head is pitched forward, it cannot continue moving forward until you fall forward. Instead, what it will do is try to bring your pelvis in line with your head by rocking it underneath you. It will literally roll your pelvis under and back, taking the natural curve of your lower back out, which forces your hips to not work as proficiently as possible.

I've worked with young athletes who, when examined from the side, were missing the small (the natural curve) in their lower back—and parents thought that was normal! But that is merely the body compromising its posture to match how its head is positioned. What their body is attempting to do is bring itself into balance, when what it's really doing is changing those children's alignment to survive the environment and negatively affecting practically every single movement their body is capable of pulling off.

Muscle malfunction: Finally, kids are spending too much time seated when using tech; extended periods of sitting also places pressure on certain muscles (particularly the gluteus muscles) and shuts them down. When these primary muscles deactivate, the body has little choice but to force the quadriceps muscles (the muscles along the front of the thigh) to take on more of the burden. Each time those young athletes jump, sprint, or perform any activity that typically relies on the largest muscle of their body (the glutes), they end up overworking their quadriceps instead, which can place added stress on both the knees and lower back.

ALIGN THEIR SPINE TO OPEN THEIR MIND

If you need to convince your young athlete how fixing forward head carriage will drastically improve their game, try this: From a standing position, have them tuck their chin to their chest as far as possible. Sweep their arms out to the sides and up overhead (if their arms are bent, it doesn't count), and bring their palms together. Lower their arms back down to their sides and repeat four or five times.

Next, have them angle their head in a neutral position with their ears directly above where their collarbone meets their shoulder blades and perform the same actions. They should instantly feel how much easier the movement is and the difference in the mechanics of their shoulders.

Another test I'll do—if they suffer from a tilted pelvis—is to snap a picture of them from the side. Then, I'll take another picture after I've repositioned their body so that their head is in line with their shoulders. Although it may be slight, they should immediately notice their lower back is slightly more curved than it was originally.

Once those connections are made, I will have young athletes imagine how much farther or harder they could throw or kick—how much faster, farther, and more explosively they could move—if everything was placed back in line. Just getting that thought into their head, making them realize that they're not posture perfect and that by correcting it, they can tap into potential power that's been stuck in neutral all this time, has been highly effective in getting many of my athletes to take their posture seriously and correct it all day long.

It's Reducing Quality Family Time

It's a no-brainer that the more time your children spend connected to tech, the less time they probably spend connecting with you. Often, this can be a problem that sometimes doesn't seem like one, since some parents believe that clocking in time watching games and driving their kid to practice counts as family time. Others feel that as their kids get older, that pullback is only natural.

IT'S NOT THEIR EYES—IT'S THEIR PHONES

If I learn from their intake information when I first begin working with them, that children get unexplained headaches (or have recently gotten glasses), I'll address their posture by simply putting my hand on the sides of the back of their neck. And if it feels like I'm touching two solid ropes, it's possible that pain is due to having forward head carriage.

When the head is positioned down, their trapezius muscles—the long, triangle-shaped muscle that attaches at the base of their skull and connects to the back of their collarbone and shoulder blades—are kept tight (instead of remaining supple and loose). When those muscles remain tight, it creates a pain referral pattern that goes over the top of the skull and sits right over their eyes.

Many times, I've seen parents try to correct this chronic issue by getting their kids glasses, or assume their children are getting eyestrain sitting too close to a screen. The answer may be neither and may be easily self-corrected by bringing their head back into alignment.

But as it relates to minimizing injury and maximizing performance, which is why you're reading this in the first place, having enough of the right type of quality family time may outweigh anything else in this book.

Even though this book is filled with tactics to help improve young athletes, we're still talking about individuals who may feel that they don't necessarily have a choice—who may not be old enough to make decisions for themselves.

In many cases, they are still children. Children participating in something that should be considered leisure. Participating in something they should be enjoying. But the less time you spend connecting with them—really connecting with them, the fewer opportunities you have to make sure that's still the case.

OVEREVALUATING YOUR CHILD'S PERFORMANCE

When I was young, I asked my dad for the best piece of advice he would offer to a pitcher, and he said: "Front foot hits the ground—hand high."

And that was it.

There wasn't any constant analysis or overthinking such things as joint angles and force line drives. There was no year-round preparation. There was no fear of losing one's edge by stepping away from the sport to either play another temporarily—or just give oneself a break. That's all we had back then, and it subsequently produced some of the most game-changing pitchers in the sport on those simple rules alone.

In today's tech-intensive world, it's possible to scrutinize every last detail of athletes' performance. You can now evaluate every angle of every joint and clock the speed of every throw, kick, and sprint. You can virtually break down every facet of every single movement your children make, right down to the very last detail—all to shape them into a better athlete.

But just because we can doesn't always mean we should.

It Keeps Them Sympathetic Dominant

When throwing, kicking, or hitting a ball, the goal is to get the ball where it needs to go. When moving forward, backward, or side to side, the goal is to move in that direction in whatever way your sport dictates. The objective is simple, or at least it should be.

Overanalyzing their every move is making some young athletes anxious about things that most times either wouldn't make a noticeable impact in their performance anyway or could be entirely out of their control, due to how their body is constantly developing daily. All that additional stress keeps many in fight-or-flight mode, which suppresses their immune system and lowers their ability to heal faster and fight off infection.

It also makes young athletes focus more on every fail. Failure—and failing often—is just a natural part of participating in sports. Even when you're the best in any activity, there is still a high percentage of disappointments along the way. But when children have every mistake they make called out to the nth degree, some forget that there is a desired result at the other end. They spend all their time on why they are failing in a particular skill, instead of remembering why they liked playing that sport in the first place.

It May All Be Meaningless Anyway

Can training technology make a slight difference in athletes for whom everything else has been set in motion? When used with college- or professional-level athletes who are fundamentally developed, coordinated, and balanced? Absolutely—especially when squeezing even the slightest degree of improvement could mean a difference that could lead to a contract. But in young athletes that are most likely overtraining themselves, eating the wrong foods, and suffering from postural issues due to poor habits? Absolutely not.

Even if children were abiding by every rule in this book, using technology to evaluate them when they may still be in the early or middle stages of their development is simply not a fair assessment. You're trying to measure the capacity of athletes that haven't fully formed yet, who are still growing and learning how to adapt to an ever-changing body.

It Makes Them Forget the Fundamentals

There was a time when baseball scouts would watch every aspect of a potential athlete. But once the radar gun came out, it gave them something they never had before: a number. And over time, finding talent became all about what the machine said about an athlete first, then sorting out the other details later. We became obsessed with speed and not accuracy, and miles per hour instead of actual movement.

Sometimes the way training tech is used to define an athlete is no different than how biomarkers are applied in medicine. If your cholesterol numbers are high, you're at risk for heart disease, or if you're a few pounds over your body mass index (BMI), then you're overweight. But as most people know, sometimes numbers don't tell the whole story. Your cholesterol might be high, but you could still have low blood pressure. Your BMI might define you as overweight, but those extra pounds could be lean muscle.

The same rules apply when it comes to the definable numbers training tech might spit out at you. Just because a young athlete can throw 95 miles an hour doesn't necessarily mean that person would be a good pitcher. So, to decide the fate—to define the path of young athletes—by gauging them on one marker makes no sense, either.

More important, you run the risk of athletes' (and parents and coaches alike) being so obsessed with improving that number that it comes at the expense of ignoring the fundamentals. Instead of training in a way that helps them focus on all the foundational pieces that help develop and protect young athletes, they put all their effort into improving a single measurable skill.

It Could Be Skewed Just to Sell You Something Else

The next time you see a facility or event where young athletes are evaluated by a trainer, pro scout, or player, I want you to consider this:

Chances are, the facility or professional that will assess kids' potential by using today's top technology doesn't just evaluate young athletes—they also (wait for it—yes, big surprise) train them. That said, do you really think their business is built on the one-time fee of $100 to take that test, or the countless lessons and equipment they can sell you afterward, once they "pinpoint" what's supposedly wrong with your son or daughter?

As I said earlier, I feel evaluating the skills of athletes younger than college-age level isn't a fair appraisal to begin with. But now ask yourself how much more unreliable that information might be if it's coming from someone that's trying to upsell you. Not only are you getting advice your son or daughter doesn't technically need at his or her age, but it might also be followed by the wrong type of training advice that could lead to a future injury, simply to turn a profit.

PLAYING A SPORT LONGER THAN AN AVERAGE SEASON

Professional athletes—the human beings paid top dollar to participate in the sport your son or daughter is trying to excel at—do something to play at their best and extend their career, which ironically doesn't seem to be something that most young athletes want to do—and it is this: Once the season is over, they take a break.

After every season my father played pro ball, he swam a lot and probably spent just as much time throwing us kids in the pool. He shot a lot of golf, played a lot of tennis, and might've even picked up a basketball to play Horse. But baseball? My dad never picked up a ball until three weeks before spring training.

As soon as the season was over, his glove went to be relaced—and then it went in his closet. He might hold a ball—in fact, he often holds a ball when he drives—and do things that were baseball related, to keep his mind on the sport. But throwing a ball? Absolutely not. The only time he would is if I asked to play a casual game of catch. And even then, he would throw the ball back at a fraction of what he was capable of doing.

The thought of "taking time off" doesn't exist in today's young athletes. For them, there is no such thing as an off-season because they are constantly "on." And even if they wanted to take time off, they're made to feel as if they will be left behind. So, why are today's young athletes not heeding the commonsense advice of both athletes past and present to give their body a break? Welcome to the business of sports!

The Snowballing of Sport—Sound Familiar?

Remember the day you innocently signed up your children for whatever sport they were interested in—or that you thought would be right for them? At that time, it seemed easy enough to handle. You looked at the calendar, wrote down when each practice and game was, then planned your summer vacation accordingly.

You probably watched your kids play two dozen or so games or matches against other towns in your neighborhood. And if they had a good season, they were invited to be a part of a select all-star team to play another dozen or so. After that, you probably thought that was it until next year—but boy, were you wrong.

Instead, other coaches begin to pour out of the woodwork, telling you how your children have such great potential and have been "selected" to play on a travel team. "They have to play against real competition against other kids in other towns in other leagues!" the coaches will urge you—because if they don't, your children will be left behind.

Suddenly, your son or daughter is involved in as many leagues as you can sign him or her up to, manage to juggle, and most important—pay for. Then, you hear about how your kid's coach also gives lessons. So, a thought runs through your head, most likely put there by another parent: "If I take lessons from the coach, maybe he or she will play my kid more."

If the lessons take place in an indoor facility, you now unexpectedly find yourself being encouraged to have your child take on additional strength and conditioning classes, performance screenings, one-on-one training, a personalized diet regimen, and in some facilities, sports-related genetic testing to reveal what his or her true sports skills might be. All for either one lump sum or à la carte.

Now, what was meant to be a fun summer activity has turned into a full-time job that, for many young athletes today, doesn't stop when the season's over. It becomes a year-round obligation that's leaving our sons and daughters burned out, beaten up, and unable to heal properly.

The Specialization Spiral

It's been assumed—or should I say drilled into many parents' heads—that if their children devote all their time to one sport, it's a surefire way of becoming better faster. However, don't always believe what you hear.

It puts your child at risk: As it turns out, young athletes who specialize in a single sport—defined as training specifically for one sport for more than eight months per year—have a significantly higher risk of stress fractures and other severe overuse injuries, according to the largest clinical study[1] of its kind. It was found that athletes between the ages of eight and eighteen who spent twice as many hours weekly in organized sports rather than free play, particularly focused on a single sport, were more likely to be injured.

Many other studies have shown that highly specialized adolescent athletes are more susceptible to knee and hip injuries,[2] overuse injuries,[3] and even learning to hate the sport over time. After the review of twenty-one years' worth of evidence regarding sports specialization, it was concluded[4] that although some degree of sports specialization may be necessary to develop elite-level skill development, for most sports, intense single sport training should be delayed until late adolescence to minimize injury, psychological stress, and burnout.

It's not what most pros did: Sticking with one sport year-round doesn't seem to be disappearing any day soon. According to a 2017 study[5] from the American Academy of Orthopaedic Surgeons, 45 percent of high school athletes now specialize in just one sport, often playing year-round and on multiple teams. Yet ironically, the same study asked more than 1,700 professional athletes whether they would have their child specialize in a single sport during childhood or adolescence—and only 22 percent said yes.

Again, it would appear that pro athletes know what's what—and rightfully so. It's been shown[6] that among NCAA Division I male and female athletes, 88 percent participated in an average of two to three sports as a kid. Another study[7] found that on average, Olympic athletes had participated in two other sports during childhood either before or alongside their main sport. The fact remains that many experts in the field admit that very few who specialize in a single sport at a young age reach elite athlete status.

It makes them one-dimensional: Believe it or not, there is such a thing as life off the field. When your young athletes aren't participating in their sport, they should be busy involved in life, and being inside a body that's equalized, which will give them an edge toward preventing injury. The thing is, there isn't a single sport that's the perfect balance in regard to body development. Every sport works a different mix of muscles, inevitably overtraining certain ones while ignoring others.

In youth baseball alone, research[8] from the American Orthopaedic Society for Sports Medicine has highlighted how muscle fatigue (particularly of the core and leg muscles) can affect trunk rotation timing and may be behind the increasing amount of shoulder and elbow injuries occurring in adolescent pitchers every year.

Your son or daughter also has a dominant side. Whether young athletes are left- or right-footed, or left- or right-handed, most sports focus on training their dominant side through performing a variety of functional skill movements over and over and over again to excel at that skill.

Because both of these factors are constantly kept in play when sticking with a single sport, it only increases the risk of being out of balance physiologically. But having a body in balance improves posture, boosts strength and power, minimizes fatigue, prevents injury, and ensures that the athletes will be able to function at their maximum capacity as both a player and a person.

BEING TOO ENAMORED BY WHAT'S BEING OFFERED

What's turning seasons into all-year events are multiple opportunities that have emerged nowadays—things that didn't exist decades ago to the extent they do today. As a parent, it can be hard to say no, especially if you want your son or daughter to reach their full potential. But here is what you should ponder about putting your child at risk with these "opportunities."

The Truth About "Select" or Travel Teams

No matter what your children's sport may be, it's unavoidable that at some point, someone will come up to you insisting they've been selected—or must try out—for either a "select" team (also known as a premier or elite team) or a travel team, which is basically a select team that travels out of town or state to compete.

It's even happened to my dad. When I was a high school senior, he received a call out of the blue by a man he didn't know. The man told him I had been "scouted and chosen to try out" for the select Minnesota travel team, and assured my dad that joining the team would unquestionably make me a better player. And all it would take to make that happen was a small fee—of around $3,000.

With that, my dad thanked the man and told him I would rather play with the kids I went to school with—and that was that. But to any other parent, hearing their child has been scouted and chosen for something billed as a stepping-stone toward improving his or her skills sounds like an opportunity that can't be passed up. But just in case you do question the proposal, don't worry: The seller has an answer for that as well.

The angle is almost always the same, no matter what the sport: "You can't expect your child to excel if he/she haven't played—and failed—against the best!" Suddenly, the sell becomes more of a scare tactic, where you may be told that by not participating, your son or daughter won't develop at the same pace as his or her teammates. Whichever angle wins you over, just know that the privilege to join is never free. Instead, it comes with a fee to join the team, along with paying for a uniform, travel, and often additional equipment.

It can also be a huge time drain. I've heard some leagues tout that their select or travel teams are a great bonding experience due to all the traveling required. I've also watched many families complain about spending every weekend attending games, instead of going to family functions, focusing on school, celebrating holidays, and most important, giving their young athlete enough rest to recover and reduce the risk of injury.

What will always remain in question is whether your child was indeed chosen because he or she was supposedly the cream of the crop, because those organizing the team always need to bring together enough kids to turn a profit. Before you consider joining any select team, just consider this: Most times, your kid probably wasn't picked because he or she had lots of potential—but *you* had the potential to make someone else a lot of money.

Indoor Programs and Elite Showcase Facilities

Sports may have seasons—and depending on where you live, the weather may play a huge factor in making your son or daughter take a break—but the business of sports never wants there to be a time when your young athlete is out of its hands. Enter the age of massive indoor sports facilities that, as many gloat, "give athletes access to high-quality training all year-round, regardless of weather conditions!"

Run 365 days a year, these high-tech facilities not only make it possible (unfortunately) to play a sport all twelve months of the year, but they encourage a variety of other services they all happen to have under the same roof. Once your son's or daughter's season is over, most of these facilities will suggest coming in to follow up with lessons, rehab, off-season conditioning, and to participate in leagues, camps, and tournaments.

Many of these facilities are exacerbating an American-based inverted performance pyramid training process (something I'll explain in greater detail in the Rebuild section). But for now, know that most tend to focus on improving functional *skills* as opposed to functional *movements*, a mistake that's behind producing the high-ability, poorly developed (and chronically injured) youth athletes we're seeing in all sports today.

PUSHING A PASSION ON YOUR PROGENY

Throughout my years, one thing has become blatantly clear to me: at least 50 percent of the time (or more) with kids below the age of fifteen, it was the parents pushing the sport on their child, as opposed to their child's truly pursuing that sport passionately.

I'm not saying that's how it is across the board. This is just my experience as a doctor who has spent the past seventeen years seeing athletes of every level and age. It's also my experience from giving eleven thousand lessons as a former baseball coach and working with countless parents and young athletes.

When I was a coach, I was looked at to serve a role. After all, I was not only the baseball guy but the son of the legendary pitcher Tommy John. So, when kids would come in knowing all that about me, but couldn't care less to be there, that was my first clue.

But even with the ones that were less obvious, as those young athletes got to know me, they started to understand that I wasn't just a coach that could talk baseball, but we could talk about life. I would ask questions about their activities, their day, and connect with them on a different level than just a baseball coach. Sometimes, we might sit and do nothing but chat, and they would be stoked—even though no baseball lesson took place at all.

I began to discover many had parents that were completely oblivious to the fact that their kid wasn't into baseball, yet year after year, they kept signing them up. Other parents knew their children weren't very good at the sport, but kept going along with whatever they thought was best for those youngsters.

Back then, it occurred to me that maybe one reason behind the rise of injury among some young athletes isn't about overused muscles or overworked kids. But maybe we're keeping some children in the system far longer than necessary, either steering toward injury or potentially pushing them away from wanting to be active later on in life, just because no one's paying attention. That maybe—just maybe—the real reason your children are struggling in their sport, and getting injured as a result, is as simple as their not wanting to be there in the first place.

So, could that be your young athlete? The only way to know for sure is to answer all four of the following questions honestly. Mind you, I'm not saying that answering yes to any or all of these questions means your child is engaged in a sport he or she has no interest in, or that you may be pushing your son or daughter to the point of possible injury, but it's important to be aware of what possibly might be happening around you. That said:

Are Your Kids in Sports Because It's Convenient?

When I taught baseball lessons, I generally had a guilty conscience for taking money when I could tell I wasn't teaching children about baseball as much as watching them for a certain amount of time, particularly kids between the ages of nine and twelve. And often when I would raise my concern to their parents, they weren't even surprised. Instead, they would just nod their head and say, "Yeah I know—but is there anything else you can do with them?"

My feeling was always the same—why? What's your real reason? So you can still have Tuesdays through Fridays free? Maybe you're offering your children more and more opportunities to train simply because you need someone else to watch them for a certain period of time.

I no longer teach baseball, but I'm still in touch with many pros that do, along with a variety of other sports. And even now when I ask how they're doing, the most popular response is: "Oh, I'm just babysitting today." Mind you, it's top-dollar babysitting, since a one-hour private lesson can run on average between $75 and $100. But even though many instructors are passionate about what they can teach a young athlete, it is equally frustrating to them when it's clear that athlete is there for the wrong reasons.

For some parents, having their son or daughter constantly engaged in a single sport could be more about getting extra time to themselves. Between all the camps, coaching, and leagues, if you pull it off right, it's easy to turn a sport into a babysitting service.

If that's you, that doesn't mean that's necessarily a bad thing. Working with so many parents over the years, I can understand the need to keep all the plates spinning in a household, and having children in sports can help capture a few hours of alone time to focus on other essential priorities. And if they love playing anyway, then more power to you. But overusing sports in this way could come at the cost of getting them injured.

One particular study out of the Loyola University Health System[9] found that young athletes from higher-income families were not only more likely to specialize in one sport but also more likely to suffer serious overuse injuries, such as stress fractures. The reason: Researchers believe that because intense specialization in one sport can cost thousands each year (due to equipment, fees, transportation, and private lessons, for example), having the financial means may provide more opportunities for young athletes to stay involved in a single sport.

Are Your Kids in Sports Because Everyone Else's Kid Is?

No one wants to see their kids fall behind, which is why most parents will turn around and see what everybody else is doing. Before you know it, that "follow the herd" mentality has your children signed up for a series of sports and activities they may care little about but said yes to, either because they thought, "Why not?" thought they couldn't say no in the first place, or want to do them because all their friends from school are part of the team.

Sometimes, kids may gravitate toward a sport purely for the social engagement, and if that's the case, that's entirely fine. Sports are supposed to be about those type of relationships, experiencing things together—and succeeding together and failing together. As long as you're not pushing your children to be better than they might be capable of being, and they're part of a team with everyone else in the neighborhood, that's great. But if that need to socialize evolves into the need to take six lessons a week and sign up for every travel team possible, then that's a different story that can lead to injury.

Are Your Kids in Sports Only Because You Were?

Did you participate in the same sport when you were young—or wish you had? Did your children show interest in the sport simply because they wanted to follow in your footsteps? If the answer's yes to any of the above, that's understandable. The important thing, though, is to recognize to what degree you may be living vicariously through your children, or how hard they may be trying to please you.

As the son of one of the best left-handed pitchers in pro baseball, you would think I would have been forced to take the same life path as my dad. And I won't deny being proud of my dad wasn't part of the reason I tried my best to play pro ball. But I never felt pressure from my father to make it to the big leagues—the desire to participate in sports was my own. Being involved in sports was always my choice, and it should always be your child's choice as well.

Are Your Kids in Sports Because You Want Them to Turn Pro?

There's nothing wrong about dreaming. I would never say not to shoot for the stars, because I spent many years doing the same. But if the reason you have your children involved in sports is that you're expecting a big payoff from that first big contract or endorsement deal, get ready for a little honesty.

I had access to my dad's genetics and his wisdom. I had him as my coach both on various teams I played for and privately all of my life. And even I never made it to the big leagues—and chances are, neither will your children.

As much as you may have big aspirations for children, it's important to recognize the odds. According to the National Collegiate Athletic Association (NCAA),[10] as of 2017, nearly 8 million students currently participate in high school athletics throughout the United States—yet no more than roughly 480,000 ever go on to compete as NCAA athletes. As it stands right now, here are their chances:

MEN

	High school participants	NCAA participants	Overall % HS to NCAA	% HS to NCAA Division I	% HS to NCAA Division II	% HS to NCAA Division III
Baseball	488,815	34,554	7.1%	2.1%	2.2%	2.8%
Basketball	546,428	18,684	3.4%	1.0%	1.0%	1.4%
Cross-country	257,691	14,412	5.6%	1.9%	1.4%	2.3%
Football	1,083,308	73,660	6.8%	2.6%	1.8%	2.4%
Golf	146,677	8,676	5.9%	2.0%	1.7%	2.2%
Ice hockey	35,155	4,102	11.7%	4.6%	.5%	6.5%
Lacrosse	109,522	13,446	12.3%	2.9%	2.3%	7.1%
Soccer	440,322	24,803	5.6%	1.3%	1.5%	2.8%
Swimming	133,470	9,455	7.1%	2.8%	1.1%	3.2%
Tennis	157,201	8,092	5.1%	1.7%	1.1%	2.4%
Track and field	591,133	28,334	4.8%	1.9%	1.2%	1.7%
Volleyball	55,417	1,899	3.4%	.7%	.8%	1.9%
Water polo	21,857	1,014	4.6%	2.6%	.7%	1.3%
Wrestling	250,653	7,075	2.8%	1.0%	.8%	1.0%

WOMEN

	High school participants	NCAA participants	Overall % HS to NCAA	% HS to NCAA Division I	% HS to NCAA Division II	% HS to NCAA Division III
Basketball	429,380	16,593	3.9%	1.2%	1.1%	1.6%
Cross-country	222,516	15,958	7.2%	2.7%	1.8%	2.7%
Field hockey	59,793	6,032	10.1%	3.0%	1.2%	5.8%
Golf	74,762	5,293	7.1%	2.9%	2.1%	2.1%
Ice hockey	9,514	2,289	24.1%	9.0%	1.0%	14.0%

continues

WOMEN *continued*

	High school participants	NCAA participants	Overall % HS to NCAA	% HS to NCAA Division I	% HS to NCAA Division II	% HS to NCAA Division III
Lacrosse	88,050	11,375	12.9%	3.8%	2.6%	6.5%
Soccer	381,529	27,358	7.2%	2.4%	1.9%	2.9%
Softball	366,685	19,680	5.4%	1.6%	1.6%	2.1%
Swimming	166,747	12,356	7.4%	3.3%	1.1%	3.0%
Tennis	183,800	8,933	4.9%	1.6%	1.1%	2.2%
Track and field	485,969	29,048	6.0%	2.7%	1.5%	1.8%
Volleyball	436,309	17,119	3.9%	1.2%	1.1%	1.6%
Water polo	20,230	1,136	5.6%	3.3%	1.0%	1.3%

From there, even if children make it as an NCAA athlete, just a select few[11] within each sport ever move on to play professionally or compete on an Olympic level. Where do their chances go from there?

	NCAA Participants	Approximate # Draft Eligible	# Draft Picks	# NCAA Drafted	% NCAA to Major Pro*
Baseball	34,554	7,679	1,206	695	9.1%
Men's Basketball	18,684	4,152	60	44	1.1%
Women's Basketball	16,593	3,687	36	35	.9%
Football	73,660	16,369	253	251	1.5%
Men's Ice Hockey	4,102	912	211	51	5.6%
Men's Soccer	24,803	5,512	81	75	1.4%

*Figures are based on the number of draft picks made in the NFL, NBA, WNBA, MLB, NHL, and MLS drafts only.

The problem is that reality hasn't stopped the business of sports from convincing many parents from buying into the dream. But all that pressure could be having an effect on your children. Researchers[12] from the University of Kent found that the pressure that parents place on young athletes to be perfect makes them more likely to use banned substances to enhance their performance.

You may also be affecting their ability to have a career if they don't make it in professional sports. A classic study[13] out of the University of Haifa found that when parents of young athletes (seventh to twelfth grade) were asked whether they would let their son or daughter skip an exam for an important game, a surprising 75 percent said yes. By banking on an endorsement deal in the future, you might be preventing your kids from getting an education in the present.

CHAPTER 6

What Matters Most When Raising a Healthy Human Being

If you're assuming I'm going to tell you and your young athlete to go cold turkey on everything I just called out in the last chapter, you're in for a surprise. Now that you've come face-to-face with which outside factors need to be dealt with, the next step is approaching each in a way that's both feasible and practical. The following variety of changes and substitutions are realistic, reliable, and most important, may remind you of what matters above all else when it comes to raising healthy human beings.

PUT THEIR TECH IN CHECK

Not being a parent myself, I've had a few people question how I could speak from example when it comes to setting limits on tech. But I think that's where not being a parent has given me an advantage.

Through my practice (and my former school), I've had to work intimately with hundreds of families and have seen every possible family dynamic that exists in relation to sport. And of all the families that I've worked with, the ones with the most vibrant, open relationships are the ones that set limits on technology. But even more surprising is that in many instances, the kids also require the least amount of work and seem to suffer from fewer sports-related injuries.

I could attribute that resilience to how less tech has prevented them from being sympathetic dominant (so their body is perpetually healing) to how being able to communicate more with their parents causes less confusion about the kids' involvement (or overinvolvement) in their sport. Whatever the case may be, spending less time with tech shows itself in both the personality and performance of every young athlete I've worked with.

However, it's hard to compete against technology, and I accept that. That's why I culled some of the most interesting techniques I've watched applied by successful sports parents over the years. These are the tried-and-true tricks they believe were behind turning the tables on tech's effect on their son's or daughter's athletic life.

Connect how tech tires them out: Tell kids they can't do something (or do it as often), and it's sometimes the quickest way to get them to want it even more, right? The same battle awaits when discussing less tech with your young athlete, but what smart sports parents use is a technique that gets their kids to recognize exactly how too much technology affects their performance.

Before setting limits on tech, these parents will pick a neutral week with no games or tests (if during the school year) but several days of practice. Then, they will let their children double the amount of time they spend using tech for the first half of the week and have them cut their average tech time for the remaining half.

Each day, they ask their young athletes how they feel physically and mentally in the morning and all day long—particularly before, during, and after practice. Did the children feel more tired or more energized? Are certain muscles sore, less sore, or not sore at all? Was it a little harder to practice or pull off a certain skill—or did something come to them easier than expected?

The reason this remains a top tactic among parents I've talked to is that, let's face it, you can't be there to monitor every minute. But if you can get your kids to recognize that when they curb tech use, there is a definite positive aftereffect they can actually feel and see—one that improved their performance both on and off the field—it's much easier to get them to rethink what they're doing in their off time with tech when you're not around.

Make tech something earned—and not expected: The majority of smart sports families make tech a reward and not a requirement. If children already have a chore list, then make a chart so that as certain things are checked off, they also earn a certain number of minutes for each chore. If they don't, then time could be earned for good grades, finishing their homework, or anything that should take top priority in your kids' life.

The only thing I wouldn't use to earn time would be their performance in their sport. This not only could put an unnecessary amount of stress on them, but it's also counterproductive because it's conflicting by nature. After all, if using less technology makes them a better athlete, then you'll be rewarding their athleticism with something that will only affect their performance negatively.

Set a time limit—and stay tough: How much is the right amount? It depends on your household. According to the latest census report by Common Sense Media:[1]

The average tween spends just around *six hours* on some form of media each day, divided up into the following: watching TV/DVD/videos—2 hours, 26 minutes; playing video, computer, or mobile games—1 hour, 19 minutes; listening to music—51 minutes; reading—29 minutes; using social media—16 minutes.

The average teen spends nearly *nine hours* using some form of media each day, more hours than actually spent sleeping: watching TV/DVD/videos—2 hours, 38 minutes; listening to music—1 hour, 54 minutes; playing video, computer, or mobile games—1 hour, 21 minutes; using social media—1 hour, 11 minutes; reading—28 minutes.

In my opinion, less is always better. But a good place to start might be paring them back to what was considered a "light user" of media by the same census report. For tweens, that might be allowing approximately 2 hours, 16 minutes; and for teens, 3 hours, 40 minutes (spread out daily).

Position them perfectly when they punch out: By using less tech, they'll already be minimizing how often they stay in a sympathetic dominant state, so their immune system stays primed at a higher level more often. But there's one rule of thumb I also recommend to help minimize the negative effect of tech and that's this:

When you do use tech, try to only use it when either standing or lying on your stomach. (This goes, across the board, for cell phones, video games, tablets, and computer use.)

The reason this approach is sound is twofold: One, both positions are slightly less comfortable than just remaining seated or curled up on a couch somewhere—so they may be inclined to spend less time on tech. But, two, it positions them in a way that reverses some of the damage already present in their body.

When standing: Their shoulders should be down and back (not slouched forward) with their glutes and abdominal muscles tight and with whatever screen they're staring at positioned at eye level—even while texting. That means if they have to hold their phone in front of themselves at eye level (as opposed to down by their chest), so be it.

On their stomach: Have them lie flat with their head up and elbows bent to support their torso, or with their chin resting on their hand. You can have them prop pillows under their elbows to make the position more comfortable.

What this position does is reverse the misalignment of posture that regular tech use causes in the young athletes through restoring the curvature of the low back, strengthening the erector spinae muscles (located along the sides of the spine) and bringing the ears behind their shoulders.

I've had a few parents question that, in that position, it's too relaxing to possibly be effective. But, trust me, your muscles are always working, even when you believe you're at rest, which is why getting your kids to spend as much time in this position as possible will have a dramatic effect on their posture if technology has already taken its toll.

No smartphones until high school. I will admit, even this one threw me the first time I heard it. Yet when I showed surprise in front of a family that hadn't given their kid a smartphone until high school, the parents and athlete looked at me as if I had three heads and said: "Of course not. Why would we do that?"

It's not that such kids had no means of contacting their parents. They had either a flip phone or a phone with limited options (nothing more than calling or texting features). But when I asked what their friends thought, they told me point blank: "They know I take being an athlete seriously—and a smartphone would only hold me back from being the best athlete possible."

Thanks to their parents, these kids didn't just excel at their sport, they wore their flip phones like a badge of honor.

They viewed their phones as purely an emergency tool rather than an entertainment source. And some—already smartened up to the postural dangers that smartphones cause—were secretly grateful that most of their competition was tethered to their texting.

Since watching this phenomenon, I'm now a huge believer in using flip phones to reduce unnecessary screen time, minimize injury, and help young athletes excel—but not every child or parent is ready for this throwback approach. However, it may be as easy as asking your young athlete if they want an edge over the competition, and how the longer they spend on their phone, the more it negatively impacts every movement they make as both an athlete and a human being.

The choice is really up to them. But if they balk, try this tip: Remind them how their competition is devolving by using newer technology. Each time they upgrade to the latest and greatest, the athletes that your son or daughter are competing against will be taking several steps back concerning his or her own evolution.

WATCH FOR THE WARNING SIGNS WEEKLY

Knowing when a sport can be a dangerous thing for a young athlete is highly individual. If your young athletes are often injured, moody or depressed, chronically distressed from conditions that could be related to the sport (such as fatigue or soreness), or hurting academically, then you may need to rethink how much time they're spending practicing and playing a particular sport.

But just because they're not suffering now doesn't mean they might not suffer later. If all you watch for are the obvious red flags, you'll miss the not so obvious ones that could be letting you know they need to dial back what you're signing them up for. That's why every few weeks, I encourage you to do the following:

1. First, Have an Honest Heart-to-Heart

How often do you honestly talk with your kids and how long does that discussion ever last? If it's minimal, or not at all, then how can you be sure if your children still want to participate in a particular sport in the first place? Or whether they are even in it for all the right reasons? So, ask your young athletes these questions:

- **Are you in it out of boredom (or for the camaraderie)?** When I was coaching, more than half of the kids that came in enjoyed the experience. They weren't attracted to the baseball—they were attracted to simply doing something. If the answer is yes, explore a few nonsports options related to the children's interests that are equally social and build teamwork skills. This will not only give their body more time to heal during the season, but make them a more well-rounded individual.

- **Are you doing it to make me proud?** This question is a tricky one because what kids don't want their parents to be proud of them? But how they reply may give you clues about whether they are truly doing it for themselves—or only doing it for you. If it's the latter, the best approach is telling them how proud you are of their effort and enthusiasm, but that you would be equally proud of them no matter what—and much happier if they were pouring that energy and enthusiasm into something *they* actually care about, instead of something they believe *you* care about.

- **Are you feeling overwhelmed?** Kids know their limits, even though sometimes we may think we know what's best for them. Even though the answer will most likely be yes, regardless of how involved they are in their sport, ask them what's on their plate and whether there's anything they wish they could remove from it. If most or all of those activities end up tied into sport, it could be telling you something.

2. Second, Look for What They're Not Sharing

Depending on how much "suck it up" spirit your children have absorbed from you, their coaches, or their friends, they may not be as willing to tell the truth. That's when keeping a close eye on them on and off the field may reveal what they refuse to admit.

- **Do they constantly touch and rub a particular area?** If yes, it could be a source of lingering pain or soreness related to overuse due to excessive sports and may need to be looked at.

- **Are they mostly ecstatic or mostly unenthusiastic?** Many parents I work with will assume their kids are unexcited merely because, well, they're a kid! For some tweens and teens, it's not cool to show emotion, but watch their demeanor when they don't think you're observing. If they're truly there because they love the sport, it should show on their face when they're on the field or court, or among their teammates. If it doesn't, it may not be puberty—it could mean lethargy due to disinterest in the sport altogether.

- **Are your kids playing their sport when they don't have to be?** Most of us spend some (if not all) of our free time participating in the things we love to do. But if the only time you see your children engaging in their sport is when you take them to practice or a game, and they never participate or discuss the sport anytime otherwise, it's an obvious sign I've watched many perceptive parents miss.

3. Third, Prepare to Point the Finger Back at Yourself

When I see proud parents that believe in their children, it's endearing—don't get me wrong. But if that pride is causing you to keep your kids in a sport 24/7 to amplify their skills, your hopes and dreams for them may be doing them more harm than good. My job is just to make sure that you, whether directly or indirectly, aren't a part of the problem. That said, give yourself a once-over by:

- **Talking to adult family members or best pals:** Asking close friends (not involved with the sport) and family whether they think you might be pushing your young athletes too hard. Trust me, if that's you, others are aware of your actions more than you realize.
- **Listening to what comes out of your mouth:** Do you mostly praise your children's performance in sport—and little else? If that pride is mostly shown only when they play or practice, it could leave them feeling that the only way to experience that pride is to stay involved year-round, which will only lead to overtraining and pushing themselves too hard. Instead, make sure that what comes out of your mouth is a balance of many things, particularly non-sports related.
- **Looking at your day planner or calendar:** Are you the one pushing for lessons and negotiating to get your young athletes onto additional leagues, all because it allows you more time for yourself? If so, your need for downtime could be creating a situation where your children are pushing themselves too hard. Instead, figure out a different way to organize your life, and/or a different nonsports activity postseason that will give your kids time to rest.
- **Admitting it's really social time for you:** It's entirely fine to be sharing the experience of your children's sport. Seeing Mom or Dad on the sidelines cheering them on is something all kids dream of. But if every game or practice is a fun time with friends for you, you may be increasing their involvement in a sport indirectly, simply to keep that social aspect going.

UNTIL HIGH SCHOOL, STICK WITH A SPORT FOR A MAXIMUM OF SIX MONTHS ANNUALLY

Every sport is different, and I don't know what activity your children are involved in. But the definition of specializing in one sport is practicing and participating for eight months (or more) per year. That's also the amount of time that seems to be breaking down more and more young athletes each year due to overuse injuries. So, what's the best approach to bring their involvement down to a reasonable number of months?

Start when the season starts—stop when the season's over: It's my first rule of thumb for anyone younger than late high school age. Once the season's over, they can either shift to another sport (I'll explain the benefit of that later on in this chapter) or continue to work on the foundations presented in this book.

One loophole parents try to use is to have their kid on two teams at the same time during the season. Absolutely not. Instead, during the season, if kids want to play with their friends in a nonleague setting, then go for it. For example, in baseball, which typically runs from February/March through July/August, that's the time period your children should be practicing and playing. If their season wraps up early, and they want to try a little travel league until those six months are up, that's fine, too. But after that, it's over.

Say no to private lessons—for now: I know—this is coming from someone who sold eleven thousand of them in his time. But remember, it was through those lessons paralleled with my practice where I realized the ramifications of too many lessons the hard way.

When we're talking about developing athletes (kids that don't have the basics down quite yet) I still don't ever think it's time for lessons. Even once they've learned the basics through regular practice, their body needs to develop so that the basics can be expressed even more so. That expression doesn't start to take place in an athlete until mid-to-late high school (around sixteen years of age or older). Then and only then could lessons be helpful.

If I can't stop you from having your kids take specific lessons, and you're following everything else regarding the Tommy John Solution, then I would say at least be smart about it. My recommendation: Only have them take lessons during their season and for 30 to 60 minutes a week—and no longer—to allow their body enough time to heal.

Skip the indoor programs and sports facilities altogether: The reason I say this is simple. Typically, these extracurricular training opportunities are more tempting during the off-season because they're more doable during the off-season. After all, during the season, your young athletes are probably too busy playing their sport to be involved with much more than that.

Instead, if you want them to participate in anything an indoor facility may have to offer, just try it within the actual sports season. Other than that, you'll be doing their body more benefit and preparing it for next year by allowing it to heal during the off-season, instead of their being misled that they are being left behind.

FIND OTHER OPTIONS TO STAY ACTIVE

Just because I want your kids to take time off each year doesn't mean I'm suggesting they remain inactive. In fact, their body will benefit by doing the exact opposite. There are plenty of ways to keep them moving that still help minimize overuse injuries and burnout that can simultaneously make them a more efficient athlete.

Let them enroll in another sport: As I mentioned earlier, 88 percent of NCAA Division I male and female athletes participated in an average of at least two or three sports when they were kids, so let your kids try on a different sport for size in the off-season. If they eventually want to settle with one sport, most experts agree that they should wait until late high school before locking down on a single one.

To offer you the perfect prescription of how many sports is too much would be impossible, since every young athlete is uniquely different. But through this book, as you begin to minimize or eliminate certain habits, and introduce new healthier habits that will allow you to discuss things more with your children, it will make it easier to see where those limits might be.

But a final reason I prefer young athletes to think multisport (beyond the fact that every sport engages different muscles, which allows their body to recover from their primary sport) is this: They may find another sport they love even more, which will give them a better understanding in regard to how their body functions differently—and at a different level—depending on the sport.

Let them play with no pressure: Many experts believe that young athletes should never spend more than twice as much time playing organized sports as they spend being involved in unorganized play—with good reason. Research is showing that when young athletes play more for fun (playing pickup games, for example), they tend to be more injury resistant, according to a Loyola University medical study.[2]

Let them enroll in nonsports youth organizations: Earlier in the book, I explained all the positive perks about sport that can help your children develop into a more well-rounded human being. But I've also watched the reverse happen, particularly when it comes to young athletes' personality.

I work with kids across every possible activity, and when I ask most about their sport, they light up. But if I switch subjects, you can see the light dim with some of them, particularly if they specialize in a single sport year-round. They suddenly become a deer in the headlights, so focused in one particular area of interest that even on the slightest of levels, they're unable to discuss any other topic of interest without difficulty.

You can see this phenomenon with certain professional athletes once they retire from their sport. Even if your young athletes manage to avoid injury throughout their careers, by putting all their eggs into that one basket, they aren't getting exposed to a plethora of other experiences at a young age when those skills may have the most impact long term.

That's why smart sports parents I work with also have their children signed up for various organizations, such as the Boy Scouts of America, the Girl Scouts of the USA, Junior Lifeguards-U.S.L.A., 4-H, and other nationally or locally known clubs that teach team building, build confidence, and promote other life skills that their primary sport may teach, but minus the wear and tear.

ENJOY THE SPORT FROM AN ENTIRELY DIFFERENT ANGLE

If children are passionate about their sport, then the very thought of taking time off from it will not only feel foreign to them—it may just infuriate them. For some young athletes, knowing they won't be participating in lessons unnecessarily or being involved in indoor facilities throughout the wintertime and off-season may be met with apprehension, anger, and/or anxiety.

But just because they have to take time to heal doesn't mean they have to take time off from their sport. There are several ways to continue to develop their body, mind, and spirit for sport in the off-season—*without actually playing it.*

Swap lessons for a library card: The greatest tool your young athletes have—the tool that will help them go the farthest in their sport and in life—is their mind. Taking the time to read books related to their sport can give them a different understanding of the game or activity that they hadn't considered.

Try looking for books that are age appropriate, but also be considerate about the content itself. I tend to advise parents to stay away from books that are focused on techniques and skills, and have the children search for other titles about the defining moments of a sports history, or memorable players within the sport. That way, what they read will keep their enthusiasm about the sport fed without causing undue stress about taking time off.

Switch out travel teams for traveling—period! If you think of the endless hours you've probably spent going to attend out-of-state competitions and tournaments throughout the year, it's time and money that could have been put to better use. In fact, it could be spent traveling to keep your athletes immersed in their sport, but in a noncompetitive way. A way that will give their body a break, but their mind a leg up on the competition, because they will be connected to their sport at a different level.

Because I'm not sure what sport your kids play, and every athlete is an individual, it's hard to recommend which places might interest your young athletes most. Still, I make the following suggestions to parents to get them thinking about all the possibilities:

- Plan a trip to the hometown of their favorite athlete.
- Try to visit a different stadium each year.
- Make a point of traveling to a museum or facility dedicated to their sport, such as:
    - The Baseball Hall of Fame and Museum in Cooperstown, New York
    - The National Ballpark Museum in Denver, Colorado
    - The ASA National Softball Hall of Fame in Oklahoma City, Oklahoma
    - The Pro Football Hall of Fame in Canton, Ohio
    - The Hockey Hall of Fame in Toronto, Ontario, Canada

- ° The United States Hockey Hall of Fame Museum in Eveleth, Minnesota
- ° The International Swimming Hall of Fame and Museum in Fort Lauderdale, Florida
- ° The National Wrestling Hall of Fame and Museum in Stillwater, Oklahoma
- ° The National Football Museum in Manchester, England
- ° The Naismith Memorial Basketball Hall of Fame in Springfield, Massachusetts

THE RIGHT MUST-HAVES IN PLACE

Have . . . an off-season. If your children are involved in several sports throughout the year, make sure they're arranged so there's some sort of three- to four-month break throughout the year.

Have . . . a clue about their coach. If you're the type that simply drops off the kids to practice, do your homework on the individuals that are putting your kids through the paces. Besides talking to your children and other parents, look online for reviews about each coach to see whether there might be a problem you're not aware of.

Have . . . the right attitude. Even though it's fun to watch young athletes succeed, the less you focus on winning and the more you concentrate on wanting them to just enjoy the moment, will always keep them in the right attitude and less likely to overwork themselves.

Have . . . the right ratio. If possible, some experts feel that young athletes should never spend more hours per week playing sports than their age.

TJ'S MVP LIST—RETHINK (IN A NUTSHELL)!

1. **Rely on tech as little as possible.**
   Why?

   • It suppresses their immune system.
   • It makes them less aware.
   • It shuts down certain muscles.
   • It's destroying their biomechanics.
   • It's reducing quality family time.

2. **Never overevaluate your children's performance.**
   Why?

   • It keeps them sympathetic dominant.
   • It may all be meaningless anyway.
   • It makes them forget the fundamentals.
   • It could be skewed just to sell you something else.

3. **Don't let your kids play a sport longer than an average season.**
   Why?

   • It puts them at risk.
   • It's not what most pros did.
   • It makes them one-dimensional.

4. **Avoid being too enamored by what's being offered.**
   Such as:

   • Select, elite, or travel teams
   • Indoor programs
   • Elite showcase facilities

5. **Don't push a passion on your progeny.**
   Warning signs:

   • Are your children in sports because it's convenient?
   • Are your children in sports because everyone else's kid is?
   • Are your children in sports only because you were?
   • Are your children in sports because you want them to turn pro?

continues

TJ'S MVP LIST—RETHINK (IN A NUTSHELL)! *continued*

6. **Put their tech in check by . . .**

   - Connecting how tech tires them out
   - Making tech something earned—and not expected
   - Setting a time limit—and staying tough

     For tweens, 2 hours, 16 minutes maximum daily
     For teens and up, 3 hours, 40 minutes maximum daily

   - Positioning them correctly when they do use tech:

     When standing: Their shoulders should be back and down (not slouched forward) with their core muscles tight and with whatever screen they're staring at positioned at eye level—even while texting.
     On their stomach: Have them lie flat with their head up and elbows bent to support their torso, or with their chin resting on their hand.

7. **Say no to smartphones until high school.**

8. **Watch for the warning signs weekly.**

   First, have an honest heart-to-heart and ask them:

   - Are you in it out of boredom (or for the camaraderie)?
   - Are you doing it to make me proud?
   - Are you feeling overwhelmed?

   Second, look for what they're not sharing.

   - Do they constantly touch and rub a specific area?
   - Are they mostly ecstatic or mostly unenthusiastic?
   - Are they playing their sport when they don't have to be?

   Third, prepare to point the finger back at yourself.

   - Talk to adult family members or best pals.
   - Listen to what comes out of your mouth.
   - Look at your day planner or calendar.
   - Admit whether it's really social time for you.

continues

TJ'S MVP LIST—RETHINK (IN A NUTSHELL)! *continued*

9. **Until high school, your children should stick with a sport for a maximum of six months annually.**

   - Start when the season starts—stop when the season's over.
   - Say no to private lessons—for now.
   - Skip the indoor programs and sports facilities altogether.

10. **Find other options to stay active.**

   - Let them enroll in another sport.
   - Let them play with no pressure.
   - Let them enroll in nonsports youth organizations.

11. **Enjoy the sport from an entirely different angle.**

   - Swap lessons for a library card.
   - Switch out travel teams for traveling—period!
   - Plan a trip to the hometown of their favorite athlete.
   - Try to visit a different stadium each year.
   - Make a point of traveling to a museum or facility dedicated to their sport.

PART II
Replenish

Nourishment of our young athletes is at an all-time low.

The problem is, if certain materials aren't being presented through the right foods, the body can never build itself into what it needs to become—or heal itself from the damage caused by sport itself.

CHAPTER 7

Don't Be Foolish When It Comes to What Fuels Them

When I used to give baseball lessons, I would have every kid start by simply swinging a bat thirty times—just thirty times. And more often than you would imagine, I've watched some young athletes become thoroughly exhausted—totally tapped from something that should never have left them feeling that way in the first place.

All it took to figure out why they gassed out was asking them a simple question: *"What did you eat today?"*

And depending on the answer, instead of grabbing a ball, I would grab breakfast with them instead of grueling through an hour-long training session. Other times, I'd either limit what we would cover that day or, in some extreme cases, I would simply send them home.

I didn't do that to be cruel. I did it because when athletes came to me malnourished, I knew it would be a waste of both my time and theirs. I realized that even if I had some idea of a training program in play, I couldn't carry it out because they wouldn't have the energy to do the fundamentals, let alone any specific advanced work. I understood that there wasn't a single workout, lesson, or drill we could perform that day that would help them reach their goals if the right foods weren't already present in their body beforehand.

Not having a solid base nutritionally affected their performance in every possible area, from their speed and timing to their ability to focus and retain what I was trying to teach them. But beyond that, it greatly affected how efficiently they were able to recover after our session was over.

What many parents fail to understand is that any workout (that includes every practice) is principally "controlled damage" placed on their kid's body so that it may evolve. For that evolution to take place, their sons and daughters need not just any food, but the right kinds of foods, so that controlled damage can be met and adapted to, so that their bodies can continue to grow and evolve.

When your young athletes step onto the field, court, or gym malnourished—due to not eating enough, or eating the wrong kinds of foods—they're approaching their sport in a constant catabolic state, meaning that their body is literally breaking down. Instead of having the nutrients needed to encourage their muscles to repair and grow after a hard practice, their body is left with little choice but to tear down muscle tissue to find the nutrients needed just to make it through their next practice.

The bad news is that most young athletes today are in a chronic catabolic state, preventing their body from ever developing toward their true potential, and instead increasing their risk of injury. The good news: it's a state that's easily balanced by eating certain foods that help replenish the body. The steps to preventing the damage being done by training, improving every aspect of your young athletes' performance, and keeping them injury-free are easy—if you come into it with an open mind.

WHY IT'S IMPORTANT—AND WHY IT GOES IGNORED

It's no secret that the American diet has left our children overfed, undernourished, and improperly hydrated in epic numbers. According to the President's Council on Fitness, Sports & Nutrition, the prevalence of obesity since the early 1970s has quadrupled in children aged six to eleven years—and tripled among kids between twelve and nineteen years of age.[1]

Yet when I first approach parents about the importance of proper nutrition, I admit, it's not always met with instant acceptance—despite the fact that it's possibly the most significant portion of the program.

The same "whatever it takes" parents that never flinch at the thought of showering their kids with extra lessons, off-season training, and top-of-the-line equipment were suddenly silent, putting marginal—if any—effort into the nutritional habits of their sons and daughters.

Early in my career, that sense of reluctance never made sense to me. At first, I attributed it to the fact that many parents of young athletes simply assume their kids are active enough—so what would be the point? They think that if their children are burning a lot of calories at practice, and aren't presently struggling with weight issues, then why focus so much attention on nutrition, right?

Truth be told, even though your son or daughter may come home exhausted from practice, it's most likely due to poor nutrition, along with a lack of sleep and bad lifestyle habits—rather than from being wrecked from a good workout. That's because it's been proven that youth sports, in general, don't offer nearly as much exercise as once believed.

Recent research[2] performed at San Diego State University/University of California, San Diego, has discovered that only one quarter of all kids participating in organized sports were actually getting the government recommended amount of exercise (60 minutes of moderate to vigorous physical activity daily) during their team practices. As it turns out, much of their time may be spent being inactive—due to listening to instruction and waiting their turn—making youth sports practices less than optimal in regard to boosting their physical activity.

But even when I get a parent to acknowledge their children may not be as active as they assume, getting them to turn the corner to modify what their young athletes eat can still be a struggle.

Why would parents that had no problem micromanaging their kids' training to the nth degree minimize—or much worse, ignore—their kids' nutrition? Why was suggesting smarter food choices that keep their children not only growing toward their full greatest potential but helping their body heal and protect itself from injury such a difficult choice to make?

After working with hundreds of parents over the years, I found it always comes down to three distinct causes:

Cause #1: Convenience Is King

For the first time in history, we have food available at all times with the least amount of effort involved. Yet our kids are malnourished not because they lack access to food, but lack what the body considers food.

According to data from the National Health and Nutrition Examination Survey, a whopping 40 percent of the total calories the average two- to eighteen-year-old eats every day comes from empty calories (calories derived from food containing absolutely no nutrients whatsoever). Even worse, half of those empty calories were shown to come from six specific sources: soda, fruit drinks, dairy desserts, grain desserts, pizza, and whole milk.[3]

Decades ago, the thought of soda, commercial chain foods, and other prepackaged unhealthy fare in schools would have been absurd. Now, in many schools, it's what's become the norm because of convenience, leaving today's kids at the mercy of what's being served more than ever before.

Cause #2: Diet Has Become a Four-Letter Word

In recent years, it's become politically incorrect to use the word *diet* with a child. Behind closed doors, I've had plenty of parents admit to me how they fear bringing up the subject of "how to eat" with their kids. Most believe that it could be seen as a form of food shaming, something that might lead to fueling an eating disorder or other issues in their children down the road.

I can understand that mentality. The only problem: It's made many parents afraid to discuss the subject of proper nutrition with their kids. By being afraid to point out their options, many parents are potentially preventing their sons or daughters from having the nutritional materials their body needs to develop, function, and heal as they were intended to.

Cause #3: It's a Team Effort—and That Means You, Too

I've saved this final one for last because it may be the most critical piece of the puzzle. That's because I believe what may be the biggest motive behind why nutrition remains an area often left neglected is that once a parent has to acknowledge its importance—*then, who's in charge of that?*

For some parents, focusing on their kids' diet from an athletic perspective can be overwhelming—and I get that. Their plates are already full staying on top of their young athletes' sport, from getting their kids to every practice, keeping the family schedule on track, and finding the time to be their children's greatest fan in the stands.

But for other parents, I think it's a matter of not wanting to admit that they don't want to take it on—and if that's you, I understand.

- Maybe you think it will require more work than you've bargained for.

- Maybe you're afraid you'll need to lead by example and have to sit down to certain meals that aren't necessarily things you would want to eat.
- Maybe you don't have a handle on your own nutritional habits, and with so much misinformation floating out there, you're simply afraid of getting it wrong, so it's been easier to ignore your child's diet rather than address it.
- Or maybe you figure, "If I make that for them, they won't eat it—so what's the point?"

No matter where you may fall in this list of excuses, if you're in there somewhere, just know you're completely covered with the Replenish portion of the Tommy John Solution. How so?

Replenishing is easier than you think! What I'll be proposing isn't some complicated diet that requires a lot of effort. It's simply a collection of reminders of certain nutrients that young athletes need, as well as warnings about which bad foods to stay away from.

Replenishing is tastier than expected! Many of the foods I'll be recommending are foods your young athletes' body already craves to help it heal. And in many cases, foods they love (such as bacon and eggs) but have shied away from, due to assuming those foods would have an adverse impact on their overall performance.

Replenishing is an easier sell—if sold the right way! When some parents tell me it's pointless because their kids will only turn down certain healthy foods, I believe that might be true the first twelve times. But by the thirteenth time, if the right lineup of foods is all that exists in the house—and that's all Mom or Dad are serving for dinner—you'd be surprised what they would be receptive to.

But the older your athletes are, the less control you may have over what they eat when you're not around. That's when I suggest speaking to them in the same way I do with all of my teenage, college, or pro athletes—and yes, even the parents—that I work with.

To really get the Replenishing techniques in this section to stick, it's important to help your children recognize any differences in how they feel and perform as they make each subtle change to how and what they eat. It could be as simple as reminding them:

- The reason they did so well on their math test was that they received a brain-boosting amount of healthy fats, thanks to the slice of avocado they had with their breakfast.
- They jumped higher during practice because of the magnesium-rich leafy salad they had at lunch—a key nutrient that plays a major role in muscle recovery, and has been shown to increase the vertical leap of volleyball players by as much as 3 cm.[4]

Even if that slice of avocado probably wasn't the main catalyst for crushing that math test, and even if that salad might not have been the one thing that made them play better that day, it's just about getting in the habit of associating what they eat with how they perform in all aspects of their life. Once your young athletes finally begin to see the connection between food and function, getting them to eat healthier when out of your supervision will become that much easier.

BEFORE YOU BEGIN—DON'T START JUST YET

Among the four parts of the Tommy John Solution, Replenish is the only one I want you to hold off on until you've spent at least one full month using the Rethink, Rebuild, and Recover sections.

One full month?

I know what you're thinking.

Wait—what? TJ . . . you've just spent pages explaining why replenishing the body is one of the most important components of the Tommy John Solution. So, why shouldn't you begin making these changes with your son or daughter right now?

You could. In many facilities like mine that address the performance, health, and wellness of a human being, young athletes are immediately given some sort of a meal plan or told to keep a food log, right on Day 1. But I've found with the athletes I work with that by jumping into a strict diet plan, all that does is create another thing that the children have to worry about—another worry that triggers their fight-or-flight response, leaving them in a state of sympathetic dominance—only this time, it's being created around food.

Just as their sport itself shouldn't be a stressful thing in young athletes' life, neither should what they eat. After all, this isn't about calorie counting—it's just about making sure that whatever calories they are eating actually count. This isn't about fat loss—this is about explaining what is lost through sport and what is needed to replenish and replace viable nutrients along the way.

When young athletes walk into my office, I may focus on everything from their reason for seeing me and identify the dysfunctions they have, to how we'll correct those dysfunctions together through the right training options and lifestyle habits. But instead of hitting them right from the start with some nutritional program that feels too brutal to tackle, I never make any changes to their diet that first day.

All I ever do is explain what is important regarding nutrition (all of which I'm about to share with you in this section), offer a few sources they can research on their own, then tell them to table all those things—*at least for now.* Then, as we go, I begin to make certain suggestions, such as how they may need to increase their intake of clean protein or healthy fats. But I always keep it general—and never specific.

One reason I do it this way is that, contrary to what many diet and lifestyle programs may tell you, there really isn't one way to eat. Every single person that walks into my office is different, and I love watching athletes young and old find their own nutritional habits.

But here's something you wouldn't expect.

More often than not, as young athletes progress through the Tommy John Solution, many of them will approach me before I can make my first suggestion because *they* want to take their nutrition to the next level. It's a phenomenon that used to surprise me, but now I've come to expect it.

That's because as they finally begin moving their body in the ways that they were intended and designed for, as they start to give their body adequate time to recover, and slowly remove many of the harmful lifestyle habits that have been holding them back, then, all of a sudden—their body begins to crave certain things naturally. I've had young athletes suddenly craving butter, bacon, cabbage, and other foods that seemed strange to them at the time, but I understood what's going on. It was just their body looking for certain building blocks necessary to evolve and grow.

So, when it comes to the following foods, *I want you to wait a month, then slowly begin to suggest certain changes.* With each change, make your children aware of the connection between what they're eating with how they're feeling or performing. Do it right, and you will help those healthy habits stick not just through each season, but for the rest of their life.

THE LOSING LINEUP THAT ALWAYS FAILS

As I mentioned, I don't believe in strict diets for young athletes. But I do stand by getting them to reconsider what they're putting into their body.

Within this list of "watch out for" foods, some may seem obvious—others may surprise you—but by getting your kids to either reduce or eliminate the following types of foods, they'll be that much closer to removing what's holding them back from performing at their best and increasing their risk of injury, both in and out of their sport.

Foods That Don't Rot (or Last Longer Than They Should)

When food starts to spoil, it may be annoying for the parent, who most likely paid for it. But it's a natural process to be thankful for, especially if your goal is getting your children to make wiser food choices when you're not around.

You see, trying to get younger athletes to understand why processed foods pumped full of preservatives are unhealthy—then expect them to read food labels and understand what to look for—pretty much ensures that they won't. After all, if most adults have a difficult time interpreting food labels, what chance do you think your son or daughter has?

I found that it's not high on a kid's priority list to care much about the effect processed foods may be having on them, despite the alarming research that's out there regarding children. Beyond the obvious negatives—increased risk of obesity and diabetes, increased risk of high blood pressure[5] from excess sodium, and encouraging food addiction and addictive-like eating[6]—processed foods have been shown to have a staggering effect on children's overall development across the board.

From lowering their IQ[7] to potentially having a link to autism—one notable study published in *Clinical Epigenetics*[8] discovered that the high consumption of additives typically found in processed foods (such as high-fructose corn syrup) contributes to mineral deficiencies that could contribute to autism spectrum disorders—the list is potentially endless.

Could you take the approach of having your children avoid foods that have ingredients they don't recognize on the label? You could, but I wouldn't. Should you give them a list of the countless ways the word *sugar* is disguised on food labels, so that they have no clue how much they're eating when it's called by such terms as corn sweetener, evaporated cane juice, crystal dextrose, carbitol, and maltodextrin?

Again, you could, but it's pressure they don't need to put on themselves. It's also a guaranteed way to make sure they don't do it, no matter how much you push them.

That's why I keep it simple with my young athletes. I explain how all it takes is the right mix of moisture, oxygen, and the right temperature, for microscopic bacteria to multiply and begin breaking down food. Then, I ask this question: If there are certain foods that even bacteria won't touch—*do you think they know something you don't?*

Making that connection to which foods to avoid is as simple as taking a lesson from nature itself. It's as simple as having them look at the food they're about to throw back and ask themselves: "*Will this rot if I leave it out for a while—or will it pretty much look the same in a week?*"

WHAT'S BRIGHT MAY BE DIMMING

Like a bee to a flower, artificial colors are usually added to certain foods to attract us—especially kids. Over time, these brighter and bolder colors begin to trigger a digestive response, which makes children crave them even more. But even if your young athletes have a handle on their hunger, those artificial colors could be affecting them in ways you're not aware of.

The negative effects of artificial food coloring (AFC) have been studied for more than thirty-five years.[9] A now-classic study from the University of Southampton[10] found that among young children (ranging from three to eight years old), consuming artificial food colors (along with the preservative sodium benzoate) caused an increased level of hyperactivity—behavior defined by increased movement, impulsivity, and inattention. Within as little as six weeks, researchers noticed that children given a drink that contained food colors and sodium benzoate were significantly more hyperactive than children that consumed additive-free fruit juice.

To stay on the safe side, especially during a critical time in the development of your children's brain (when certain neurological patterns and habits are being formed that will carry them throughout life), remind them that what may be attracting their attention *now* could prevent them from achieving *later*.

Most of the stuff they shouldn't be eating is the stuff that never goes bad and can sit there forever. It's the stuff that comes in a box or bag. It's that energy bar they opened and left in their training bag, only to find it unchanged three weeks later. It's any food they've never seen wilt, rot, or spoil because it's been processed and made not to. It's making them realize that nature never makes mistakes, so if nature doesn't want it, your body doesn't need it.

Overhydration—the Myth of "Health Through Water"

It's a scenario I saw time and time again when giving baseball lessons, and it's something I still see at every game and every practice I go to, no matter what sport and no matter what age the athlete: Parents practically trip over themselves, racing to get their children their water bottle so they can stay properly hydrated.

When I train young athletes, and they ask me during their session whether they can have some water, I'll often say no and tell them that they're okay. Because quite honestly, believe it or not, they are.

Instead, I have them channel that craving and discomfort toward being present with what they're doing right then and there, then let them know they can have water as a reward afterward. I essentially shut down that need to hydrate and prove to them that they can function just fine without water at that moment.

I know this somewhat flies in the face of convention since one of the biggest trends today is "health through water." I also get that inadequate hydration is a very real issue for kids today. According to the first national study[11] of its kind out of the Harvard T. H. Chan School of Public Health, more than half of all children and adolescents in the United States are not getting enough hydration, a situation that could have significant repercussions for their physical health and their cognitive and emotional functioning.

When researchers looked at data on more than four thousand children and adolescents between six and nineteen years old, they found that boys were 76 percent more likely than girls, and non-Hispanic blacks 34 percent more likely than non-Hispanic whites, to be inadequately hydrated. The assumption is that kids aren't drinking enough water. But personally, I think it may be the other way around.

See, I barely drink water unless I'm thirsty or sitting down for a meal—and my healthiest clients do the same. But what surprises many is that my hydration levels (and those of my clients) are roughly 15 percent higher than those of people that make it a point to drink as much water as possible throughout the day. Even more shocking: when I've used a body fat scale that measures water with clients in my office, I've clinically observed over the years that the least hydrated people tend to be the ones that drink the most water.

I'm not saying that water isn't great for the body—just the opposite. Staying properly hydrated is crucial for maintaining every single system throughout your children's body. But throughout many sports today, many kids are trying to earn health by killing water. In a nutshell, they're overdoing it, yet strangely enough, they're also dehydrated as a result.

So . . . what exactly is going on?

1. Not enough water-rich foods: In the United States, it's estimated[12] that about 22 percent of water comes from our food, which is lower compared to European countries, such as Greece, whose residents enjoy a higher intake of healthy fats, along with fruits and vegetables in their diet. Why that is important to know is related to how your children's body was naturally meant to absorb water.

What's not widely known is that our body is naturally designed to take in water primarily from the foods we eat. Think about it: Historically, our ancestors weren't walking around with bottles of water strapped to their hips, sipping exactly 8 to 12 ounces every fifteen minutes at all times, in fear of dehydration. They may wet their mouth when they got hot, or used water to wash down food when they ate meals, but when you're eating the right foods, hydration is automatically taken care of.

The main reason water-rich foods are a smarter way to hydrate is how they make your young athletes' body more efficient at getting water where it needs to go. You see, when your kid eats a water-rich food, such as a fruit or vegetable, they aren't just taking in water—they're also taking in nutrients. Whenever water is attached to something (such as vitamins and minerals), the body quickly takes those nutrients where they're needed, using whatever water is attached to help shuttle those nutrients throughout the body.

When water acts as a carrier for nutrients, it's able to be implemented into cells more efficiently. It's why, for the most part, I don't believe many kids are necessarily dehydrated—I simply think it's a matter of young athletes' being malnourished.

2. Too much water—and nothing else: The bottled water industry has done such a fantastic job at getting us to believe that H_2O is vital for athletes, that not drinking it constantly will hurt their performance. When the reality is, their body doesn't necessarily know what to do with all that extra water after they drink it.

When your kids take in plain water that's not accompanied by anything else, their body brings it in and—for the most part—pushes it right back out. Most of that water finds its way into the stomach, and don't get me wrong, some of it does get absorbed into the body. But for the most part, the balance of that liquid passes through because taken in that way, your body's ability to absorb it simply isn't as efficient. It's the reason why so many young athletes are operating on a half-tank at all times, even though they are consuming large amounts of water before, during, and after practice or games. They are making the mistake of trying to solve their hydration problem through liquid alone.

All that unnecessary water can also lead to hyponatremia, an overhydration of the cells that dilutes the concentration of minerals in the blood. Among young athletes, overhydrating can specifically lead to exercise-associated hyponatremia (EAH),[13] a condition that occurs when the body has too much water relative to sodium. As the salt level in a person's blood drops far below normal, it can lead to significant neurological problems ranging from mild (difficulty thinking, headaches, and vomiting) to the severe, with symptoms ranging from severe confusion, seizures, coma, and even death.

3. Too much reliance on sports drinks: Quick question—when was the last time your children ever sweated red or blue?

Exactly! So, first and foremost, if they're drinking something that is intentionally putting artificial food coloring into their body—something shown to cause hyperactivity in kids—then what else is in there that they don't necessarily need?

If that's not enough to convince you to have your young athletes forsake sports drinks entirely, think about this: The very point of a sports drink is to replace water and certain key minerals and electrolytes lost during long bouts of intense activity. When they were developed decades ago for athletes, they were designed for athletes engaging in a minimum of sixty minutes of continuous activity in high-heat conditions.

But if you think that's your kid, then think again.

A popular cross-sectional study[14] that compared the physical activity during youth sports practices found that the average amount of time spent doing moderate to vigorous physical activity during practice is about forty-five minutes total. Overall, only 24 percent of the participants in this study met the minimum guidelines of at least sixty minutes of moderate to vigorous physical activity, with fewer than 10 percent of eleven- to fourteen-year-olds and 2 percent of girl softball players hitting those guidelines.

Another misconception is that sports drinks provide energy. When I hear parents tell me that their child has been so down and out that they've been fueling them with sports drinks (or even worse, energy drinks), I immediately ask their kids why they feel down in the first place. Almost every time, if I'm dealing with young athletes with low energy, it's not that they're lethargic because they need more sports drinks in their diet—it's a matter of their being malnourished.

Yet thanks to endless marketing, much of which is directed toward kids, sports drinks are more popular than ever with young athletes—and even kids not participating in sports at all. One recent study[15] out of Cardiff University found that among twelve- to fourteen-year-olds, half of the kids surveyed consumed sports drinks purely for social reasons, with taste being the primary reason (90%), compared to the 18 percent that claimed they drank them for their perceived performance-enhancing effect.

That dependence is causing a lot of issues in youth today, including increasing their risk of diabetes (since many leading brands typically have as much as two-thirds the sugar of soda) and obesity. One study published in the journal *Obesity*[16] discovered that young people who drank as little as one sports drink daily gained more weight over a three-year period than did their classmates who chose other beverages. Among girls, each daily serving of a sports drink saw a 0.3 increase in their body mass index (BMI) over two to three years. (Males were roughly the same, with each daily serving causing a 0.33 BMI jump over the same amount of time.)

For something your children don't even need in the first place, sports drinks are even doing damage where you least expect it. According to the Academy of General Dentistry,[17] the alarming rise in the consumption of sports and energy drinks, particularly among adolescents, is even causing irreparable damage to teeth. In one study,[18] when enamel and root surfaces of healthy permanent molars and premolars were exposed for twenty-five hours to different beverages (including Gatorade, Red Bull, Coke, 100% apple juice, and Diet Coke), it was the sports drink that caused the most erosion to both enamel and roots.

FORGET THE SODA—FOR THEIR SAKE

Even though it's hard to avoid at most sporting events, soda is another obvious off-the-table option. But my reasoning goes way beyond the fact that it's packed with empty calories and excess sugar. It's now due to the dangers it may be causing young athletes, especially if they are turning to soda as a way to rehydrate during long hot games or practices.

A 2016 study[19] published in the *American Journal of Physiology— Regulatory, Integrative and Comparative Physiology* found that among rats, drinking soft drinks to rehydrate worsened dehydration and kidney injury. The rats that drank fructose-glucose water (the content of an average soft drink) after repeated heat-induced dehydration were found to be more dehydrated (and had worse kidney injury) than those that consumed either plain water or water with stevia.

Fruit and Vegetable Juice

In general, when speaking to parents, I never have to sell the role fruits and vegetables play in their young athletes' overall development. But what I do have to remind many is how it's less about *which* fruits and vegetables their children eat, compared to *how* they serve those fruits and vegetables.

There's a common belief among many parents that if they can't get vitamins and minerals into their kids by feeding them healthy fruits and vegetables, then the next best alternative is juice. Even worse, I've had parents come to me believing they were benefiting their child by offering them capsules that contained the same healthy equivalence of vitamins and minerals found in vegetables and fruits.

But I don't support shortcuts—and neither should you.

If you're worried about your young athletes' not getting their fill of fruits and vegetables by taking juice off the table, then don't—I'll explain how to solve that problem later in this section. But for now, I want you to understand why I encourage every parent not to serve their kids juice.

The first reason is the obvious one that some parents recognize, which is how the juicing process removes most—if not all, depending on the machine—of the fiber contained in produce. Some argue that's a good thing, claiming that helps the body absorb nutrients more efficiently and gives the digestive system a break. However, according to the Mayo Clinic,[20] "there's no sound scientific evidence that extracted juices are healthier than the juice you get by eating the fruit or vegetable itself."

But it's the removal of fiber from kids' diet that's more frightening. The amount of fiber young athletes need each day depends on their age:[21] 4 to 8 years old, 17 grams female/20 grams male; 9 to 13 years old, 22 grams female/25 grams male; 14 to 18 years old, 25 grams female/31 grams male. Yet according to national data, dietary fiber intakes are inadequate in most US children, with teenagers being even less likely to meet their recommendation than younger children.[22]

The second reason: Even if your son or daughter isn't fiber deficient, juicing removes a natural process that's essential for proper digestion. When parents ask me whether I have a blender or juicer, I tell them I do—then I point to my mouth.

The original blender or juicer is our teeth, saliva, and jaw muscles, all working together to break down our foods. Every time we chew, it triggers a neural connection with our stomach, telling it to get hydrochloric acid ready for digestion because something is coming down that needs to be broken down and assimilated.

But by "drinking" fruits and vegetables, our body never gets that signal, nor does our saliva begin the process of predigesting our food. As those foods reach our stomach, they never get digested properly, so more of it passes through our system, preventing as many essential nutrients from being absorbed. Basically, by making the process easier to get healthier foods into your kids, you're making it easier for those healthier foods to pass through their system at a quicker pace, preventing as many essential nutrients from being utilized.

Also, breaking down fruits and vegetables into juice form makes it easier not only for your young athletes to consume excess calories, but it allows all the sugar naturally found in those foods to get dumped into your children's system at a much faster pace. That sugar rush triggers an abnormally large release of insulin (the hormone responsible for stabilizing blood sugar levels) which immediately stores all that excess sugar as glucose within the body. The problem: That quick response can cause your kids' blood sugar to drop quickly, leaving them reaching for more sugar.

The result: It creates a vicious roller coaster of energy highs and lows, leaving your young athletes either jittery or sluggish, but never at an even level that is ideal for peak performance.

Drinking Cow's Milk

I used to be a huge milk drinker (especially when I was young), for the reasons I'm sure you understand all too well as a parent. When your entire focus as a kid is to become a better athlete, cow's milk was that one thing you could pull out of your fridge that made you believe you were building an unstoppable body with every glass.

Why is that exactly? The main reason is that the dairy industry has done a fantastic job of making us believe cow's milk is one of the best, most convenient, and highly efficient sources of protein (to build muscles), calcium (essential for growing strong bones), and vitamin D (which, among other jobs, promotes the absorption of calcium). Those three reasons alone make cow's milk one of the hardest things to reconsider for some parents that I work with.

First things first: Although cow's milk has all three of those essential nutrients, if your children are eating right, they are most likely getting those nutrients in abundance through other sources:

- The 8 grams of protein in one glass of milk can easily be found in other foods, including beans, eggs, nuts, and meat (a single ounce of chicken, beef, pork, or fish typically contains just as much—if not more).
- Calcium is also found in many other sources besides milk, including beans, greens, and nuts (especially almonds).
- Vitamin D (an essential nutrient that doesn't occur naturally in milk—it's added) is free, since it's also synthesized within the body whenever your kids are exposed to ultraviolet rays from sunlight.

Fortunately, I'm beginning to see a shift with parents' being aware more than ever that milk from cows isn't necessarily good for their children, although many still aren't sure why it's such a poor nutritional choice. The first concern they have is what's being injected into cows, such as the growth hormone IGF-1, which is an issue up for debate. But even if your children are drinking cow's milk that is hormone-free, there's still the issue of extra calories and sugar. In a 2014 study,[23] the *Archives of Disease in Childhood* discovered that preschoolers who drink three or more servings of milk a day were likelier to be taller, but also just as likely to be obese and overweight.

Another issue finally being brought up is whether or not cow's milk even lives up to its claims, with new research debating whether milk actually makes children's bones any stronger. A twenty-two-year-long study[24] published in the journal *JAMA Pediatrics* investigated whether drinking milk during one's teens (ages 13 to 18) reduced the incident of hip fracture as adults. The answer—not only did it not reduce the risk, but it discovered that each additional glass of milk consumed daily during their teenage years increased the risk of hip fracture as adults by 9 percent.

But beyond the data that continue to come out about cow's milk, it comes down to one thing: Your children's body was never meant to consume it in the first place.

We are one of the only species on the planet that drink another animal's milk— milk that by design is produced by an animal with four stomachs for a baby cow that also has four stomachs. Think about that. It's designed to be digested by an animal that has a four-stomach system.

Whenever a parent comes to me and tells me that their kid is lactose intolerant, it doesn't surprise me, because—guess what?—we all are. Your kids' body is supposed to be. When people are lactose intolerant, it's because they can't digest the main sugar found in milk (lactose) because the enzyme needed in their body to make that happen (lactase) stops being produced by their body between the ages of two and five. Once children finally have the teeth needed to break down solid food, their body naturally shuts down the production of lactase.

The fact that many kids can digest milk after they no longer produce lactase is merely a genetic adaptation. In fact, being able to digest milk at all is so strange that many scientists believe that we're not necessarily lactose intolerant, but that many people have become "lactase persistent," meaning that their body is continuing to produce lactase like an infant, solely so that they can continue to drink milk. It's yet another example of how kids today are holding onto processes that should be eliminated in infancy but kept in play unnecessarily through their youth and even through adulthood.

CHAPTER 8

The Best Foods That Nourish, Boost Performance, and Promote Healing

The Tommy John Solution is far from a diet—it's only a simple series of easy-to-incorporate suggestions of foods that help reverse
the damage caused from being overfed and malnourished. Foods
that work in tandem with the other three portions of this book to help
boost performance, promote healing, and make your son or daughter a
better all-around athlete.

If you were looking for exact measurements (grams, ounces, you
name it) with some of my starting lineup foods, then look somewhere
else. You'll be as disappointed as some parents I work with—parents that
expect an exact plan because they're worried about getting it wrong.
But again, the reason I never get that specific isn't just because this isn't
a diet—it's because what I'm about to suggest is relatively foolproof.

For the most part, unless I tell you otherwise, your kids can eat as
much of each as they like, depending on which foods they begin to
crave as they go through the Tommy John Solution. Because of how
effective most are concerning satiety, it's fairly hard to overdo the foods
I'm about to recommend. In fact, they would almost have to make it
their job to do so.

That said, here's my all-natural approach to performance nutrition
that puts young athletes that much further ahead of their competition.

HAVE ESSENTIAL HEALTHY FATS
WITH EVERY MEAL OR SNACK

I don't care about how many grams of healthy fats they have at each serving or which foods they get it from. *I just tell young athletes to have some form of healthy fat present at every meal or snack.* How much doesn't matter to me—and it shouldn't to you, either. As long as it's there in front of them, that's half the battle. Besides, the minute they have to measure something or think too hard about it, you've lost them.

You see, there's a massive lack of healthy fats in young athletes' diet today, and it can be blamed on the diet industry. Fats have gotten a stigma as being the enemy, a label that's only become more believed as the growing number of overweight and obese kids in this country continues to rise. But the right type of healthy fats is crucial for brain growth, nerve development, and hormone balance—and plays a major factor when it comes to children's overall sports performance.

Right now, they are in a period of their life when their central nervous system (CNS)—the complex of nerve tissues that controls every activity of the body, and the system responsible for triggering the release of essential hormones—is beginning to fully develop. This is the wiring, if you will, that carries information from their brain through the body and vice versa.

That wiring, by the way, relies on fat.

Believe it or not, the fattest organ in kids' body is their brain, which is made up of roughly 60 percent fat.[1] When they get enough healthy fats in their diet, it improves synaptic transmission, cognitive ability, and creates a positive brain environment for overall health by involving molecules that act on metabolism and synaptic plasticity, according to researchers.[2] But when they don't get enough, the exact opposite happens, which result in a body that's out of sync with itself from head to toe.

Today's young athletes' body and brain are starving for essential fatty acids. The ironic thing I tell clients is there are two populations of people that need healthy fats the most—children and the elderly. It's at the tail ends of our life that we need healthy fats the most. Yet when I share with parents some of the foods their kids should be eating (such as grass-fed butter, coconut oil, egg yolks, nuts, bacon—and, yes, I'll say it—cooking in old-fashioned lard), their expressions are priceless.

But if you care about your young athletes' development, incorporating this important nutrient back into their eating habits is key. Here are just a few ways they can do it that take little effort.

Grass-fed Butter

Compared to butter produced by grain-fed cows, not only does grass-fed butter contain five times[3] as much conjugated linoleic acid (CLA)—a fatty acid believed to have anticancer benefits—but it's also higher in omega-3 fatty acids. When it comes to your young athletes, research has shown that omega-3 fatty acids run the gamut when it comes to improving sports performance, ranging from developing faster reaction times in athletes,[4] reducing inflammation,[5] preventing delayed onset muscle soreness,[6] and even aiding in building more muscle.[7]

How to add it to your kids' diet: Getting them to eat grass-fed butter shouldn't be a problem, since they can spread it on whatever they would normally use butter with and it tastes virtually the same. But if you're looking for a way to sneak it into their diet, this recipe that I recommend to my clients never fails:

CINNAMON TOAST BITES

1 slice sourdough bread
1 tablespoon raw organic honey
1½ teaspoons grass-fed butter
1 to 2 teaspoons organic Ceylon cinnamon
Pinch of Himalayan salt

➤ Toast the sourdough bread.
➤ Combine the honey, grass-fed butter, cinnamon to taste, and salt in a small saucepan over medium heat, then stir until melted.
➤ Pour onto the toasted bread and let the mixture soak in for 2 to 3 minutes.
➤ Cut into small pieces.

Coconut Oil

Long considered unhealthy (because around 90% of its fat is saturated fat), coconut oil is also made up of mostly medium-chain triglycerides (MCTs), which are processed slightly differently by the body than other dietary fats.

From young athletes' perspective, MCTs have been shown to improve the regulation of blood sugar,[8] giving athletes an even source of energy throughout the day, and they curb hunger, making the children less likely to reach for bad-for-them impulse foods.[9] Also ongoing research is being done to see coconut oil's effect on balancing hormone levels and helping support the immune system.

Just be aware there are several types of coconut oil that you can purchase. Your best bet: always choose an unrefined (a.k.a. virgin) oil, which contains more phytonutrients (meaning plant-based nutrients) and flavor. Otherwise, you're probably buying a refined coconut oil, which is bleached and though less pure, it's safer to cook with at higher temperatures.

How to add it to your kids' diet: I recommend to parents that instead of using other oil or butter when cooking foods (especially vegetables), switch to using a little coconut oil instead. This trick not only ensures they have a little fat in their meal, but it sweetens the taste of vegetables that may seem bitter to their kids.

Because of its high melting point, coconut oil stays solid at room temperature, making it hard to mix into many things. I've had parents ask whether their children could just scoop it into their mouth—and the answer is yes. I've personally done it, but if kids aren't used to digesting that much fat, it could cause a negative response, such as cramps or loose stools. But I've had more success introducing it into young athletes' diet in the following ways:

- Spread it on a piece of whole-grain toast.
- Add ¼ teaspoon to a small handful of nuts and sprinkle cacao nibs on top.
- Take a tablespoon of organic unsweetened peanut butter, then drizzle some coconut oil on top.
- Melt together a tablespoon each of honey and coconut oil, mix in a pinch of Himalayan salt, then drizzle over an apple. (The honey and coconut combined become an amazing caramel.)

Organic Pastured (Cage-free) Eggs

Getting young athletes to eat eggs is usually never a problem, but breaking them of the habit of tossing the yolks sometimes is. But both came together in the egg, and you should eat them together—it's as simple as that. Not only does the yolk contain half of an egg's total protein, but it's rich in omega-3 fatty acids, seven vitamins (including vitamin D, B_6, and B_{12}), along with carotenoids that protect your children's eyes from losing the ability to correctly focus light.

Egg yolks are also one of the richest sources of choline, an essential nutrient that plays a significant role in brain development, cell signaling, nerve impulse transmission, and lipid transport and metabolism. It's crucial for boosting sports performance, but unfortunately, most of us—especially kids—aren't getting enough on a daily basis,[10] according to a recent study published in the *Journal of the American College of Nutrition.*

How to add them to your kids' diet: Instead of treating eggs as only a breakfast food, boil a dozen at the start of the week, so they're always within arms' reach. Or treat them like the convenience food they are and throw one in your children's sports bag for a midpractice snack.

Raw Nuts and Seeds

Whatever the kind, all nuts and seeds are a fantastic source of polyunsaturated fats, along with fiber, magnesium, antioxidants, and protein—all of which are indispensable in promoting healing, building lean muscle, and improving the performance of young athletes both physically and neurologically.

Better still, just one serving daily could extend not only their sports career but their life. In a recent project[11] that involved 819,000 subjects across twenty-nine international studies, it was found that eating less than an ounce of nuts (roughly what would fit in a child's palm) reduced the risk of cardiovascular disease, total cancer, all-cause mortality, and mortality from respiratory disease, diabetes, and infections.

How to add them to your kids' diet: Eating nuts and seeds isn't the problem, since having a handful as a snack is about as easy as it gets for kids. However, if children aren't particular, don't just stick with one type. I recommend buying as many different kinds of nuts and seeds as possible, then mixing them all together. This can give the young athletes' an added edge in their sport since certain nuts and seeds have different performance perks. Beyond the more traditional nuts (almonds, walnuts, peanuts, etc.), here are just a few other types I encourage all athletes to mix in:

- **Pumpkin seeds:** Rich in leucine—an amino acid that can help promote fat oxidation and endurance, they're also packed with vitamin K (which contributes to bone growth and healing).
- **Brazil nuts:** A single 1-ounce serving has over one quarter of the recommended daily allowance for magnesium (which plays a key role in how muscles function and how efficiently your children's body both breaks down protein and absorbs energy from foods). The nut also contains one quarter of the recommended daily allowance (RDA) for copper, critical for building, maintaining, and protecting both bone and connective tissue.
- **Cashews:** Teeming with magnesium and copper, cashews also have a healthy amount of iron, essential for producing red blood cells, which carry oxygen throughout the body for energy.
- **Pecans:** In addition to supporting young athletes' cardiovascular system, among all nuts, pecans have the highest ORAC (oxygen radical absorbance capacity) score, which measures a food's ability to squash free radicals, the unstable molecules in the body that damage cells and contribute to disease.

Avocados

High in monounsaturated fat, avocados are also teeming with antioxidants, fiber, and twenty vitamins and minerals that speed up recovery times, prevent muscle cramps, and naturally reduce inflammation—and that's just a few of the immediate effects on your children.

By getting them used to eating more of this superfruit on a regular basis, you'll also be helping them live a long and healthy life. That's because a new 2017 study[12] concluded that eating avocado daily may prevent metabolic syndrome (the term for a group of risk factors, such as high blood pressure, abnormal cholesterol, and excess body fat around the waist, that increase the risk of diabetes, stroke, and heart disease).

How to add them to your kids' diet: Before you do, if your young athletes are allergic to latex, talk to their doctor before adding avocado to their diet as an essential healthy fat. (It's been shown that individuals with a serious allergy to latex may also experience symptoms after eating the fruit.) If the answer's no, and if eating a slice straight is too much effort, the fruit can be introduced in a number of easy ways.

- Spread half of an avocado over a piece of whole-grain toast and add a pinch of Himalayan salt.
- Add it as a topping on a lean hamburger or over eggs.
- Use it as a condiment to replace mayonnaise, cream cheese, mustard, or ketchup.
- Chop it up into tiny chunks and mix into a fruit salad.
- Turn it into guacamole and keep it handy as a dip for fresh vegetables.

Pasture-Raised Bacon and Lard

I'll admit it—these are the two recommendations that confuse parents the most to get more fat into their young athletes' diet. Back when fat became the enemy in the early 1990s, both bacon and lard began to be looked at negatively. But when a pig is fed in the right way—hormone-free and pasture-raised (free-range)—its meat is much healthier to eat (in moderation of course). Plus, lard is one of the highest food sources around of vitamin D. Just 1 tablespoon from a pasture-raised pig contains roughly 1,000 IU worth, whereas olive oil has absolutely none.

How to add them to your kids' diet: First, if you can't find pasture-raised bacon or organic lard in the store, visit localharvest.org, which will help you locate a farm in your area. After that, serving up a slice of bacon isn't difficult, but adding a little lard into children's diet takes a little effort—although it's easier than you would expect. (Note: I personally recommend wallacefarms.com, which ships to all 50 states and internationally, because it's highly transparent in its practices—and its bacon is the absolute best.)

When cooking with either oil or butter, switch to a tablespoon of lard instead. It's not just for the added flavor it infuses into vegetables and meats (which I've found makes it easier to get young athletes to eat even more veggies) but also due to how it protects food from losing as many nutrients when being cooked. Cooking with high heat with such oils as canola, corn, or olive actually changes a food's structure, destroying nutrients while causing the release of free radicals (which can cause inflammation). However, the chain of fatty acids within lard helps protect food and minimizes that denaturing, so your foods retain more nutrients.

Eat Only Clean Animal Protein

Protein is the building block behind every cell in your children's body. It's not only used to make and grow bone, meniscus, cartilage, tendons, ligaments, muscles, and blood, but to repair all of the above as well. It's also the macronutrient that plays a huge role in helping their body maintain fluid, in addition to producing enzymes, hormones, and other important chemicals that assist with function, growth, and development.

With all those jobs and all that responsibility, doesn't it just make sense to have your kid eat the best protein possible?

Many parents I work with swear that they never have a problem getting their kids to eat protein. What they're less clear about is the difference between having them throw back a few hot dogs versus eating clean animal protein, such as grass-fed beef, pastured pork, free-range organic chicken, or wild game or fish.

But then I explain protein's major role and how it's behind the growth and repair of every single square inch of their kids' body. I remind them how their kids are in a constant state of development, growing and maturing so rapidly that their body can barely keep up. I educate them about how playing and training for sports basically break down their children in a controlled setting, causing microtraumas throughout their body that need to be repaired to bring them back to homeostasis.

Finally, I ask them: "Your kids' body desperately needs protein for repair, recovery, and regeneration so they will always come back to the field or court an even better version of themselves than when they walked off it—so, which building blocks are you going to give them? A processed hot dog filled with who knows what—or a clean, hormone-free source of animal protein that will give their body the best building blocks possible?"

How to add it to your kids' diet: As long as the meat your children are eating is organic, pastured, and/or grass-fed, I don't care what source they prefer—whether it's grass-fed beef, pastured pork, free-range organic chicken, or wild game or fish.

Beyond their being free of antibiotics and hormones, new research[13] has shown that organic meats contain 50 percent more omega-3 fatty acids than conventionally produced products, so the kids win no matter what they eat.

Just be cautious of any meats that are labeled "grass-fed" (but are missing the "organic" label). Certain manufacturers are using a loophole that allows them to feed scraps of GMO (genetically modified) corn (left over from ethanol processing) to cattle. Because those scraps are technically not the original GMO corn, they're not required to stamp "grain-fed" onto the product, and consequently those companies may say "grass-fed" on their label, even though their livestock was fed GMO corn residue.

BUT TOMMY—I'M ON A BUDGET!

I get that—me, too. Many are on some sort of budget where we have to prioritize what we buy, especially when it comes to what we eat. However, I always will stand behind the belief that you should never—ever—be cheap when it comes to buying anything animal related.

If you're buying nonorganic vegetables, that may not be as optimal, but it's not that bad. But with animal products, it's the unknowns regarding how much (and which types) of hormones and/or antibiotics are used that aren't worth the risk. You need to remind yourself that eating organically isn't about following a trend—it's the fact that whatever was injected or ingested into an animal is going right into your children when they eat it. That said, if you only have a limited amount of spend on organic foods, put those dollars toward anything animal-based.

Another money-saving trick: Visit localharvest.org to locate farms in your area. Sometimes, a farm may be organic, but because the process to have its food stamped "organic" can be too pricey for some farmers, they may opt out. Once you find a farm, take a visit to see how the farmers raise their livestock—you may end up finding a great source for healthy meat that's cheaper than you might expect.

GET HYDRATED THE RIGHT WAY

Before I start, you may notice something as your children begin eating the right foods and removing the wrong ones. After a short while, you'll find they are drinking water less often. That's because as they begin to eat more foods that naturally hydrate their body, their need to reach for a water bottle will become less and less. But when they're thirsty, how and what they drink at that moment will either give them a competitive edge—or leave them with less than their body bargained for.

How to add more fluids to your kids' diet: Some coaches tell their athletes to drink a certain number of glasses per day, whereas others might say to take a few sips of something every fifteen minutes of practice or game time.

Me? I personally believe that every practice and competition is different—and that every young athlete is different—so an amount that may be ideal for one kid could easily be too much or not enough for another. I also don't believe in causing stress by telling athletes they must consistently analyze how much they're drinking every waking quarter, inning, or minute. It's yet another trigger that keeps them in a sympathetic dominant state all day long.

Instead, *I just want them always to have at least 16 ounces of some form of water-based drink accessible at all times* (such as tea, infused water, and other options I'll show you next), I also insist that anytime your kid sits down for a meal, there should always be a water-based drink present as well. That way, they can grab a sip whenever they need one—for the most part, their body will tell them when it's time.

What to Drink?

As I mentioned earlier, drinking plain water without anything attached to it makes it less effective for hydration.

Herbal tea: Many times herbal tea gets the label of being a drink only for adults. But making your own herbal tea and keeping it in the fridge is a terrific grab-and-go hydration option that not only refreshes but has just enough nutrients attached to it that your body knows what to do with that water.

Water—with a pinch: If your children insist on having a bottle of water, add a pinch of Himalayan salt, so it turns it into something. Himalayan salt is a natural source of sodium revered for its mineral content (84 minerals total), including iron, magnesium, phosphorus, calcium, potassium, and chloride, all of which are necessary for bodily health and replacing the electrolytes lost during activity.

Tip: They'll know they have the right combination when they take a sip and are just on the verge of tasting something salty, yet have to think about it for a second. For some kids, that might mean a tiny pinch or a few pinches. But even if they add just a few grains, their water will be a bomb of minerals, so it doesn't take a lot of salt.

TJ'S PRIME-TIME LEMON-LIME AID!

With so many kids hooked on sports drinks, I teach young athletes how to make their own, if their true reason for drinking them in the first place is replacing what sports take out of them.

This simple recipe not only mimics the taste of lemon-lime Gatorade, but provides potassium, sodium, plus eighty-six other trace minerals that help replace the electrolytes lost during activity. But the best part is that they can drink as much of it as they need without fear of overconsuming calories or fat-soluble vitamins. Here's all you need:

12 ounces filtered water
1 tablespoon organic apple cider vinegar
1 to 2 tablespoons raw organic honey
Juice of ½ to 1 lemon, strained of seeds
Pinch of Himalayan salt

➤ Shake for 20 to 30 seconds. Chill or pour over ice. Boom!

Kombucha: This fermented drink made by mixing bacteria, yeast, sugar, and either black or green tea, then letting it sit for several weeks, is finally getting its due—and I'm thrilled. Personally, I've been drinking kombucha for years, and when I bring it into my office and have young athletes try it (without telling them what it is or what it does), they love it because its bubbly, tangy taste almost reminds them of a version of soda.

Why do I hold back first telling them what it is or does? When I first introduce this by name to young athletes and parents, they flinch because kombucha gets a bad rep for being some crazy health tonic. That assessment's half right, in that it has been tied to everything from more energy and repairing joints to curing cancer (although the research on most claims is thin).

But what isn't disputable is that kombucha contains a healthy amount of probiotics, the good-for-you bacteria that aid in digestion and work to restore symbiosis between the harmful and the helpful bacteria in your children's gut. When that balance of bacteria shifts to "the bad," it may affect digestive health and impact their immune system. That's why I recommend having just a tiny glass of kombucha either first thing in the morning, right before bed, or simply to wash down their dinner.

TJ'S HOMEMADE KOMBUCHA RECIPE

What you'll need

1 gallon filtered or spring water (not tap water—it could contain chlorine, which can limit or prevent beneficial bacteria and yeasts from growing)

6 to 8 organic black or green tea bags

1 to 2 cups of starter kombucha

1 cup organic granulated cane sugar

1 large, wide-mouth glass container (you could use a 1-gallon mason jar, or even a large glass pitcher)

1 SCOBY (short for "symbiotic culture of bacteria and yeast"; you can purchase one from a health food store or online. Shaped like a giant mushroom, this is the colony of friendly bacteria that ferments the tea.)

1 clean dishcloth (or T-shirt)

Rubber bands

continues

TJ'S HOMEMADE KOMBUCHA RECIPE *continued*

How to make it

➤ Bring the gallon of water to a boil in a large pot. Drop in the tea bags, remove from the heat, then let steep for 20 minutes.

➤ Remove the tea bags, then add the sugar. Let the mixture cool, stirring sporadically to help the sugar dissolve.

➤ Once the mixture is room temperature (that's key—if it's still too hot, the heat could kill some of the live bacteria and yeasts in your SCOBY), pour it into the container.

➤ Add the SCOBY and the starter kombucha.

➤ Cover the top of the container with the cloth and secure it with a rubber band.

➤ Place the container in a dark place (such as a pantry or cabinet) for 7 to 14 days.

➤ After that, it's done. They can drink it as is, or you can add different flavors by removing the SCOBY, pouring the finished kombucha into an airtight bottle, adding in a few flavorings—ranging from fresh ginger and turmeric to fresh fruit, then letting it sit for another few days.

EAT AS MANY ORGANIC FRUITS/ VEGGIES AS POSSIBLE

This obvious suggestion sometimes earns me an eye roll from parents, since most already know fruits and veggies are a fantastic natural source of antioxidants, fiber, vitamins, minerals, and other nutrients—all of which help improve sports performance. Some are even aware of some of the new science emerging, including how nitrate[14]—a compound found in leafy greens, such as spinach—may actually change muscle fiber composition, and in some cases, make the heart stronger.[15]

The real challenge isn't convincing young athletes why they should eat more fruits and vegetables—it's just getting them to do it in the first place. In a perfect world, I would have every young athlete eating the widest variety possible across the spectrum of colors. The richer and brighter a vegetable is, the more nutritionally dense it typically is. But that's a perfect world—and the main reason why most aren't eating more of these superfoods as they should be.

It's too much pressure for a parent, let alone a kid, to figure out the best combination to eat, since every fruit and vegetable has a certain balance of different vitamins and minerals. That's why to get young athletes to eat more of each, I focus on overturning the excuses that might be holding them back from throwing more fruits and vegetables into their sports bag.

Excuse #1: "I Hate Vegetables!"

Whenever I talk to a group of kids, I love asking them to raise their hand if they don't like vegetables. Inevitably, every hand goes up in the room. But when I ask them to raise their hand if they like one vegetable, again, everybody raises a hand. And as I go around the room and ask what that vegetable is, it always—every single time I do this experiment—varies from kid to kid.

The solution: Know that any fruit or veggie counts. Whatever the fruit or vegetable your children love to eat, just let them eat it—even if all they like is celery and grapes. Even though variety is important and can be presented over time, immediately trying to wean kids off the few fruits and vegetables they love and replace them with others is the fastest way to ensure they stop eating them altogether.

If you're worried about vitamin or mineral deficiency, know that as they eat other healthy foods in the Replenish program, those nutritional gaps will automatically be taken care of. Besides, if they seem to prefer certain fruits and vegetables one day and different ones the next day, it might be for a reason. Even if they aren't deficient in any area, the nutrients within that food may be exactly what their body needs for development at that exact period of time.

Excuse #2: "Some Have Too Much Sugar!"

Today, many parents view sugar as the enemy, just as they had decades ago in regard to fat. I have a problem with these extremes, especially because sugar by nature is meant to be utilized by the body, but only in certain forms.

Despite that fact, I've watched some nutritionists make parents nervous about the sugar content of certain vegetables and fruits. It's gotten to the point where some children are afraid to eat carrots because the vegetable is higher in natural sugar compared to other vegetables. Carrots! I'm sorry, but we've officially gone overboard with worrying too much in this particular area.

The solution: Unless they're diabetic—forget the glycemic index: Many fruits and vegetables contain simple sugars (such as fructose and glucose), but they also have less sugar by volume along with plenty of fiber, which slows down digestion and how quickly sugar is absorbed. Those perks alone make it much harder—if not impossible—to achieve the same sugar surge that refined sugars found in processed foods can cause.

Also, when your children get sugar from a natural source, their brain and body recognizes that source and knows what to do with it, so it's processed by the body more efficiently. When that source is unnatural—such as a refined form of sugar— the body's reaction is not the same, which is one reason that refined sugars should be consumed in moderation. With all the nutrients stripped out, the body doesn't know what to do with the sugar being dumped into its system.

In short: As long as your children aren't allergic to anything, have any food sensitivity issues, or are diabetic, then potatoes, bananas, corn, watermelon, pineapple, beets, carrots, and any other high-glycemic fruit or vegetable that has gotten an unnecessarily bad reputation is considered fair game.

Excuse #3: "I'm Afraid They'll Eat Too Much!"

When I hear that statement, I always ask this: "When was the last time you saw anyone obese on a talk show say they became that way by eating too many fruits or vegetables?"

Why that question is always answered with a "never" is because of how the body interprets what it's eating. If your children eat food with no nutritional value, their body will often keep sending a signal to your brain to continue to eat until it gets what it needs. Thanks to the wide variety of artificial, nutrient-less foods that exist on the market today, it's one reason that kids tend to consume more and more unhealthy foods and never feel quite full.

The solution: Let them eat what they like until satisfied: So long as they're getting their fruits and vegetables from the right sources—fiber-filled and fresh, not canned or processed—their body will know when it has everything it needs much faster, signaling their brain that all needs have been met.

How to add more to your kids' diet: The only rule I have is that every time they sit for a meal, there should be a portion of vegetable present (and if possible, make vegetables the majority of the meal). Other than that, your children should simply eat them as often as possible,

- **Make them as convenient as possible.** Having foods that are easy to take on the go (clementines, bananas, apples, or carrots, for example) is one solution. Having others ready in the refrigerator is another, whether that's preparing a fruit salad, having veggie kebabs on hand, or just a bowl of snap peas handy.
- **Pay attention to texture.** Sometimes, kids don't necessarily prefer certain foods because of their texture (crunchy, smooth, juicy, etc.) and not necessarily their taste. If they prefer a specific texture, find other foods that match it.
- **Prepare a vegetable in every way possible**—steamed, roasted, grilled, sautéed, baked, or raw (when possible). Since each style of cooking can bring out a different flavor, your children may discover they don't hate a vegetable—they just prefer a veggie cooked a certain way.

Personally, I'm a big fan of fermenting vegetables, which not only changes the taste of veggies to something young athletes have never tried before, but fortifies them with healthy enzymes and good bacteria. They're also incredibly easy to make, and it's a process that lets children help out if they choose to.

RAW HONEY

I often suggest young athletes have a spoonful of raw honey every day, but not necessarily for any of the antibacterial and anti-inflammatory properties some claim it contains. Even if you're skeptical about the healing properties of honey, the main reason I recommend it is that it's a great natural form of sugar that's also loaded with enzymes and illness-fighting antioxidants.

If you're a honey expert, you might think I'm being hypocritical, since I warned your kids to steer clear of foods that don't rot. Because of its low moisture content and composition, when sealed properly, honey can basically last forever—and it's my only exception to my "rot rule." Actually, it's because it keeps so well that it makes a great emergency energy source for your children's gym bag or locker.

How to add more to your kids' diet: Most store-bought honey that's clear (and pours at room temperature) is processed, lacking in nutrients compared to raw

REPLACE THEIR WATER BOTTLE—WITH AN APPLE?

We live in a society where parents are constantly reminding their children not to forget their water bottle. But I would be thrilled to finally see the day when parents begin to say, "Don't forget your apple."

The fiber-packed fruit isn't just an all-natural appetite regulator, but the nondigestible compounds inside apples (particularly dietary fiber and polyphenols) have been recently shown[16] to act as food for the good bacteria in your children's gut. That way, if your young athletes aren't into fermented foods or drinks, this can be another way to improve their performance by bringing balance to their belly.

However, I like apples because they are around 84 percent water, which is why I call them nature's water bottle. Plus, the natural sugar inside them delivers an even stream of energy that's sustaining for a very long time. If your kids don't like apples, a pear is a good high-fiber, water-rich alternative.

honey. That's why I prefer raw honey, which isn't heated or filtered, so it retains all of its amino acids, vitamins, and minerals, including calcium, iron, potassium, and all the B-complex vitamins (among many other nutrients). Also, color matters, so pick the darkest type you can find. Research[17] has shown that the darker the honey, the more antioxidants it has inside.

With the young athletes I work with, I find having a spoonful of raw honey in the morning right before they head to school gives them a sustainable form of energy that lasts until lunchtime. Suddenly, many find they no longer want the usual junk foods they typically crave in between breakfast and lunch.

Another perfect time: right before practice when they won't be eating dinner until a few hours later. I prefer this to the typical approach many parents take, which is slipping their kids an energy bar. By having a small jar of honey (properly sealed) in their locker or bag, all it takes is one scoop bombed with a little water to wash it down, and now, they have a quick form of immediate and sustainable all-natural, prepractice energy.

INSTANT ENERGY BAR ALTERNATIVE!

Many clients come to me asking for a homemade solution to energy bars, which are nothing more than hyped-up candy bars processed with unnecessary sugar, calories, and artificial ingredients that impair—not improve—sports performance, in my opinion.

My solution is what I call Fastballs. These homemade energy bites take minutes to make and are packed with all-natural ingredients that provide young athletes with a clean source of consistent energy that doesn't trigger either an insulin surge or hypoglycemia.

FASTBALLS

Makes 6 servings

1 cup organic raw oats
⅓ cup organic coconut flakes
½ cup organic raw almond butter
½ cup ground flaxseeds
⅓ cup raw organic honey
1 tablespoon chia seeds
1 teaspoon raw vanilla extract
½ teaspoon organic Ceylon cinnamon
1 teaspoon raw organic cocoa powder
Several pinches of Himalayan salt

➤ Mix together all the ingredients in a bowl. Roll spoonfuls of the mixture into small spheres and place in the freezer. Boom!

IF THEY MUST HAVE MILK—MAKE IT COW-FREE

Even though I've made it clear earlier why I prefer young athletes to eliminate milk altogether, I understand that may be impossible for some parents to pull off. I'm also not a big fan of giving parents too much of a leash because I find when I do that, they will use all of it. But if that's you, then just know that you do have alternatives—it's all about substitution.

If you're not sure which alternative to try to switch your children to, my preference would be to go in the following order (from most preferred to least preferred):

- Coconut milk
- Hemp milk
- Almond (or any other nut) milk
- Raw grass-fed goat's milk (Although goats and cows both have four stomachs, goat's milk has less lactose, making it easier to digest.)
- Grass-fed goat's milk (pasteurized)
- Grass-fed raw cow's milk (Laws vary from state to state regarding the sale of raw milk, so check your state laws and regulations before you buy.)

If you're having trouble getting children to accept these alternatives—and you can pull it off—I suggest playing with the ratios to acclimate them to the taste. Instead of pouring a full glass of milk, fill it three quarters of the way, then top it off with an alternative milk.

The difference in taste will be negligible, and as they slowly adjust to it, you can either continue lessening the amount of cow's milk added, or do what I've had other parents do: just show them the container of what they've been drinking. Trust me, sometimes the battle to make the switch is the uncertainty. But once they realize that milk made from hemp or almonds isn't half bad, getting them to make the change for performance's sake is a much easier sell.

MAKE THEIR SOUP SUPER!

One dietary staple I insist every young athlete try is bone broth. Mainly soup stock with a higher bone-to-meat ratio, it's cooked slowly (around 24 to 72 hours, on average), which pulls joint-healthy gelatin and collagen from the bones, along with other nutrients, such as anti-inflammatory fats, muscle-building amino acids, electrolytes, and assorted vitamins and minerals. Not only is the broth a meal in itself, but with each sip, it helps strengthen bones, protects joints, and has even been shown to boost energy, promote restful sleep, and improve gut health, among other benefits.

Having a cup every one to two days is usually enough to get the job done. You can buy it in a box, but it's just as easy to make your own in a slow cooker, using either leftover bones from a meal or buying bones from a local butcher. Any bones will do, so feel free to mix and match, so long as they are from grass-fed beef or lamb, or organic chicken, turkey, game, or pork. Here's just one way to do it:

3 pounds bones with marrow (raw or leftover cooked)
3 quarts filtered water
1 tablespoon organic apple cider vinegar
1 tablespoon Himalayan salt, plus more to taste

> Place the bones, water, vinegar, and 1 tablespoon of the salt in a slow cooker—remember how high the water level comes to—and cover.
> Bring to a boil, then lower the heat to LOW and let simmer for 24 to 48 hours.
> As it cooks, fat and gelatin will rise to the surface. Don't remove it—that's the nutritious part. Add water as needed to bring the level of the broth back up to the starting level as it evaporates.
> When done cooking, remove from the heat, allow the broth to cool, then discard the bones.
> Add additional Himalayan salt to taste.
> Use the broth within 1 week, or freeze it for up to 2 to 3 months. For even more flavor, try throwing in whatever leftover organic vegetables you may have, or your choice of spices.

TJ'S MVP LIST—REPLENISH (IN A NUTSHELL)!

Wait at least one month after beginning the Tommy John Solution, then slowly begin to suggest the following easy-to-incorporate food suggestions. With each change, talk with your young athletes to make them aware of the connection between what they're eating with how they're feeling throughout the day or performing in their sport.

1. **Eliminate or reduce the following types of foods/drinks:**

   - Any foods that don't rot (or that last longer than they should)
   - Any foods that use artificial food coloring
   - Plain water (with nothing attached to it)
   - Sports (and energy) drinks
   - Soda
   - Cow's milk
   - Fruit or vegetable juice

2. **Add or increase the following types of foods/drinks:**
   Essential healthy fats (with every meal or snack)
   Examples include:

   - Organic grass-fed butter
   - Organic coconut oil
   - Organic pastured (cage-free) eggs
   - Raw nuts and seeds
   - Avocados
   - Organic pasture-raised bacon (in moderation)
   - Organic lard (in moderation)

   Clean animal protein
   Examples include:

   - Organic grass-fed beef
   - Organic pastured pork
   - Free-range organic chicken
   - Wild game
   - Wild fish

continues

TJ'S MVP LIST—REPLENISH (IN A NUTSHELL)! *continued*

At least 16 ounces of some form of water-based drink accessible at all times

Examples include:

- Herbal tea
- Water—with a pinch of Himalayan salt
- Prime-time Lemon-Lime Aid (page 103)
- Kombucha (page 104)

As many organic fruits and veggies as possible

One spoonful of raw honey before school—or immediately after breakfast

If you must have milk—replace it with:

- Coconut milk
- Hemp milk
- Almond (or any other nut) milk
- Raw grass-fed goat's milk
- Grass-fed goat's milk (pasteurized)
- Grass-fed raw cow's milk

1 cup of bone broth every 1 to 2 days

DON'T TURN PRO (-BIOTIC) TOO FAST

As you've probably noticed, the Replenish section relies on a few different types of probiotic foods. All are generally safe for most people, although if a young athlete suffers from any immune system issue (or any other serious health condition), consult a doctor before trying them.

Even if your children aren't sensitive to probiotics, there is a possibility of doing too much—even though they honestly would have to make a job of it. In my experience, eating too many probiotic foods may cause mild side effects, such as an upset stomach, diarrhea, gas, and bloating (which in many ways isn't any different than overdoing soda, cow's milk, and other unhealthy foods). To be on the safer side, try introducing the probiotics in smaller amounts to see whether your children have any issues with them.

SAMPLE NEXT-LEVEL MEALS

If introducing the starting lineup of foods I'm suggesting your young athletes eat to boost performance and encourage healing seems difficult, you just might not be thinking about all the possibilities. Here are just a few recipes I pass on to my clients to show them not only how easy it is to incorporate what's best for their young athletes' body, but just how tasty it can be as well to take meals to the next level.

SAMPLE BREAKFAST: NEXT-LEVEL EGGS AND SAUSAGE

Makes 1 serving

Several pieces of pastured sausage
2 pastured, organic eggs
Pinch of chopped fresh garlic (optional)
Pinch of ground turmeric (optional)
Freshly ground black pepper (optional)
Himalayan salt
1 slice sourdough bread
1 teaspoon grass-fed unsalted butter or coconut oil

➤ Cook the sausage first in an ungreased skillet, then use the leftover rendered fat to cook the eggs (any style).

➤ If desired, add the garlic, turmeric, pepper, and/or Himalayan salt.

➤ Broil or toast the bread, spread the butter on top, then add a pinch of Himalayan salt on top.

➤ Lay the eggs over the top of the bread (or serve on the side).

SAMPLE LUNCH: NEXT-LEVEL CHICKEN BACON CLUB
Makes 2 to 4 servings

Marinade:

½ cup olive oil

Freshly ground black pepper

Himalayan salt

2 to 4 raw garlic cloves, diced

½ to 1 tablespoon ground turmeric

Sandwich:

1 pound organic pastured chicken (¼ to ½ pound per sandwich)

3 to 5 slices organic pastured bacon per sandwich

2 slices whole-grain bread per sandwich

1 teaspoon unsalted grass-fed butter per sandwich

3 to 4 organic lettuce leaves per sandwich

1 organic tomato, chopped, per sandwich

1 slice avocado per sandwich (optional)

➤ Prepare the marinade: Mix together all the marinade ingredients in a bowl.

➤ Cut the chicken into pieces or long strips, then poke holes into each piece, using a fork.

➤ Let soak in the marinade for 20 minutes or up to a day, if desired.

➤ Bake the chicken and bacon separately in a 365°F oven until fully cooked (save the rendered bacon fat in a mason jar to cook with later).

➤ Toast the bread (or leave it untoasted), then spread with the butter.

➤ Assemble the sandwiches, adding the lettuce, tomato, and avocado.

SAMPLE DINNER: NEXT-LEVEL BURGERS AND FRIES

Makes 4 servings

Hamburgers

1 pound grass-fed organic ground beef (the fattier, the better)
2 tablespoons coconut oil
1 tablespoon ground turmeric
1 teaspoon dried oregano
Freshly ground black pepper
Himalayan salt

➤ Put the ground beef in a large bowl.

➤ Melt the coconut oil and pour into the bowl.

➤ Add the turmeric, oregano, pepper, and Himalayan salt, then knead all the ingredients into the beef.

➤ Divide the beef into four patties, putting a thumb indention in the middle of each to prevent shrinkage.

➤ Heat a skillet over medium heat and cook the patties until they acquire the desired doneness.

Home Fries

1 medium-size to large organic Idaho potato
1 medium-size to large sweet potato
2 tablespoons coconut oil
1 tablespoon ground turmeric
Freshly ground black pepper
Himalayan salt
1 to 2 teaspoons dried oregano
2 to 6 raw garlic cloves, chopped (if your child hates garlic, substitute
    1 organic onion, chopped)

➤ Chop both potatoes into fry-size pieces.

➤ Make a sauce by melting the coconut oil in a small pan, then mixing in the turmeric, pepper and Himalayan salt to taste, oregano, and garlic.

➤ Mix the potatoes and sauce together in a bowl until the potatoes are coated.

➤ Lay the potatoes in a pan and bake in a 365°F oven for 35 to 40 minutes, or until done. (I personally like them crispy, so I'll finish for the last couple of minutes on HIGH BROIL.)

SAMPLE SNACK: HONEY ALMOND CARAMEL CLUSTERS

Makes 4 to 6 servings, depending on the size of the mold

1 to 2 cups dark or organic milk chocolate (or both)
¼ cup coconut oil
½ to 1 cup organic almonds (or whatever nut you prefer)
⅓ cup raw organic honey
Caramel-flavored stevia
Pinch of Himalayan salt

➤ Melt the chocolate and coconut oil in a double boiler, then add the almonds and stir.
➤ Spoon out the mixture into cupcake molds. (If you're using an average-size mold, fill each one-quarter to one-half full. You should have enough to fill between four and six molds.
➤ Melt the honey: Put the honey into a small jar, boil water in a saucepan, then remove from the heat. Place the jar in the pan and allow to heat until the honey turns liquid.
➤ Add a few drops of caramel-flavored stevia and the Himalayan salt to the honey, stir, then drizzle over the top of the almond clusters.
➤ Place in the fridge to chill for at least 24 hours.

PART III
Rebuild

What I have found in dealing with injuries of all kinds in all levels of human beings is that most of the specific causes of injury stem from the simple gains we once had as children that we've now lost.

We've become overstimulated and less aware, overcoached and less prepared, and perhaps, worst of all, overtrained and less developed.

CHAPTER 9

The Decisions That Lead to De-evolution

After every season—and a closet filled with too-small uniforms, jackets, and outfits kept purely for nostalgia's sake—it's hard not to notice your young athletes growing. But what most parents don't realize is that their children aren't evolving right in front of their eyes. They are devolving every single day as a direct result of what's being practiced and encouraged today in sports, particularly in regard to exercise and training.

They're losing what they should have: Athletes aren't born with the skill sets to just run, jump, climb, sprint, throw, kick, or turn on a dime. In fact, at birth, they start almost paralyzed before finally beginning to explore motion. Over time, certain limbs coordinate with other limbs in a certain way, and before you know it, they have a pattern.

One of the most intrinsic patterns we all have within ourselves is the cross-crawl—the simple act of simultaneously moving the right leg and left arm forward, then moving the left leg and right arm forward. It's a pattern ingrained within your young athletes to prepare them for locomotion, from walking to eventually being able to run—whether that's around the bases, up the field, or down the court.

It's a pattern we count on for movement. But when many people experience a tight low back, or their knee bothers them as they walk, often it's not just muscular fatigue that's to blame—it's most likely a misfire of this pattern that should be automatic within each of us. That chronic misfiring is something I often see in my practice with injured adults in their fifties and sixties. But today, it's a phenomenon I'm repeatedly seeing in athletes as young as eight years old.

When asked to perform a simple march—one that has them lift each knee up as high as possible while simultaneously reaching the opposite arm of whichever knee is raised up to the ceiling—an interesting thing occurs. What should be a clean, beautiful motion that's effortless quickly turns into a misfire, and they're even fatiguing much faster than they should be—in as little as seventeen seconds into marching. As they fatigue, the athletes start firing on the same side (meaning that they raise the arm and knee on the same side of their body instead of alternating them), or worse, they'll stop to remind themselves how to perform the motion.

They actually have to stop—and concentrate—on something that's been ingrained in them since birth.

They're holding on to what they should let go of: We all begin life with many primitive reflexes that naturally subside as we develop. But now in many young athletes, two reflexes in particular don't seem to be fading into the background.

The first—the **spinal Galant's reflex**—kicks in at birth and is present to encourage movement, as well as assist in the development of range of motion in the hips. It reveals itself whenever the skin along the side of an infant's spine is stroked. When that area is stimulated by touch, the body will automatically flex toward the side of stroking, and that hip will rise toward the touch.

It's a reflex that should disappear in around twelve months, but it's being retained in today's youth. Quite often, kids will come to my office, sit on a chair, and suddenly, they start rocking back and forth! I've had their parents yell at them for not sitting still, or worse, tell me such children have a learning disability (such as ADHD) and that they're on medication for it. But what they don't understand is that if that reflex is still present, it's being activated every time the children sit and the chair touches their back. They aren't defiant or impatient—their brain is simply still hardwired to react a certain way.

The second—the **asymmetrical tonic neck reflex**—starts around one month of age. It's triggered whenever an infant's head is turned to the side, which causes the arm and leg on that same side to straighten and the opposite arm and leg to bend. This reflex should disappear even sooner (about six months after birth), but I still see it present in many young athletes today.

I'll ask them to stand with their eyes shut, head upright, and their arms straightened out in front of them like a zombie. Then, when I go behind them and turn their head manually to the side, instead of keeping their body pointed straight ahead, they turn in the direction of their head. It's no different than when you look over your shoulder as you're driving, but your body rotates in the same direction. It shouldn't—the two moves should be separated to allow more complex movements in life. But connected, it makes certain intricate actions much more difficult—or in some cases impossible—to perform.

Having a body out of balance is your young athletes' #1 enemy. And if you're now following the advice in the Rethink section, you're already on your way to eliminating forward head carriage, pelvic tilt, and the absence of a cervical curve in your children. But their postural problems are far from over if your goal is to have them injury-free and performing at their absolute best.

Certain training methods they may be performing right now may not only be preventing their brain from being in sync with certain movements, but causing them to retain reflexes they no longer need—and erasing a key pattern that should stay present.

THE LOSING LINEUP THAT ALWAYS FAILS

In my professional opinion, the "de-evolution" of young athletes caused by training is a culmination of three factors that create the perfect storm of disproportion in their body. Without a body in balance, one that operates exactly as it was always meant to perform, being able to pull off many of the complex movements that all sports require—both as perfectly as possible and as safely as possible—is quite simply, well, impossible.

The more imbalanced these children are, the more incapable they become at executing the movements and skills that decide whether they grow into an exceptional athlete or stay an average one. But most important, remaining out of balance makes them more likely to end up on the injured list not just more often, but more likely with an injury that could keep them out of the game for good.

SPENDING TOO MUCH TIME JUST IN SPORTS

By implementing what I showed you in the Rethink section, you're not only improving your children's posture, you're already removing one of the key reasons that young athlete's body is no longer in balance—and that's specializing in only organized sports.

Even if their chosen sport is a full-body affair that seems to challenge their muscles from head to toe, it's still an activity that favors certain muscles over others. So, if the only way their body is challenged is by a single sport, it naturally causes certain muscles to become stronger or overworked, and others to become weaker and more susceptible to being the weakest link in the movement chain.

I especially see this chronically in young athletes playing baseball, softball, tennis, soccer, and golf, due to the constant use of one side of their body over the other. These types of same-side sports only exacerbate an imbalance in our young, making them more prone to injury in an even shorter period of time. Even worse, spending more time focused on one side of the body more than the other creates survival patterns that become so locked in that the cross-crawl pattern meant to balance them is no longer ingrained.

ASSUMING SPORTS ARE ALL YOU NEED TO STAY ACTIVE

The biggest reason certain reflexes are sticking around and a key pattern is being dimmed is because young athletes simply aren't moving their body enough to either establish or eliminate what they started with since birth.

I have parents confused by this notion often, since they figure that since their children are in sports, their kids are already constantly moving. They are, but the movements that are essential for eliminating these reflexes and reestablishing the cross-crawl pattern are motions that need to take place on all different planes and a variety of surfaces. Motions that involve kids' exerting themselves both at a low intensity and a high intensity—and all points in between.

The randomness and volume required to bring back a sense of balance simply aren't present in any one sport. No matter how many hours young athletes practice their sport, they are still practicing a very focused set of skills, as opposed to a variety of movements that take place on different planes on a variety of surfaces—moves that also work both sides of the body evenly from head to toe. Every sport, for the most part, works certain muscles, but it's impossible to get away with training every muscle equally.

Other factors contributing to this imbalance include the removal or reduction of physical education from the school system, as well as the diminishing amount of responsibility we seem to be placing on kids today. According to one poll reported by the *Wall Street Journal*,[1] 82 percent of American parents admitted they did chores regularly as kids, yet only 28 percent make their children do chores. I've even watched (on more than one occasion) parents carry their kids' equipment for them, like a personal caddy, into practice or to a game!

Beyond the obvious developmental benefits that chores teach, they also provide children with a physiological benefit that indirectly keeps everything even inside them. Shoveling the walk, carrying groceries, doing yard work, and other daily physical responsibilities that were once a normal part of a kid's life are simply not there anymore, due to parents not wanting to burden their children, or assuming their kids may get hurt and miss a practice if they try to help out around the house.

But my biggest concern is how a lack of daily movement—the right kind of movement—is impeding their mind-muscle connection. You see, the human brain needs sensory stimulation and movement for normal growth and development. As children begin to crawl and move about, every repetitious motion helps stimulate and organize neurons, allowing their brain to control such cognitive processes as comprehension, concentration, and memory.

It's these sensory experiences that build the foundational neural networks that eventually govern all young athletes' higher-level brain development. But because they're not being stimulated as often in a balanced way—when there's less development of the brain from proprioceptive nourishment, integration, and stimulation through general body movement—then their focus, attention, cognitive retention, creativity, and the ability to even desire to want to learn, are just a few areas that are kept dim.

RELYING ON LOPSIDED TRAINING AND EXERCISE PROGRAMS

When it comes to the American Way, it's always about being able to deliver the most impressive and immediate results. We want to be the best—and we want it right now.

That philosophy is now a part of youth sports in a big way, where it's become all about making our young athletes bigger, stronger, and faster. It's become all about teaching sports skills as soon as possible—before bothering to build these athletes' foundation first. It's become about developing six-year-old boys or girls into an NCAA tennis player by having them hit a ball incessantly as hard as possible, whereas, in other countries, that same six-year-old would never pick up a ball or racquet for years.

So, what's so bad about that?

It Makes Them Strong and Speedy—but Not Sustainable

How the human body adapts to exercise is both a blessing and a curse. Stimulate it by lifting weights, and the body will respond by becoming bigger and expressing more strength and speed. Numbers go up (such as weight loads, reps, and sets), and it's believed that the higher they go—that by making our kids bigger, stronger, and faster—we're building a better athlete.

However, many young athletes are only just beginning to learn body awareness and how to coordinate and balance themselves when they're first introduced to weights and other aggressive forms of training. They may get bigger, stronger, and faster, but because they are building their body upon a weak foundation, their body can't sustain that. By not going about things in the correct order, these training techniques provide an immediate expression of power or speed, but it leads to inevitable repercussions.

The way young athletes are being trained today, it's as if they're coming into an athletic facility to learn how to spell their name. When they leave, they may be able to write faster and press down harder when writing their signature—while spelling their name completely wrong.

What is supposed to happen (and what is done in other countries) is that before you ever add weight to any exercise, such as the squat, that move needs to be mastered first. Look at some of the best squatters in the world, and they will retouch the basic movement pattern by performing a squat with nothing more than a wooden stick on their back, then doing one thousand good squats—before even considering going under a bar with weight.

Instead, most coaches and trainers will sidestep this to get an immediate response by adding some type of stimulus (in this case, weight)—and that response is muscle growth. They will train a specific area and build specific muscles to express an athletic trait—such as power, speed, or strength—which it will because the body adapts. But without building a solid foundation first, the power, speed, and strength created by overdeveloping muscles can't be sustained for very long before the surrounding underdeveloped muscles, joints, and ligaments eventually fail to support them.

This imbalance is something I'm seeing not just in young athletes but across the board. Most amateur and pro athletes that come into my office are the equivalent of Ferraris with a moped engine under their hood. They may look athletic, but underneath—when you dive into how their body is functioning—they're not doing well at all, which is why we see injuries on the rise.

Because of how they're being trained—the same methods that more and more young athletes are using nowadays—most have a larger chest and enormous trapezius muscles, and they are quad dominant (meaning that the front of their thighs are stronger than the hamstring muscles in the back of their thighs and their glutes). But they also have weak feet, the middle and lower portions of their backs are less developed, and when you walk behind them, their shoulder blades are spread apart wider than normal.

Try to imagine the chaos those muscular imbalances can cause. When your muscles are proportionate to one another, with opposing muscles working with each other in harmony, every movement you make is like a dance. But what's happening now through the overdevelopment of certain muscles and underdevelopment of others, it's like watching a bodybuilder and a child trying to dance the tango.

They're Sacrificing Solid Foundation for Short-Lived Skill

At your children's next practice, I want you to time something for me. But before you do, let me introduce you to the Performance Pyramid:

- At the bottom of the pyramid is **functional movement**, such as the squat, the lunge, any basic pushing and pulling movements (push-up or pull-ups, for example), or basically, any nonweight movement that helps develop endurance, posture, body awareness, balance, and coordination. These movements aren't related to any sport—they are simply the movements we learned as kids and should have a history of doing over and over again for extended periods of time to build a solid foundation throughout our body.
- The middle portion of the pyramid is **functional performance**, which is when we take those functional movements, but add resistance to express these basic moves at a higher velocity, with greater acceleration, or more power.
- The top of the pyramid is **functional skill**, which is when we start combining and altering those movements to perform a sports-specific skill, such as hitting a baseball, shooting a basketball, kicking a ball, throwing a punch, etc.

The best way to build a balanced body is by starting from the bottom up—but that's not the priority of many coaches today.

Remember when I asked you to time something for me? The next time you watch them practice, watch your kids and ask yourself where they fall along the pyramid. Did they spend any time working on functional movements, or even functional performance exercises—or are they specifically focusing on building functional skill? I don't need the numbers from you because I already know the answer.

Because velocity, speed, and power have become such important markers to measure an athlete's performance among both coaches and parents, boosting each is easily achievable by training athletes starting from the top down. They have essentially inverted the Performance Pyramid. The problem is, you can't sustain it through the top down.

What's also a problem is that we are getting kids to express their maximum capabilities too soon. You see, you can't necessarily teach something like speed, for example, because you're born with a certain level. Meaning that I can't turn your kids into a 95 mph thrower, simply because there's a limitation in their genetic ability.

But by inverting the pyramid, what a coach can do is get your children to express their maximum capabilities earlier than they are supposed to. That's what's happening with many young athletes today. They might seem as if they are "ahead of the curve," but all many children are doing is reaching their maximum potential at much younger ages—without bothering to create a foundation using functional movement that can protect their body from sustaining injury.

WEARING SHOES THAT ARE WORKING AGAINST THEM

More than 90 percent of the young athletes that come through my office injured all suffer from collapsed arches. That's because many are walking around in shoes they believe will make them a more functional athlete, but that are secretly destroying the foundation of their feet.

Have you ever seen a broken arm or leg after the cast comes off? Within as little as six weeks, the muscles within that limb suffer from disuse atrophy due to not using them. The problem with today's high-tech footwear is that all that extra cushioning and arch support they come with is creating the same effect in young athletes' feet. In other words, those $150 shoes are $150 casts that are taking away the responsibility of what their feet are naturally supposed to do.

It works like this: Worn long enough, people's brain begins to communicate with their feet regarding which areas down below are being supported and cushioned. In turn, the brain spends less energy worrying about the strength of certain ligaments and muscles, because after all—the shoes have it covered.

They're just feet—who cares! I've had parents say that to me, believing it's one less thing to worry about. That's until I ask their children to demonstrate just one single movement or skill from their sport. In almost every instance, whether it's a swing, throw, kick, push-off, jump, you-name-it—it requires creating force through the ground. And what's the first thing that touches the ground that your child's muscles integrate through?

It's their feet.

What's happening today in some athletes is that you have all these overdeveloped muscles stacked upon these two points of contact—two points that aren't developed as they should be. Yet this small square footage is so vital for reacting with the ground that if it doesn't do its job properly, that if it's not conditioned enough to support the mass above it and how that mass moves in all planes of motion, then all that synchronicity falls apart, leading to a decrease in performance—or worse, a possible injury.

BREATHING AS IF THEY'RE SCARED INSTEAD OF SERENE

As I mentioned in the Rethink section, when young athletes come into my office, I observe everything about them, especially how they breathe. Most people—and not just young athletes—breathe through their mouth and fill their chest instead of through their nose and into their diaphragm (or belly).

In fact, it's rare when I see someone breathe the right way. Those that do it correctly almost appear as if they're going into a trance, readying their body for what is about to come. They don't even know they are doing it—it's just instinctual.

Why do most young athletes breathe improperly, despite the fact that we know that chest breathing draws in less air and only uses roughly the upper two thirds of their lungs? Is it a pride thing? Is it a "let me puff out my chest" thing that's preventing most from taking deeper, fuller stomach breaths that have been shown to allow more oxygen to enter through the blood—extra oxygen that gives young athletes more energy, concentration, and mental sharpness?

I believe it all ties back to a previous point about how most kids today have become sympathetic dominant. When people are frightened, their natural reaction is not to take a big, clearing breath through their nose. Instead, their shoulders rise, their neck muscles flare, and they instinctively gasp through their mouth. Because kids today are primarily sympathetic dominant, that instinctive need to take shallow breaths stays in the "on" mode, making it much harder to teach them how to breathe correctly with practice.

CHAPTER 10

Bringing the Body Back into Balance

Eliminating stuck reflexes and reestablishing lost patterns requires movement. Bringing a body back into balance, so that every muscle works with precision with one another, also requires movement. But to help athletes improve their athletic ability to pull off technical and tactical skills more successfully, make them less susceptible to injuries, and fortify their body to survive the demands of any sport—it takes the right *kind* of movement.

IMPLEMENTING LTAD INTO YOUR ATHLETES' LIFE

The healthiest cities in the world (such as Okinawa and Vancouver) aren't blessed with better foods, greater access to gyms, or fresher air. The residents excel in health because being active is a natural part of their daily lifestyle. But more important, Japan and Canada (along with Russia and certain other countries) understand the importance of implementing long-term athletic development techniques (LTAD), a system that describes the things athletes need to be doing at specific ages and stages—and *only* at specific ages and stages.

In countries that have adopted LTAD, training, competition, and recovery programs are designed around young athletes' developmental age—meaning that the physical, mental, and emotional maturation of an individual—instead of their chronological age. As a result, their injuries are lower, their overall health is envied worldwide, and there's a lifelong engagement in physical activity and sport.

With LTAD, the guidelines are so broad that everybody fits them and progresses at his or her own pace. There isn't any worry about kids' "not being where they should be," as is seen in America, just because they aren't performing at a certain standard. Instead, each athlete is exactly where he or she naturally should be at that moment—instead of being viewed as flawed, different, or behind.

It's a system that should be used with youth who choose to participate in sports at a younger age, but it's rarely seen. Is this type of training available in America? To a degree, but more so in the private sector, such as places like my facility. But typically, when it's implemented by coaches or trainers, they have reinvented the formula to put their own sexy, immediate spin to it.

After all, you can't sell a program that takes years—one that doesn't instantly give a young athlete strength and power early on. You can't get most parents to understand how a natural progression of development needs to occur, starting off with such attributes as stability, mobility, spatial awareness, balance, coordination, and agility. And then—and only after those abilities are developed—should they ever consider working on strength and power.

REINFORCING THE THREE AREAS OF DYSFUNCTION

What I've come to discover over the course of time is that almost every injury mainly comes down to dysfunction in one (or several) of three distinct and separate areas: the **shoulder blades/scapular stabilizers**, the **hips/gluteal muscles**, and the **anterior lower leg/foot complex**.

The job of all three areas, like that of all muscles of the body, is to absorb force. If muscles don't absorb force, that force has to go somewhere because that's simply what force does. It's unyielding, and it will go until it's absorbed. But if any of these three areas is weak, due to inactivity, trauma, nerve interference, specializing in sports, or because of muscular imbalance created by improper training, instead of absorbing force into capable, integrated, strong, supple muscles, the force has little choice but travel into ligaments, joints, discs, meniscus, fascia, and bone.

That's the basis of all injuries—the body's inability to absorb force. But these three areas, in particular, are not absorbing force on a majority of young athletes across the board, and the result is varying injuries of many different degrees throughout all forms of sport.

When I first point out these areas of dysfunction, the greatest challenge is getting parents to understand their young athlete has a problem in the first place. Most times, they won't equate an issue with their child unless there's pain involved in a given area. But it's paramount to understand that the dysfunction is not sensed by pain initially. Pain is typically the last thing to show up—and the first thing to go away.

That said, here is how these three areas of dysfunction may be holding your young athlete back from being his or her best:

The shoulder blades/scapular stabilizers: Performance-wise, the shoulder is the anchor for an accelerating hand. Whether that's to swing a tennis racket, hit an overhand serve in volleyball, push off a defender, support the body during a handspring, throw a ball, or perform a swim stroke, it's the elbow that's powerfully pulling back and pressing forward—and that elbow is anchored through the muscles of the shoulder blades and scapular stabilizers.

If either or both are dysfunctional and can't absorb the appropriate force, it's like shooting a cannon from a canoe—and that force continues on. In some people, it goes to the medial elbow, which could make the child a candidate for Tommy John surgery eventually. In others, that force may make its way to smaller muscles of the shoulder, or other tissue, such as the labrum (the cartilage around the ball and socket joint of the shoulder) or biceps tendon, that attaches the biceps muscle to the shoulder. Or the rotator cuff muscles themselves may just tear apart.

Even in a sport that doesn't require throwing, having any dysfunction in the shoulder blades can still cause problems below the belt. I especially see it in young athletes that run long distances, such as track, basketball, or soccer players. When they come in with toe, ankle, or knee problems, the last thing they expect to hear is that they have dysfunctional shoulders—but it all ties back to kids' losing their cross-crawl pattern.

When you run, the elbows are pulled back and released forward because the muscles of the shoulder blades—and the legs respond reflexively. When the left elbow is swung back, the left leg is flexed forward—and vice versa. But by losing that cross-crawl pattern, that synchronicity isn't in place. This can cause more dysfunction at the shoulder blades, which begins to creep down through the legs by negatively affecting their stride.

The hips/gluteal muscles: When the glutes (the gluteus maximus, gluteus medius, and gluteus minimus) are dysfunctional, force from both the ground up and from the top down isn't transmitted in sequence as it should be. If young athletes' glutes are weak, their body is less stable, which can cause inefficient movement, energy loss, and an onslaught of forces to be redirected and increase the risk of injury in other places, such as the knees, ankles, and the lower back (just to mention a few).

Dysfunctional glutes also inhibit the hips—which are crucial for stability, power, mobility, and posture, among other tasks—from functioning as effectively. Typically, the brain's natural response to weak glutes is to create inflexibility in the hip flexors to protect the muscles and structures underneath. The brain essentially places the hip flexors into lockdown mode, tightening them in a way that negatively affects young athletes' gait and shortens their stride length.

Another common issue is that it also causes the hamstring muscles to work much harder than necessary. When it comes to hip extension—the backward movement of the thigh, the glutes do most of the work. But when they're less able, the hamstrings (which assist the glutes) are called upon more to extend the hips. Young athletes can get away with this mismanagement of muscles for a while, but when they eventually become overloaded, it leads to a pulled hamstring—an injury that typically gets blamed on not warming up properly or stretching—as well as knee issues.

The anterior lower leg/foot complex: Most people look at their calf muscles and their feet as two separate portions of the body, but the calf muscles insert both underneath the foot and on top of the foot, so they should always be regarded as one.

The one obvious issue parents connect with is how running exerts force that can be as much as three times young athletes' body weight. When that force isn't absorbed properly, that multiplied amount of force transfers into their muscles, knees, legs, torso, shoulders, and elbows. But running isn't the only area that's an issue—it's an issue that affects every move the children make.

As I mentioned earlier, no matter what sport they play, movement naturally occurs in this area every time they lift their foot up and place it down. So, even if your son or daughter has no dysfunction in his or her shoulders, hips, or glutes, if this region is neglected, then none of that matters because all those areas are resting—and relying—upon strength at their base.

Performance-wise, every athlete wants to be faster, jump higher, hit or kick harder, throw farther, and so on. But pulling off every single one of those skills hinges upon the body's ability to press or pull into the ground away from itself. Young athletes can focus on any exercise or drill if they want to improve every single muscle and motion above their knees, but their overall performance with all of that effort comes down to one thing: their ability to create force off a fixed surface, whether that's a court, a field, a gym floor, a pool's edge, you name it.

INCORPORATE THE 4-1-8-1 BREATHING TECHNIQUE AT EVERY OPPORTUNITY

By sticking with all four components of the Tommy John Solution, young athletes will slowly slip out of a sympathetic dominant state. As that begins to occur, you should notice them breathing less from their mouth into their chest and more through their nose into their belly, which naturally produces a parasympathetic response, which promotes relaxation and recovery. But there is a way to make this breathing technique even more potent, a way that boosts energy-rich oxygen and secretly develops their core muscles.

1. Have your son or daughter start with his or her mouth completely closed. Begin to inhale through the nose as deeply as possible for a count of four, concentrating on filling the belly with as much air as possible. The stomach should extend outward and away from his or her body—that is the goal.
2. Next, have him or her hold his or her breath for a count of one.
3. Next, have him or her exhale out for at least double the amount of time it took to inhale. If it took a count of four to fill his or her lungs, then it should take a minimum of a count of eight to exhale. The air should feel as if it's creeping out on the body at a nice slow and steady pace. This slow pace is crucial because that it helps boost the parasympathetic nervous system response in the body.
4. Once all the air is out of his or her body, have your son or daughter pause again for another count of one.
5. Repeat the process over again for a minimum of ten times.

Do it whenever you like: The good thing about the technique is that unlike other exercises where a person could overdo it, doing more will only bring your son or daughter more benefit. A great time to practice the technique is right before bed (because it's that one time of the day when there's really no excuse not to). But honestly, the more different types of environments your child can practice the technique, the better—whether that's waiting on the field or court, sitting on the bench, paying attention in school, driving to and from either practice or a game, and so forth.

Do it when there's self-doubt: During those moments when your young athlete may have negative thoughts on the field or court or gym, that's when this technique can come in handy because it strips away some of that anxiety. Those thoughts may be present and recognized, but what the 4-1-8-1 technique does is eliminate the physical response that those thoughts create in your child.

Don't use a stopwatch: When I say 4-1-8-1, that doesn't mean it has to be exact. It helps, but counting could also make the technique feel more regimented and stressful for some kids. If that's the case, just have them count slowly in their mind. It doesn't matter if what they perceive as "one second" is a little bit longer than one second. It's all about inhaling as deeply and slowly as possible, pausing, then exhaling for a longer time than it took them to inhale, then pausing again.

Do it even longer than last time: A count of 4-1-8-1 may be the minimum, but the goal is to lengthen those numbers—so long as they always match. For how many counts it takes to inhale, it should always take a minimum of double that time to exhale. If that seems impossible, give it time and watch how quickly it will become second nature to your child. I have watched certain masters of this technique take a mere three breaths in three minutes, just to give you a sense of how far your young athlete may take this technique over time.

Finally—don't worry if kids shift back during sport: When young athletes are competing, they benefit by being in a sympathetic state because their body needs to be ready to go. The problem is that because most children are now sympathetic dominant, that initial burst of reserved energy is slightly diminished from constantly being on standby.

By spending more time in a parasympathetic state, thanks to the 4-1-8-1 technique and many of the other steps within the Tommy John Solution, when they eventually engage in sport and trigger a natural sympathetic response, the spike of energy that kicks in will be more pronounced.

PUT THE RIGHT FOOT FORWARD

To young athletes, they're just their feet. But to their muscles and mind, feet are shock-absorbing sensors that help displace the forces of activity and provide the brain with information about how that force is being transferred. So, what should your children wear to strengthen them to prevent force from being sent unnecessarily to their bones, tendons, weaker muscles, and ligaments?

Whenever possible, go shoeless: That's right—if the opportunity presents itself to be barefoot, tell them to take it. Hands down, the gold standard is simply letting their feet (and all the muscles and tendons within them) do their job so that they develop properly.

Believe it or not, that even goes for running as well. A recent study[1] out of the University of Granada discovered that barefoot running can actually decrease the risk of injury, due to the changes it makes in how the foot strikes the ground. Scientists discovered that using footwear causes runners to initiate contact with the ground heel first, whereas barefoot running causes runners to strike the ground with their forefoot first, which lessens the impact of each strike. (Note: If you decide for them to try running barefoot, phase this change into their regime slowly because the drastic switch could increase their risk of injury until their body is able to adapt, which should take a minimum of about three months.)

Within a short amount of time, they should begin to notice an improvement in both posture and balance, while you'll have the peace of mind that they're minimizing their risk of such injuries as stress fractures, torn shoulder labrums, bursitis, UCL tears, tendinitis in the Achilles tendon, Little League elbow, shin splints, and plantar fasciitis (to name a few). If they can't walk around in bare feet, but socks are an option, take it as well. But ideally, their goal should always be to get as much skin on surface time as possible—as long as the surface is safe and clean enough to do so.

When shoes are a must—think flat and wide: Look for a shoe with as little to no elevation change between the heel and the toe as possible. Also, a wide toe box is essential to keep the foot in its natural shape. Most athletic shoes are too narrow, which shuttles the toes inward and creates dysfunction. Merrell is one company that has terrific options available for young athletes (such as its Minimalist line), but stay away from any shoe that promises that "barefoot" feel but separates the toes, since again, that prevents the foot from working in the way it's supposed to.

If they have to wear something airy on their feet, opt for a sandal that wraps around the foot—but no flip-flops. Even though they might have a thin sole, the mechanics of a flip-flop prevents the foot from functioning properly. As you walk, the big toe has to dip down whenever the foot leaves the ground, to hold the flip-flop on the foot. Unfortunately, the big toe isn't meant to flex downward as you walk—it should pull itself up. A thin-soled sandal that wraps around the foot prevents that from happening, so their feet flex as they're meant to.

TJ'S MVP LIST—REBUILD (IN A NUTSHELL)!

1. **Don't spend too much time in just sports.**

2. **Never assume sports is all you need to stay active.**

3. **Avoid relying on lopsided training and exercise programs.**

4. **Don't wear shoes that are working against you.**

5. **Never breathe as if you're scared instead of serene.**

6. **Try to implement LTAD into your athlete's life.**

7. **Reinforce the three areas of dysfunction.**

   • The shoulder blades/scapular stabilizers
   • The hips/gluteal muscles
   • The anterior lower leg/foot complex

8. **Use the 4-1-8-1 breathing technique often.**

   • Do it whenever you like.
   • Do it when there's self-doubt.
   • Don't use a stopwatch.
   • Do it even longer than last time.
   • Don't worry if you shift back during sport.

9. **Put the right foot forward.**

   • Whenever possible, go shoeless.
   • When shoes are a must—think flat and wide.

THE RE-EVOLUTION REGIMEN

Throughout my years of training athletes of every age—from amateur to pro—certain movements, drills, and programs have never failed me. And more important, they have never failed my clients.

The **Re-evolution Regimen** is a culmination of those athlete-tested techniques, based upon the LTAD approaches being used by countries around the world. It's a routine that addresses and corrects all three centers of dysfunction while simultaneously helping to restore connective tissue, bring blood into the joints, flush out impurities, and shuttle nutrients throughout the body where they're needed most.

But most important, it's a game plan that goes beyond making your son or daughter a better athlete—it's designed to make him or her a better human being, both physiologically and neurologically.

For Athletes Younger Than Eight Years Old

This portion of the book is not for them. Instead, my exercise prescription is simple—I want them to play.

If you're worried about how your youngest young athletes will evolve, especially if you've noticed dysfunction in them by taking the Tryout Test, don't worry. The changes you'll be making in their life using Rethink, Replenish, and Recover will be equally impactful on them until they reach eight years of age. In fact, when they're ready for this portion of the program, they will be healthier, more resilient, and primed, so when they eventually take it on, the effects will be even more extraordinary.

Because some parents may be unsure what activities might be best to do with their young children, I asked Jeremy Frisch, owner and director of Achieve Performance Training in Clinton, Massachusetts, and former assistant strength and conditioning coach for the Holy Cross athletic department, for just a few ways to make mini obstacle courses that are fun, easy to set up, and most important, extraordinary at working young athletes through a random mix of forgotten movements that will help their body evolve.

His top picks that always click with kids include having them:

- Walk/jog/sprint around cones, chairs, trees, bushes, through hula hoops or tires, over hurdles or logs, up steps or small hills.
- Perform animal/gymnastic movements for short distances, such as a bear crawl, crab walk, log roll, or somersault.
- Jump/hop over cones, small hurdles, rocks, logs, ropes on the ground, sticks, or piles of leaves.
- Climb/crawl under tables or bushes, through old boxes, on gymnastic mats, on top of fallen trees, or up and down small hills.
- Jump rope (can be done for repetitions, for time, or even traveling for distances).
- Lift rocks, pick up or stack light firewood, pick up or drag a light sandbag, or carry buckets of water.
- Throw different objects (such as a ball, water balloon, small rock, or sticks) either toward a target or for distance.

THE RULES BEFORE THEY RE-EVOLVE

The Re-evolution Regimen is divided into three separate routines: Beginner, Intermediate, and Advanced.

1. Always start with the Beginner routine, no matter how old your young athlete is, or how well they scored on the Tryout Test.

Why? Even though I asked you to test your young athletes using the Tryout Test and score them according to their biological age, the beauty of the Re-evolution Regimen is that it solely focuses on functional age.

Because this is a routine that most young athletes have never experienced, no matter how well developed they may be, they are still starting from square one. How quickly they move up to intermediate or advanced will be up to their body and how quickly they develop naturally.

Note: Even if your son or daughter aced every exercise in the Tryout Test, and you feel compelled to have him or her start at the Intermediate level, I won't tell you that you can't. However, try to remember that this portion is just that—it's just a portion of the entire Tommy John Solution. If your child were my client, I would still have him or her start at the Beginner level and naturally progress, and expect he or she would probably do so at a much faster pace.

2. Stick with the Beginner program for three months, but have the child retake the Tryout Test at the end of every month.

If your son or daughter hasn't shown any improvement after three months . . .

Don't worry—because it will come. It may take longer, depending on how much dysfunction needs to be corrected. You may be in the process of reversing an entire lifetime's worth of damage, so know it takes time. That said, I want you to also ask yourself this:

- Is your child in the middle of a season that may be adding more activity to his or her schedule?
- Is your child putting in as much effort as he or she is expected to put in?
- Are there any other factors that may be keeping him or her from moving forward?

Regardless of the answers, have your child continue with the Beginner routine for another month, then take the Tryout Test each month afterward until he or she shows improvement.

If your son or daughter has shown improvement . . .

But is still finding his or her way through the Beginner routine, stick with it until your child feels ready to progress to Intermediate.

Alternatively, if he or she no longer feels as challenged by the Beginner routine, move on to the Intermediate routine.

3. Once a child has reached Intermediate, the same rules still apply. Stick with the Intermediate program for three months, but have him or her retake the Tryout Test at the end of every month.

If your son or daughter hasn't shown any improvement after three months . . .

Ask yourself:

- Is your child in the middle of a season that may be adding more activity to his or her schedule?

- Is your child putting in as much effort as he or she is expected to put in?
- Are there any other factors that may be keeping your child from moving forward?

Regardless of the answers, have the child continue with the Intermediate routine for another month, then take the Tryout each month afterward until they show improvement.

If your son or daughter has shown improvement . . .

But is still finding his or her way through the Intermediate routine, stick with it until your child feels ready to progress to Advanced.

Alternatively, if he or she no longer feels as challenged by the Intermediate routine, move on to the Advanced routine.

4. Once your child has reached Advanced, he or she has the option of doing any of the following:

Use the Advanced program for as long as he or she likes. Or, switch back to the Intermediate or Beginner programs every so often (such as once a week or month), to revisit the fundamentals.

Finally: Hey, TJ—Can I Dial This Back a Bit?

You can, but first, remember this: The Re-evolution Regimen is a program I use with clients because it gets the job done. If you believe that sidestepping certain exercises will accomplish the same goals, you'll be shortening their workout but limiting their potential. In other words, if you do 75 percent of the regimen, you can expect to see 75 percent of the results—or less.

If it seems like a huge commitment, I understand that reaction. But if they are following every part of the Tommy John Solution, the time that used to be spent on extra activities that were damaging the children's body will be recouped, allowing your young athlete to have more free time overall by using a regimen that will improve their performance and heal them from within.

That said, I get it—life happens. I would never presume there won't be times when it's harder than others for your children to perform the Re-evolution Regimen.

DON'T BE DISCOURAGED—BE EXCITED!

What your son or daughter is accomplishing using the Re-evolution Regimen is "rehabbing" their body from head to toe, taking everything that's dysfunctional and making it functional.

If you're hoping for a quick fix, ask yourself how long it takes to heal a bone or bring mobility back to a frozen joint. You would never expect a broken bone that takes 4 to 6 months to mend in a month, or expect a joint that might typically take 6 to 9 months to achieve complete mobility to have a full range of motion within 2 or 3 months.

Truth be told, if young athletes never break free of the Beginner routine for any reason, even if that reason is as simple as them feeling comfortable with it and not wanting to change, that is entirely fine. They will still be doing more for themselves on a daily basis than most people (let alone athletes) ever do.

The most important thing to remember is that *this isn't a race*—it's simply about mastering every movement in the routine to the best of that athlete's ability.

BEST TIME TO DO IT

It doesn't matter whether children prefer to get their workout out of the way first thing in the morning, like to do it right after school, or opt to work out before bedtime as a way to get a good night's sleep. Their body is always ready to go, so the best time is when they have a moment to be distracted by nothing. The best time is whenever they can be "on it." That way, they can pour all their attention and focus into the workout from beginning to end.

However, that doesn't mean they should ever skip a workout if they miss that perfect window of opportunity. If for some reason, they feel less energetic than other days, then that's okay. They don't necessarily have to be primed and well rested when stepping into a session. All it means is that they should expect to move a little slower or less efficiently, or that they won't be able to hold a move for as long of a period of time. The point is: as long as they do it, it's getting done. Boom.

WHAT YOU'LL NEED

Many of the bodyweight-only exercises in the Re-evolution Regimen require no equipment at all, but a select few do. Know this: If you don't have a single piece of equipment needed to perform the Re-evolution Regimen (and chances are, you have a few lying around—trust me), the expense will probably be in the range of $100–$200 for a few pairs of hand weights, a pull-up bar, and a pair of push-up bars.

Also, every piece of equipment I'm recommending has a shelf life that will extend far beyond young athletes' sports career, meaning that they will be able to use these pieces of equipment throughout their teenage years through college and long after they retire their shirt or jersey for good.

Footwear: Ideally, young athletes should perform every workout in the Re-evolution Regimen either barefoot, or at the very least, wearing minimal footwear that brings their feet as close to the floor/ground as possible.

But if certain portions feel impossible to complete on certain days, then you have the following options:

Shorten the session: Instead of doing two or three circuits of a set of exercises, try two or just one. It will be less impactful, but at least you'll be doing it.

Spread out the session: If they can't do all the exercises in one session, then try spreading them—in order—throughout the day. For example, they can start the routine before school, do one or two exercises while waiting for the bus, do another one or two on the playground, do a few before dinner, and finish right before bed.

Skip to the end: If they absolutely cannot do a session for any reason, then I insist they at least do the Spinal Hygiene Complex, which is the final portion of every workout (no matter what level).

This seven-move complex takes little time, requires no equipment, and specifically addresses maintaining the strength, endurance, immobility, nourishment, and protection of the most important system in your kids' body—the central nervous system (CNS)—the brain, brain stem, and spinal cord. Simply put, it's a routine that protects the system that controls every other system in their body, because if their CNS isn't at its healthiest, every system within their body is at its mercy.

If it's so vital, then why is it at the end of each workout—instead of being first in line? The way I phrase it to my patients is this: "When an artist is done painting a picture, it's sprayed with an acrylic spray to lock it in." That's what the Spinal Hygiene Complex does. It acts as a form of cool-down that virtually seals in all the positive changes your son or daughter will have made by using the program until the very next day.

THE RE-EVOLUTION ROUTINES

Beginner

The Rules

- The Beginner routine is split into two workouts: Session 1 and Session 2.

- Your child will start with Session 1, then perform Session 2 the next day. After that, he or she will continue to alternate back and forth between Sessions 1 and 2.

- Although I don't prefer it with my athletes, if your child requires a break during the week, he or she can take a day off once a week as needed.

- If your child does take a day off for any reason, I still recommend that he or she does the Spinal Hygiene Complex (found at the tail end of each workout).

- If your child needs to stop at any point during an exercise, have him or her stand in place for one or two deep breaths through the nose, then continue. The child may pause for a breather as many times as he or she needs to, as long as only one or two deep breaths are taken each time.

- If your child is ambitious (and has the energy), doing both sessions in one day is also acceptable, so long as he or she waits at least six hours in between each session.

SESSION 1

Warm-up

Start by doing all 12 exercises in order, one after the other, without resting in between.

- Calf Jumps (30 seconds)
- 15 Arm Shakedowns
- 5 to 10 Push-ups (kneeling or up on toes)
- 20 Prisoner Squats
- Calf Jumps (30 seconds)
- 15 Spinal Rotations
- 5 to 10 Push-ups (kneeling or up on toes)
- 20 Prisoner Squats
- Calf Jumps (30 seconds)
- 15 Toe Touches
- 5 to 10 Push-ups (kneeling or up on toes)
- 20 Prisoner Squats
- Rest for a minimum of 3 minutes to 5 minutes maximum before continuing the program.

Workout A

Do all exercises in order without resting in between.

- 3-Way Hip Circles (25 reps in both directions [clockwise and counterclockwise] in all 3 positions: leg forward, leg to the side, and leg back. Repeat for each leg.)
- Rest for a minimum of 3 minutes to 5 minutes maximum before continuing.

Workout B

Do all exercises in order without resting in between.

- Squat Holds—supported if necessary (30 seconds)
- 30-yard March
- Casually walk backward to your starting point, then repeat the circuit twice more (for a total of 3 circuits).
- Rest for a minimum of 3 minutes to 5 minutes maximum before continuing.

TIPS:

- When marching, if you can't measure distance, just count the number of steps. Do 15 steps for each leg—left and right—for a total of 30 steps.
- If you're doing the workout indoors, then march in place for the same number of steps—15 per leg. Instead of walking backward, rest by standing still for 30 to 60 seconds before repeating the circuit.

Workout C

Do all exercises in order without resting in between.

- Squat Holds—supported if necessary (30 seconds)
- 30-yard A-Skips
- Casually walk backward to your starting point, then repeat the circuit twice more (for a total of 3 circuits).
- Rest for a minimum of 3 minutes to 5 minutes maximum before continuing.

TIPS:

- Again, if you can't measure distance, just count the number of steps. Do 15 steps for each leg—left and right—for a total of 30 steps.
- If you're doing the workout indoors, then skip in place for 15 skips per leg. Instead of walking backward, rest by standing still for 30 to 60 seconds before repeating the circuit.

Workout D

Do all exercises in order without resting in between.

- Push-up Hold Bottom (kneeling or up on toes) for 30 seconds
- 20 Statue of Libertys (each arm) using 0- to 1-pound weights
- Rest for 1 to 2 minutes, then repeat the circuit twice more (for a total of 3 circuits).
- Rest for a minimum of 3 minutes to 5 minutes maximum before continuing.

Workout E

Do all exercises in order without resting in between.

- Push-up Hold Bottom (kneeling or up on toes) for 30 seconds
- 20 Scap Reps

- Rest for 1 to 2 minutes, then repeat the circuit twice more (for a total of 3 circuits).
- Rest for a minimum of 3 minutes to 5 minutes maximum before continuing.

TIP:

- If your child can't do a Scap Rep, due to not having a chin-up bar, you can substitute Single-Arm Bent-Over Lateral Raises instead (do 20 repetitions each arm using 0- to 1-pound weights).

Workout F

Do all exercises in order without resting in between.

- Calf Raises (50 reps—pause at top and bottom)
- Immediately continue to the Spinal Hygiene Complex without resting.

Spinal Hygiene Complex

- Neck Rotation (15 reps each way)
- Neck Lateral Flexion (15 reps each way)
- Neck Flexion/Extension (15 reps each way)
- Spine Rolling (15 reps)
- Spine Lateral Bends (15 reps each way)
- Spine Rotations (15 reps each way)
- Cross-Crawl Supermans (100 reps each side)

SESSION 2

Warm-up

Same as Session 1, then rest for a minimum of 3 to 5 minutes maximum before continuing the program.

Workout A

- Standing Leg Curls (50 reps left leg)
- Rest for a minimum of 3 minutes to 5 minutes maximum.
- Standing Leg Curls (50 reps right leg)
- Rest for a minimum of 3 minutes to 5 minutes maximum.

Workout B

Do all exercises in order without resting in between.

- Lunge Holds (30 seconds, left leg forward)
- 20 Swings (holding a 1-pound weight)
- Lunge Holds (30 seconds, right leg forward)
- Rest for 1 to 2 minutes, then repeat the circuit 5 more times (for a total of 6 circuits).
- Rest for a minimum of 3 minutes to 5 minutes maximum before continuing.

Workout C

Do all exercises in order without resting in between.

- Push-up Hold Bottom (kneeling or up on toes) for 30 seconds.
- 20 Front Delt Rebounds (each arm; use 1-pound dumbbell)
- Rest for 1 to 2 minutes, then repeat the circuit twice more (for a total of 3 circuits).
- Rest for a minimum of 3 minutes to 5 minutes maximum before continuing.

Workout D

Do all exercises in order without resting in between.

- Push-up Hold Bottom (kneeling or up on toes) for 30 seconds.
- 20 Scap Reps
- Rest for 1 to 2 minutes, then repeat the circuit twice more (for a total of 3 circuits)
- Rest for a minimum of 3 minutes to 5 minutes maximum before continuing.

TIP:

- If your child can't do a Scap Rep, you can substitute Single-Arm Bent-Over Lateral Raises instead (do 20 repetitions each arm using a 0- to 1-pound weight).

Workout E

- Calf Jumps (perform for 60 seconds, rest 60 seconds, then repeat for 60 seconds)
- Immediately continue to the Spinal Hygiene Complex without resting.

Spinal Hygiene Complex

- Same as Session 1.

Intermediate

The Rules

- The Intermediate routine is split into three workouts: Session 1, Session 2, and Session 3.

- Your child will start with Session 1, perform Session 2 the next day, then Session 3 on the third day. After that, he or she will continue to perform a session in that order for each day.

- If your child requires a break during the week, he or she can take a day off once a week as needed, then immediately restart the routine with whichever session is next in order.

- If your child does take a day off for any reason, I still recommend that he or she does the Spinal Hygiene Complex (found at the tail end of each workout).

- If your child needs to stop at any point during an exercise, have him or her stand in place for one or two deep breaths through the nose, then continue. The child may pause for a breather as many times as he or she needs to, so long as only one or two deep breaths are taken each time.

- If your child is ambitious (and has the energy), doing two sessions in one day is also acceptable, so long as he or she waits at least six hours in between each session, and continues to do the sessions in the order presented. For example, if a child wants to do Sessions 1 and 2 on one day, then Session 3 and 1 the next day, then Sessions 2 and 3 the following day, that's fine.

SESSION 1

Warm-up

Start by doing all 14 exercises in order, one after the other, without resting in between.

- Calf Jumps (60 seconds)
- 15 Arm Shakedowns
- 15 Y's
- 5 Rebound Push-ups (kneeling or up on toes)
- 5 Squat Jumps
- 15 Spine Rotations
- 15 Spine Lateral Bends
- 5 Rebound Push-ups (kneeling or up on toes)
- 5 Squat Jumps
- 15 Groiners
- 15 Scorpions
- 5 Rebound Push-ups (kneeling or up on toes)
- 5 Squat Jumps
- Calf Jumps (60 seconds)
- Rest for a minimum of 3 minutes to 5 minutes maximum before continuing.

Workout A

- Standing Leg Curls (100 reps left leg)
- Rest for a minimum of 3 minutes to 5 minutes maximum before continuing.
- Standing Leg Curls (100 reps right leg)
- Rest for a minimum of 3 minutes to 5 minutes maximum before continuing.

Workout B

Do all exercises in order without resting in between.

- Squat Hold (Loaded) (30 seconds)
- 30 Lunge Bounces (each leg)
- Rest for 1 to 2 minutes, then repeat the circuit 4 more times (for a total of 5 circuits).
- Rest for a minimum of 3 minutes to 5 minutes maximum before continuing.

Workout C

Do all exercises in order without resting in between.

- Squat Hold (Loaded) (30 seconds)
- 30-yard sprint
- Casually walk backward to your starting point, rest for an additional 1 to 2 minutes if needed, then repeat the circuit 4 more times (for a total of 5 circuits).
- Rest for a minimum of 3 minutes to 5 minutes maximum before continuing.

TIPS:

- If you can't measure distance, just count the number of steps. Do 15 steps for each leg—left and right—for a total of 30 steps.
- If you're doing the workout indoors, then do 15 Speed Russian Lunges for each leg instead. Afterward, rest by standing still for 2 to 3 minutes before repeating the circuit.

Workout D

Do everything in order without resting in between.

- Push-up Hold Bottom from feet (10 seconds)
- Do 9 full repetitions.
- Push-up Hold Bottom from feet (10 seconds)
- Do 6 full repetitions.
- Push-up Hold Bottom from feet (10 seconds)
- Do a final 3 full repetitions.
- Rest for 2 to 3 minutes, then repeat the circuit twice more (for a total of 3 sets).
- Rest for a minimum of 3 minutes to 5 minutes maximum before continuing.

TIP:

- If your child hits a point of failure when doing repetitions, don't have him or her stop. Instead, simply have the child drop to his or her knees to finish the number of repetitions, then return to a regular position (up on toes) for the hold positions. It's important that young athletes don't stop—they will eventually build strength and endurance over time.

Workout E

Do everything in order without resting in between.

- Biceps Curl Hold (10 seconds)
- Do 9 Quick-Style Biceps Curls.
- Biceps Curl Hold (10 seconds)
- Do 6 Quick-Style Biceps Curls.
- Biceps Curl Hold (10 seconds)
- Do a final 3 Quick-Style Biceps Curls.
- Rest for 2 to 3 minutes, then repeat the circuit twice more (for a total of 3 sets).
- Rest for a minimum of 3 minutes to 5 minutes maximum before continuing.

TIPS:

- Finding the best weight to use for each athlete can be tricky. The first time your child tries this circuit, start with a light weight. If this portion of the workout feels too easy, increase the weight by 2.5 to 5 pounds each time the child tries it, until he or she finds a weight load that fatigues his or her muscles after three sets.
- As the exercise is performed for repetitions, each time the weight is lowered, make sure your child never locks his or her arms at the bottom.

Workout F

- Single-Leg Calf Raises (50 repetitions each leg)
- Immediately continue to the Spinal Hygiene Complex without resting.

TIPS:

- For each calf raise, have your child pause at the top, then pause at the bottom.
- Something that happens in many dysfunctional young athletes is that their quadriceps and gluteal muscles will "shut off," so as they raise themselves up, their knees will bend and their hips will drop back. This is an injury pattern that shouldn't exist. To prevent it, have your child lock his or her knees, as well as lock his or her hips forward, for the duration of the exercise.

Spinal Hygiene Complex

- Neck Rotations (30 reps each way)
- Neck Lateral Flexion (30 reps each way)
- Neck Flexion/Extension (30 reps each way)

- Spine Rolling (30 reps)
- Spine Lateral Bends (30 reps each way)
- Spine Rotations (30 reps each way)
- Cross-Crawl Supermans (200 reps each side)

SESSION 2

Warm-up

Same as Session 1, then rest for a minimum of three minutes to five minutes maximum before continuing the program.

Workout A

- 3-Way Hip Circles: left leg (50 reps in both directions [clockwise and counterclockwise] in all three positions: left leg forward, left leg to the side, and left leg back)
- Rest for a minimum of 3 minutes to 5 minutes maximum.
- 3-Way Hip Circles: right leg (50 reps in both directions [clockwise and counterclockwise] in all three positions: right leg forward, right leg to the side, and right leg back)
- Rest for a minimum of 3 minutes to 5 minutes maximum before continuing.

Workout B

Do all exercises in order without resting in between.
- Lunge Holds (Loaded) (30 seconds, left leg forward)
- 10 Squat Jumps
- Lunge Holds (Loaded) (30 seconds, right leg forward)
- Rest for 1 to 2 minutes, then repeat the circuit 9 more times (for a total of 10 circuits).
- Rest for a minimum of 3 minutes to 5 minutes maximum before continuing.

Workout C

Do all exercises in order without resting in between.
- Push-up Hold Bottom (60 seconds)
- 50 Front Delt Rebounds (each arm; use 2-pound dumbbell)
- Rest for 1 to 2 minutes, then repeat the circuit once more (for a total of 2 circuits).
- Rest for a minimum of 3 minutes to 5 minutes maximum before continuing.

Workout D

Do all exercises in order without resting in between.

- Push-up Hold Bottom (60 seconds)
- 50 Lateral Raise Rebounds (each arm; use 2-pound dumbbell)
- Rest for 1 to 2 minutes, then repeat the circuit once more (for a total of 2 circuits).
- Rest for a minimum of 3 minutes to 5 minutes maximum before continuing.

Workout E

Do all exercises in order without resting in between.

- Push-up Hold Bottom (60 seconds)
- 30 Pull-ups/Scapular Rebounds
- Rest for 1 to 2 minutes, then repeat the circuit once more (for a total of 2 circuits).
- Rest for a minimum of 3 minutes to 5 minutes maximum before continuing.

TIP:

- Here's how the Pull-up/Scapular Rebound works: Start by doing as many pull-ups as you can in one shot, take a one- to two-breath pause, then continue. Once you reach the point where you are unable to pull your chin over the bar for at least three repetitions, finish the remainder of the 30 repetitions by performing scapular rebounds.

Workout F

- Calf Jumps (3 minutes)
- Immediately continue to the Spinal Hygiene Complex without resting.

Spinal Hygiene Complex

- Neck Rotations (30 reps each way)
- Neck Lateral Flexion (30 reps each way)
- Neck Flexion/Extension (30 reps each way)
- Spine Rolling (30 reps)
- Spine Lateral Bends (30 reps each way)
- Spine Rotations (30 reps each way)
- Cross-Crawl Supermans (200 reps each side)

SESSION 3

Warm-up

Because of the way this workout is designed, and how each exercise is performed, your child won't require a warm-up. It's a combination of warm-up, workout, and recovery all in one.

Workout

Your child will perform each of the following exercises for a single repetition, holding each exercise at the greatest range of motion and fight against gravity for three minutes.

If he or she fails with any exercise and needs to stop before the three minutes are up (which is certain to happen), have your child take a deep breath without stopping the clock, then immediately continue with the exercise. The goal is to perform each exercise *without breaking form* while taking as few breathers in between as possible. I don't care if the child can last for three minutes without taking a break if his or her posture isn't optimal throughout. It's better to fail with perfect form than last for three minutes out of position.

- Standing Straight Leg Raise (left leg); rest for 3 to 5 minutes
- Standing Straight Leg Raise (right leg); rest for 3 to 5 minutes
- Squat Hold (Loaded); rest for 3 to 5 minutes
- Standing Eccentric Hamstring; rest for 3 to 5 minutes
- Lunge Hold (Loaded), left leg forward; rest for 3 to 5 minutes
- Lunge Hold (Loaded), right leg forward; rest for 3 to 5 minutes
- Push-up (Loaded); rest for 3 to 5 minutes
- Scap Hang (Loaded); rest for 3 to 5 minutes
- Single-Leg Calf Raises (Loaded), left leg; rest for 3 to 5 minutes
- Single-Leg Calf Raises (Loaded), right leg

TIPS:

- While becoming more proficient at this routine, your young athlete will feel he or she doesn't need to rest for as long in between each exercise. Your child is free to reduce the amount of time between exercises to under 3 minutes as he or she adapts to the program, so long as the child reaches a level where he or she can hold both exercises (the one before the rest and the one after the rest) for a straight 3 minutes.

- What's more important to your young athlete's development is being able to hold each of these exercises for 3 minutes each. Until he or she can do that, reducing the rest times in between the exercises will only interfere with your child's ability to do so.

- Why are we doing these moves like this? Doing each exercise in this way places young athletes' muscles under tension while they are in a lengthened, stretched state. It works this way: A muscle's only job is to contract eccentrically (whereby a muscle lengthens while producing force), concentrically (whereby a muscle shortens while producing force), or isometrically (whereby a muscle produces force, but never changes length).

Performing each exercise at this incredibly controlled pace addresses vital mobility without the negative effect of stretching statically, which lowers power output. What we're doing is teaching the body how to efficiently absorb and create force many times over, which is the key to injury prevention and performance in sports and life.

Plus, it gives your young athlete the added bonus of earning strength through the greatest range of motion possible, which will increase mobility rather than just flexibility. A flexible, weak athlete is at more of a disadvantage, thus more injury-prone, compared to an athlete who is strong and mobile—mobility trumps flexibility in sports every time!

Advanced

The Rules

- The Advanced routine is split into four workouts: Session 1, Session 2, Session 3, and Session 4.

- Your child will start with Session 1, perform Session 2 the next day, Session 3 on the third day, then Session 4 on the fourth day. After that, you'll continue to perform a session in that order for each day.

- If your child requires a break during the week, he or she can take a day off once a week as needed, then immediately restart the routine with whichever session is next in order.

- If your child takes a day off for any reason, I still recommend that he or she at least do the Spinal Hygiene Complex (found at the tail end of each workout).

- If your child needs to stop at any point during an exercise, have him or her stand in place for one or two deep breaths through the nose, then continue. The child may pause for a breather as many times as he or she needs to, so long as only one or two deep breaths are taken each time.

- If your young athlete is ambitious (and has the energy), doing two sessions in one day is also acceptable, so long as he or she waits at least six hours in between each session, and continues to do the sessions in the order presented. For example, if he or she want to do Sessions 1 and 2 on one day, then Session 3 and 4 the next day, then Sessions 1 and 2 the following day, that's entirely fine.

NOTE: Even if your young athlete found the energy/time to handle two sessions a day when going through the beginner and intermediate portions, these advanced sessions are definitely more intense, so sticking with one session per day is still commendable.

SESSION 1

Warm-up

Start by doing all 11 exercises in order, one after the other, without resting in between.

- Calf Jumps (30 seconds; medium intensity)
- 30 Arm Shakedowns
- 30 Y's
- Calf Jumps (30 seconds; done aggressively)
- 20 Spine Rotations
- 20 Spine Lateral Bends
- 20 Toe Touches
- Calf Jumps (30 seconds; attack the ground and jump as high as possible)
- 20 Groiners
- 20 Scorpions
- 20 Rollover to Hamstring
- Rest for a minimum of 3 minutes to 5 minutes maximum before continuing.

Workout A

- 3-Way Hip Circles: left leg (100 reps in both directions [clockwise and counterclockwise] in all three positions: left leg forward, left leg to the side, and left leg back)
- Rest for a minimum of 3 minutes to 5 minutes maximum before continuing.
- 3-Way Hip Circles: right leg (100 reps in both directions [clockwise and counterclockwise] in all three positions: right leg forward, right leg to the side, and right leg back)
- Rest for a minimum of 3 minutes to 5 minutes maximum before continuing.

Workout B

- Squat Hold (Loaded) (10 seconds, with maximum weight)
- 10 Speed Russian Lunges (each leg)

- Squat Hold (Loaded) (10 seconds, with maximum weight)
- 10 Russian Lunges (left leg forward)
- 10 Russian Lunges (right leg forward)
- Squat Hold (Loaded) (10 seconds, with maximum weight)
- 10 Squat Jumps
- Rest for 3 to 5 minutes, then repeat the circuit twice more (for a total of 3 circuits).
- Rest for a minimum of 3 minutes to 5 minutes maximum before continuing.

TIP:

- For the Squat Hold (Loaded), pick a weight that's a challenge to hold for 10 seconds. If the weight feels too light—or doesn't have the child close to failure after 10 seconds—then add more weight as necessary.

Workout C

- Standing Eccentric Hamstring (hold for 3 minutes)
- Rest for a minimum of 3 minutes to 5 minutes maximum before continuing.

TIP:

- If your child needs to stop before the 3 minutes are up, have him or her take a deep breath without stopping the clock, then immediately continue the exercise. The goal is to perform each exercise while taking as few breath-long breaks in between as possible.

Workout D

- Lunge Hold (left leg forward) (2 ½ minutes)
- Rest for a minimum of 3 minutes to 5 minutes maximum before continuing.
- Lunge Hold (right leg forward) (2 ½ minutes)
- Rest for a minimum of 3 minutes to 5 minutes maximum before continuing.

Workout E

- 100 Kneeling Drop Push-ups (no handles)
- Scap Hang (3 minutes)
- Rest for a minimum of 3 minutes to 5 minutes maximum before continuing, only if needed.

TIP:

- For Scap Hangs, if your child needs to stop before the 3 minutes are up, have him or her take a deep breath without stopping the clock, then immediately continue the exercise. The goal is to perform each exercise while taking as few breath-long breaks in between as possible.

Spinal Hygiene Complex

- Neck Rotation (50 reps each way)
- Neck Lateral Flexion (50 reps each way)
- Neck Flexion/Extension (50 reps each way)
- Spine Rolling (50 reps)
- Spine Lateral Bends (50 reps each way)
- Spine Rotations (50 reps each way)
- Cross-Crawl Supermans (300 reps each side)

SESSION 2

Warm-up

Same as Session 1, then rest for a minimum of three minutes to five minutes maximum before continuing the program.

Workout A

Do all exercises in order without resting in between.

- Push-up Hold Bottom (2 minutes)
- 100 Front Delt Rebounds (each arm; use 3-pound dumbbell)
- Rest for a minimum of 3 minutes to 5 minutes maximum before continuing.

Workout B

Do all exercises in order without resting in between.

- Push-up Hold Bottom (2 minutes)
- 100 Lateral Raise Rebounds (each arm; use 3-pound dumbbell)
- Rest for a minimum of 3 minutes to 5 minutes maximum before continuing.

Workout C

Do all exercises in order without resting in between.

- Push-up Hold Bottom (2 minutes)
- 100 Bent-Over Lateral Rebounds (each arm; use 3-pound dumbbell)
- Rest for a minimum of 3 minutes to 5 minutes maximum before continuing.

Workout D

Do all exercises in order without resting in between.

- Scap Hang (60 seconds)
- 30 Quick-Style Biceps Curls
- Rest for 2 to 3 minutes, then repeat the circuit twice more (for a total of 3 circuits).
- Rest for a minimum of 3 minutes to 5 minutes maximum before continuing.

Workout E

- 100 Depth Drop Squats
- Rest for a minimum of 3 minutes to 5 minutes maximum before continuing.

Workout F

- Single-Leg Calf Raises (left leg) (5 minutes)
- Rest for a minimum of 3 minutes to 5 minutes maximum before continuing.
- Single-Leg Calf Raises (right leg) (5 minutes)
- Rest for a minimum of 3 minutes to 5 minutes maximum before continuing.

TIP:

- Your child shouldn't be able to hold his or her heel above parallel for the entire 5 minutes. I want him or her to fail at some point below parallel—meaning that I want his or her calf muscles to fatigue to the point where the heel eventually is lower than the toes. If that doesn't happen within that 5-minute window, then add more weight the next workout (2.5 to 5 pounds) until you find the perfect weight load to use.

Spinal Hygiene Complex (only one exercise)

- Cross-Crawl Supermans (300 reps each side)

SESSION 3

Warm-up

Same as Session 1, then rest for a minimum of 3 minutes to 5 minutes maximum before continuing the program.

Workout A

- 3-Way Hip Circles: left leg (100 reps in both directions [clockwise and counterclockwise] in all three positions: left leg forward, left leg to the side, and left leg back)
- Rest for a minimum of 3 minutes to 5 minutes maximum before continuing.
- 3-Way Hip Circles: right leg (100 reps in both directions [clockwise and counterclockwise] in all three positions: right leg forward, right leg to the side, and right leg back)
- Rest for a minimum of 3 minutes to 5 minutes maximum before continuing.

Workout B

Do all exercises in order without resting in between.
- Supported Squats (3 minutes)
- Russian Lunges (left leg forward): You'll start by doing the exercise for 1 repetition, then rest for 10 seconds. After that, you'll immediately repeat the exercise, but do it for 2 repetitions, then rest for 10 seconds. Keep repeating the exercise (adding 1 more rep than you did before, then resting for 10 seconds) until you eventually do the move for 10 repetitions. Rest for 2 minutes, then immediately repeat the exercise, but subtract one rep each time (so 9, 8, 7, 6, and so forth, resting for 10 seconds after each) until you end up doing only 1 repetition at the end.
- Rest for a minimum of 3 minutes to 5 minutes maximum before continuing.

Workout C

Do all exercises in order without resting in between.
- Supported Squats (3 minutes)
- Russian Lunges (right leg forward): You'll start by doing the exercise for 1 repetition, then rest for 10 seconds. After that, you'll immediately repeat the exercise, but do it for 2 repetitions, then rest for 10 seconds. Keep repeating the exercise (adding 1 more rep than you did before, then resting for 10 seconds)

until you eventually do the move for 10 repetitions. Rest for 2 minutes, then immediately repeat the exercise, but subtract one rep each time (so 9, 8, 7, 6, and so forth, resting for 10 seconds after each) until you end up doing only 1 repetition at the end.

- Rest for a minimum of 3 minutes to 5 minutes maximum before continuing.

Workout D

Do all exercises in order without resting in between.

- 100 Statue of Libertys (each arm) using 3-pound weights
- Scap Hang (2 minutes)
- Rest for a minimum of 3 minutes to 5 minutes maximum before continuing.

Spinal Hygiene Complex

- Neck Rotation (50 reps each way)
- Neck Lateral Flexion (50 reps each way)
- Neck Flexion/Extension (50 reps each way)
- Spine Rolling (50 reps)
- Spine Lateral Bends (50 reps each way)
- Spine Rotation (50 reps each way)
- No Supermans

SESSION 4

Warm-up

Same as Session 1, then rest for a minimum of 3 minutes to 5 minutes maximum before continuing the program.

Workout A

Do all exercises in order without resting in between.

- Push-up (Loaded) (hold bottom for 10 seconds)
- 10 Rebound Push-ups (up on feet)
- Push-up (Loaded) (hold bottom for 10 seconds)
- 10 Rebound Push-ups (up on feet)
- Push-up (Loaded) (hold bottom for 10 seconds)
- 10 Rebound Push-ups (up on feet) (Beast Mode)

- Rest for 3 to 5 minutes, then repeat the circuit twice more (for a total of 3 circuits).
- Rest for a minimum of 3 minutes to 5 minutes maximum before continuing.

TIP:

- For the Rebound Push-up, if your child reaches a point where he or she is unable to complete a full 10 repetitions from the standard push-up position (up on his or her feet), your child can finish the set by dropping his or her knees to the floor instead—just keep the child moving throughout the exercise as quickly as possible without sacrificing form.

Workout B

Do all exercises in order without resting in between.
- Biceps Curl Hold (10 seconds)
- 10 Quick-Style Biceps Curl
- Biceps Curl Hold (10 seconds)
- 10 Quick-Style Biceps Curl
- Biceps Curl Hold (10 seconds)
- 10 Quick-Style Biceps Curl
- Rest for 3 to 5 minutes, then repeat the circuit twice more (for a total of 3 circuits).
- Rest for a minimum of 3 minutes to 5 minutes maximum before continuing.

TIPS:

- Ideally, I have young athletes use two different bars/dumbbells for this circuit: a heavy weight that causes their biceps to fatigue after 10 seconds when held in the bottom curl position (for the Biceps Curl Hold), and a much lighter weight load to perform the Quick-Style Biceps Curl.
- If you don't have that option (and can only round up one weighted bar, or a single pair of dumbbells), there's a solution: Choose a lighter weight your child can curl for 30 reps—this should be a good baseline to start with to perform the Quick-Style Biceps Curl, although your child can always raise or lower the amount after trying this circuit a few times to gauge his or her strength. Then, to compensate for not having heavier weights to do the Biceps Curl Hold, have the child do the exercise using the same barbell/dumbbells, but have a

partner press down on the weight(s) and apply manual pressure. It should be just enough so that your son or daughter is fatigued after 10 seconds.

Workout C
- Vertical Jump to Lunge (50 each side)
- Rest for a minimum of 3 minutes to 5 minutes maximum before continuing.

Workout D
- Calf Jumps or skip rope (5 minutes)

Spinal Hygiene Complex (only one exercise)
- Cross-Crawl Supermans (300 reps each side)

THE MOVEMENTS

3-WAY HIP CIRCLES

SETUP: Stand straight with your arms crossed over your chest. Extend your right leg out in front of you so that your right heel is suspended just above the floor. Your right knee should be locked with your toes pulled up.

EXECUTE:

1. Maintaining your balance, rotate your right heel clockwise for the required number of repetitions, then counterclockwise for the required number of repetitions.
2. Next, extend your right leg out to the side—keeping your knee locked and heel just above the floor—and repeat (both clockwise and counterclockwise) for the same required number of repetitions.
3. Finally, extend your right leg out behind you—again keeping your knee locked and toes just above the floor—and repeat (both clockwise and counterclockwise) for the same required number of repetitions.

Once finished, repeat the entire drill once more with your left leg.

TIPS:

- Go as fast as you can without losing your balance. If you keep having to catch yourself or keep pausing the exercise to get back into position, slow down the pace to one you can maintain consistently—no matter how slow that speed may be.
- As your quadriceps muscles tire, the knee of your extended leg is going to want to relax—keep your knee locked in position at all times.
- When the move becomes easy, try locking your fingers behind your head (this variation will challenge your stability even further).

3-WAY NECK CHECK

Stand straight and tall with your chest up for all three movements. When performing each move, it's very important that you go to your extreme position each time, meaning that you need to move your head as far as you possibly can using only your neck muscles.

1. **Neck Rotation:** Slowly turn your head to one side as far as you possibly can (using only the muscles of your neck and spine), then slowly turn your head to the opposite side. Looking to the left and the right counts as one repetition.

TIP: Your shoulders shouldn't rotate as you go. To prevent your shoulders from following the direction of your head, concentrate on keeping them pinned downward with your chest up.

2. **Neck Lateral Flexion:** Slowly bring your ear down toward your shoulder as far as you can, then repeat to the other side. That's one repetition.

TIP: As you do this move, your shoulder is going to want to rise to meet your ear. Concentrate on keeping your shoulder pinned so it doesn't move. It will limit your range of motion, but that's your "true" range of motion for this movement.

3. **Neck Flexion/Extension:** Finally, keeping your back straight, slowly lower your chin down toward your chest as far as possible, then slowly look up at the ceiling by bringing your head back as far as you comfortably can. That's one repetition.

TIP: This move rquires only using the anterior (front) and posterior (back) muscles of the neck. If you're moving anything else, such as rounding your shoulders or pushing your hips forward, you're doing it incorrectly.

3-WAY SPINE UNWIND

1. Spine Lateral Bends

SETUP: Stand straight with your feet hip-width apart, feet pointed forward, with your arms hanging straight down at your sides. Your feet should stay on the ground throughout the entire move.

EXECUTE: Start by leaning as far to the left as possible. As you go, allow your left arm to swing behind you and touch your right leg as far down as you can. (This trick will keep your spine open as you rotate instead of folding it forward.) Come back up to center and repeat by leaning to the right as far as possible, allowing your right arm to go behind you and touch your left leg as far down as possible. That's one repetition.

TIP: The move should almost feel as if you're doing a crunch while standing.

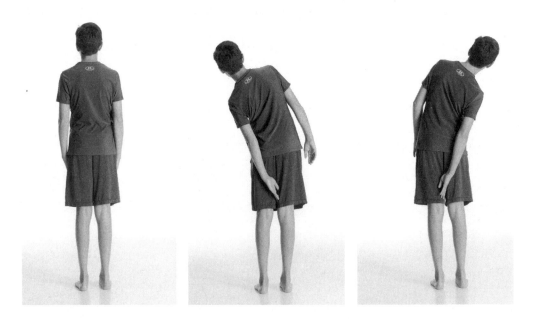

2. Spine Rolling

SETUP: Stand straight with your feet shoulder-width apart and your arms down at your sides.

EXECUTE: Start by doing the following in this order: 1. Slowly tuck your chin. 2. Round your thoracic (upper back) forward. 3. Round your lower back. 4. Bend forward and lower yourself down to the floor as far as possible. Pause, then reverse the motion in the following order: lift your head back up, pull your thoracic back, straighten your lower back, and raise yourself up into the Setup Position. That's one repetition.

TIPS:

- Imagine your spine is a worm—the entire movement should turn into one smooth, continuous motion.
- If you're overweight and have a belly that might interfere with how far down you can bend forward, simply go through as much of the movement that you can.
- If this move seems impossible standing, you can start to move in a seated position until you're ready. Sit down on a hard, rigid surface—such as a sturdy chair or box—with your knees bent and your feet flat on the floor. Spread your knees out so that you'll have plenty of room to lower your torso between your legs.

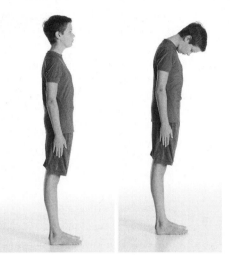

3. **Spine Rotations**

SETUP: Stand straight with your feet pointed forward, arms down at your sides.

EXECUTE: Keeping your feet flat on the floor, slowly turn your head to the left as far as possible, then continue rotating through your mid back, then finally rotate through your hips as far to the left as possible—let your head lead your body. Finally, bend your arms and cup your hands in front of your chest, close to your torso—and continue to stretch as far as you can. Return to the Setup Position, then repeat the move by turning to the right as far as possible. That's one repetition.

TIPS:

- Maintain a nice, slow pace. You don't want momentum helping you swing your torso as you go. All the movement should come from your muscles working together.
- Focus on your gluteal muscles as you go. You should notice the glute of the opposite side you're turning toward beginning to powerfully contract, which helps create an opposing force that allows for more rotation.

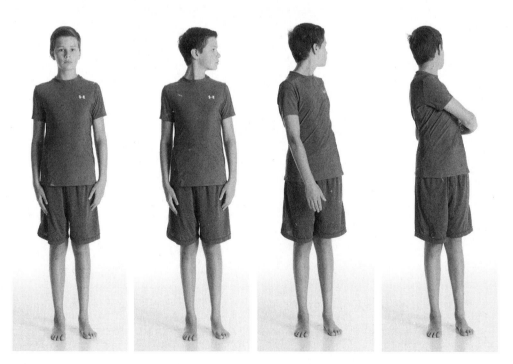

30-YARD A-SKIPS

SETUP: Stand straight with your feet hip-width apart.

EXECUTE: Keeping your back straight and your core tight, bend your arms at 90 degrees with your fists facing forward. Now, skip forward by lifting your left knee up to waist height (keeping your right leg straight) as you simultaneously swing your right arm forward and your left arm back. Land on the balls of your feet, then immediately repeat, this time by lifting your right knee up (keeping your left leg straight) as you simultaneously swing your left arm forward and right arm back. Continue alternating—left leg, right leg—for the required distance.

TIPS:

- Don't worry if you move at a slower pace to start. You'll eventually master the coordination, so go with the tempo that works for you, and concentrate on improving that tempo each time.
- With each skip, forcefully push off the ground, drive your knee high above your hip, then bring it down fast.
- If you lack the space to skip, you can do the exercise in place.

30-YARD MARCH

SETUP: Stand straight with your feet hip-width apart.

EXECUTE: Bend your arms at 90 degrees with your fists facing forward. Now, march forward—as you go, raise each knee up as high as possible, toes lifted toward your knee. Your arms should move in tandem with your legs (when your left knee is forward, your right arm should swing forward and vice versa—right knee/left arm forward).

TIPS:

- Make sure you pull each arm back as you go. This activates the posterior chain, which is underutilized in many young athletes today.
- Your arms should never cross the midpoint of your torso. Always keep them moving forward and backward along a straight path.
- If you lack the space to march, you can do the exercise in place.
- This exercise may seem basic, but neurologically, it's actually advanced. It shouldn't be something that's difficult for your young athlete to do, but it's a skill many have forgotten to do properly.

30-YARD SPRINTS

SETUP: Stand straight with your feet together.

EXECUTE: Start running forward. As you go, try to bring your knees up to your chest as high as possible while you vigorously pump your arms back and forth. Your arms should be bent at a 90-degree angle, moving in tandem with your legs (when your left leg is forward, your right arm should swing forward and vice versa—right leg/left arm forward.)

TIPS:

- Make sure your pull each arm back as you go. This activates the posterior chain, which is underutilized in many young athletes today.
- Your arms should never cross the midpoint of your torso. Always keep them moving forward and backward along a straight path.
- If you lack the space to sprint, you can do the exercise in place.

ARM SHAKEDOWNS

SETUP: Stand straight with your feet hip-width apart and reach your arms up over your head, palms facing forward.

EXECUTE: Quickly bend your elbows and throw your hands down by your sides. As you go, rotate your hands so that at the bottom of the move, your palms end up facing away from you. Quickly reverse the motion by reaching back up as high as possible, palms facing each other. That's one repetition.

TIPS:

- Imagine as if you're trying to throw your hands off your body by forcefully shaking your arms straight down in front of yourself.
- Don't worry if your arms travel past your body and behind you, due to momentum—that's entirely natural.

BENT-OVER LATERAL REBOUNDS

SETUP: Stand straight with your feet hip-width apart, arms at your sides, holding a light weight in your left hand. Keeping your legs slightly bent and knees soft, bend at the hips and lean forward until your torso is as close to parallel as possible. (If you can't lower your torso down that far, just go as far down as you can, so long as your back remains flat at all times.) Extend your left arm straight out from the side, parallel to the floor, palm facing down. (Let your right arm relax and rest your right hand along your left thigh.)

EXECUTE: With your left arm kept parallel to the floor, drop the weight. As it falls, chase it with your left hand and catch it. Once you grab it, quickly reverse the position by bringing your left arm straight up until it's parallel once more. That's one repetition. After performing the required number of reps, repeat the exercise with your right arm.

TIPS:

- As soon as you drop the weight, drive your arm down as fast as possible to catch it.
- Concentrate on dropping the weight. It should never be a throwing motion.
- The motion should only involve the working arm. You want to minimize any other movement, such as your body turning toward the falling weight.

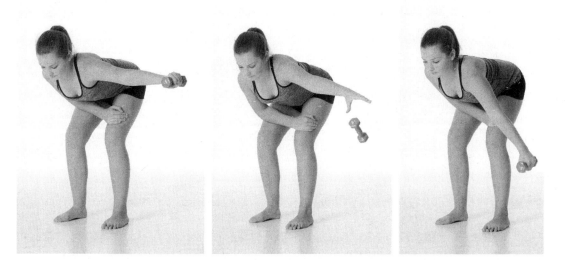

BICEPS CURL HOLDS

SETUP: Grab a barbell with an underhand grip (palms facing out) and your hands shoulder-width apart. Your arms should hang straight, so the bar is positioned directly in front of your thighs.

EXECUTE: Keeping your back straight and elbows tucked into your sides, barely raise the weight by bending slightly at the elbows with your wrists curled. Imagine that the goal is to have your arms as straight as possible *without* locking your elbows at the bottom. Hold this position for the required amount of time.

TIPS:

- If you don't have access to a barbell, just substitute a pair of dumbbells.
- There should be constant tension on your biceps. If your biceps muscles aren't flexed throughout the move, that means your elbows are locked out—instead of being slightly bent.
- Your shoulder blades must stay locked down throughout the exercise. A trick I use with athletes is having them picture an orange tucked under each armpit and that they need to squeeze them throughout the movement.

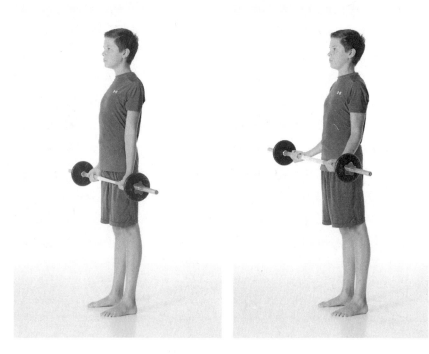

CALF JUMPS

SETUP: Stand straight with your feet hip-width apart with your arms down by your sides. Raise your heels so that you're on the balls of your feet.

EXECUTE: Pushing off to the balls of your feet, quickly jump straight up. As your feet leave the floor, don't let them point downward. Instead, the moment you leave the ground, pull your toes up. Land only on the balls of your feet, keeping your heels off the floor, and repeat.

TIPS:

- Your upper body should remain relaxed throughout the movement with your arms kept hanging down by your sides.
- Your knees should never buckle. If they do, you'll be incorporating more of your thigh muscles—instead of your feet and calf muscles—to propel you upward. Instead, keep them "soft" to help absorb each landing, but never let them buckle or bend.
- Your legs should always remain perfectly straight beneath you. If they shift forward, you're using your hip flexors instead of only your calf muscles.

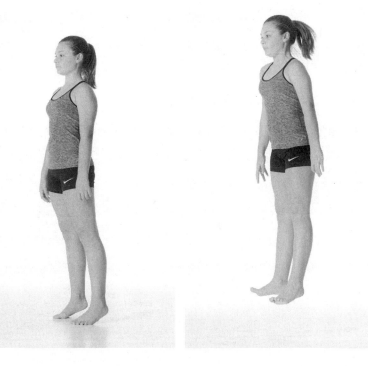

CALF RAISES

SETUP: Stand tall on a stable platform 6 to 12 inches high (such as a step or sturdy box) and place the balls of your feet on the edge of the platform so that your heels hang off the edge. For balance, place a hand lightly on something nearby, such as a railing or wall corner. Your legs can be either together or hip-width apart, whichever feels more comfortable.

EXECUTE: Maintaining your balance, slowly raise your heels up as high as possible, then lower your heels down as far as possible. That's one repetition.

TIPS:

- Stay in control of the motion the entire time. If you feel as if you're bouncing, you're using more momentum than muscles to lift yourself upward.
- Keep your knees and hips locked throughout the entire exercise.

CROSS-CRAWL SUPERMANS

SETUP: Lie facedown on a mat (or any soft surface that cushions your pelvis) with your arms and legs extended. Position your arms as close to your head as possible with your thumbs facing up. Finally, pull your toes in toward your knees so that you're not resting on the tops of your feet. (From the side, the bottoms of your feet should be perpendicular to the floor.)

EXECUTE: Keeping your arms and legs straight, simultaneously lift your left arm and right leg up at the same time. Lower them back down, then lift your right arm and left leg up at the same time—that's one repetition.

TIPS:

- Raise your arms and legs up, but don't overextend them. You want your spine to stay in a neutral position at all times. (Overdoing it will cause it to arch.)
- Your body should remain stable the entire time. If you start to rotate from side to side, you're either raising your arms and legs too high or you're not engaging your core stabilizers appropriately.
- Although you can rest your forehead on the floor, try resting on your chin instead.
- Even though it might feel more difficult to do in this position, always breathe through your nose instead of your mouth.
- Finally, once you finish, you might notice you're no longer in the same place, and that your body rotated along the way (either clockwise or counterclockwise). This rotation is caused by muscular imbalances that the program will correct over time. But a trick that can help: try imagining extending your arms and legs as you're lifting them.

DEPTH DROP SQUATS

For this exercise, you'll need a sturdy box to jump off of. The size of the box can range between 6 and 30 inches, depending on your ability. If you're unsure, start with a box no more than 6 inches high until the move feels comfortable.

SETUP: Step up onto the box and turn around so that only your toes are hanging over the edge. Raise your left knee up so that your left thigh is parallel to the floor, toes pointed upward. Let your arms hang down by your sides.

EXECUTE: Pushing off with your right foot, step off the box and bring your right knee up in line with your left knee. As you land on your feet, immediately drop into a quarter squat (your legs should end up halfway between standing straight and having your thighs parallel). Push yourself back up into a standing position. That's one repetition.

TIPS:

- It should feel as if you're doing a squat in midair, then landing to stick the move.
- It's important not to land heels first. Instead, your feet should come in contact with the floor starting with your toes, rolling back through your heels.
- At the bottom of the move, everything in your body should feel turned on, so that if somebody asked you to immediately move left or right, you'd be stable enough to do so.
- Your arms are going to naturally bend and swing forward—that's fine. This will enable you to land with more stability.

FRONT DELT REBOUNDS

SETUP: Stand straight with your feet hip-width apart, arms at your sides. Holding a light weight in your left hand, extend your left arm out directly in front of you, parallel to the floor, palm facing down.

EXECUTE: With your left arm kept parallel to the floor, drop the weight. As it falls, chase it with your left hand and catch it. Once you grab it, quickly reverse the position by bringing your left arm straight up until it's parallel once more. That's one repetition. After performing the required number of reps, repeat the exercise with your right arm.

TIPS:

- As soon as you drop the weight, drive your arm down as fast as possible to catch it.
- Concentrate on dropping the weight. It should never be a throwing motion.
- The motion should only involve the working arm. You want to minimize any other movement, such as your body leaning forward. What we're trying to do is teach the body to activate the core, glutes, and hamstring muscles each time force enters the body with every catch.

GROINERS

SETUP: Get into a push-up position; hands spaced shoulder-width apart and your legs extended straight behind you.

EXECUTE: Keeping your hands on the floor, quickly step your left foot forward and place it as close to the outside of your left hand as possible. Quickly step your left foot back as you simultaneously step your right foot forward (bringing it as close to the outside of your right hand as possible). That's one repetition. Continue alternating from left to right for the duration of the exercise.

TIPS:

- Your goal is to get your feet as close to your hands as possible (and even past them, if possible).
- Each time you step forward, drop your hips briefly.
- If you can't get the hang of moving both legs simultaneously, try doing one leg at a time to start. (Bring your left foot forward, return to the Setup Position, then bring your right foot forward, return to the Setup Position.)
- Finally, don't let your heels hit the floor—stay on the balls of your feet for the entire move.

KNEELING DROP PUSH-UPS

SETUP: Kneel down on a mat (or rolled-up towel) with your elbows bent, arms close to your body, palms facing forward. Pull your elbows slightly back so that your palms are close to the sides of your torso, shoulder-width apart from each other.

EXECUTE: Keeping your knees on the floor, let your torso fall forward and catch yourself at the bottom by quickly placing your hands flat on the floor midfall. Press yourself back up into the Setup Position. That's one repetition.

TIPS:

- The goal is to see how close to the ground you can catch yourself without your thighs, stomach, or chest touching the floor.
- At first, you'll have a tendency to reach out early out of fear—that's natural. Eventually, with practice, you'll get more comfortable with the move, as well as more conditioned to the point where you'll feel a clear, distinct moment at the bottom where every muscle turns on automatically—from your hands through your core right down to your toes.

LATERAL RAISE REBOUNDS

SETUP: Stand straight with your feet hip-width apart, arms at your sides. Holding a light weight in your right hand, extend your right arm straight out from the side, parallel to the floor, palm facing down.

EXECUTE: With your right arm kept parallel to the floor, drop the weight. As it falls, chase it with your right hand and catch it. Once you grab it, quickly reverse the position by bringing your right arm straight up until it's parallel once more. That's one repetition. After performing the required number of reps, repeat the exercise with your left arm.

TIPS:

- As soon as you drop the weight, drive your arm down as fast as possible to catch it.
- Concentrate on dropping the weight. It should never be a throwing motion.
- The motion should only involve the working arm. You want to minimize any other movement, such as your body leaning to the working side.

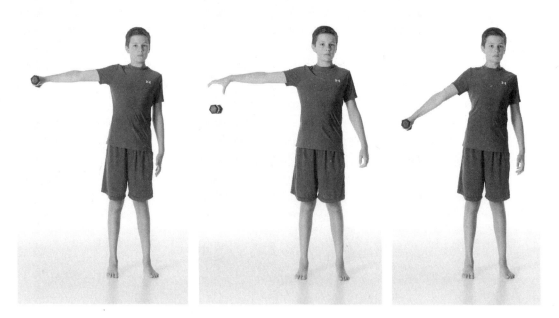

LUNGE BOUNCES

SETUP: Stand straight with your feet hip-width apart, arms down at your sides. Take a large step forward, plant your lead foot on the floor and sink into a lunge position. Your front leg should be bent at 90 degrees (thigh parallel to the floor; lower leg perpendicular) with your front heel barely off the floor. Your back leg should be as straight as possible behind you with your heel raised off the floor.

EXECUTE: Keeping your arms relaxed, quickly hop both feet off the ground simultaneously. As soon as you land, immediately hop once again and continue for the required number of repetitions. When finished, switch positions to work the opposite leg.

TIPS:

- Keep your chest up and your eyes focused straight in front of you.
- The rest of your body needs to stay relaxed throughout the movement. Involving your arms only generates momentum that robs the muscles you're trying to work of some of the effort.

LUNGE HOLDS

SETUP: Stand straight with your feet hip-width apart, arms down at your sides. Take a large step forward (don't cheat yourself—take as long of a stride as possible), plant your lead foot on the floor, and sink into a lunge position. Your front leg should be bent at 90 degrees (thigh parallel to the floor; lower leg perpendicular) with your front heel barely off the floor. Your back leg should be as straight as possible behind you with your heel raised off the floor.

EXECUTE: Maintaining this position, hold for the required amount of time.

TIPS:

- Keep your chest up and your eyes focused straight in front of you.
- Resist the urge to rest your hands on your lead leg—just let your arms hang down relaxed by your sides.
- Don't let the heel of your front foot completely rest on the floor. It should stay barely off the floor at all times.

LUNGE HOLDS (LOADED)

SETUP: Rest a barbell across the back of your shoulders, then repeat the same movements as the traditional Lunge Hold. If you don't have access to a barbell, you can use a pair of dumbbells instead. Grab a dumbbell in each hand, curl the weights up, then rest the ends along the front of your shoulders.

TIP:

- If you have a hard time holding two dumbbells by your shoulders, try the move holding a single heavier dumbbell in front of your chest with both hands, or just let your arms hang straight down.

PRISONER SQUATS

SETUP: Stand straight with your feet hip-width apart and your arms up, elbows bent, fingers laced behind your head.

EXECUTE: Keeping your chest up and your back flat, sit back into a squat and lower yourself as far down as possible. Your feet should remain flat on the floor throughout the entire move. Pushing through your heels, press yourself back up into the Setup Position. That's one repetition.

TIP:

- If you find that you're rolling your back slightly in order to sink deeper into the squat, don't. Instead, only squat down as far as you can with your back flat.

PULL-UPS

SETUP: Reach up and grab the pull-up bar with an overhand grip (palms facing away from you) with your hands slightly wider than shoulder-width apart, thumbs wrapped around the bar. Pull your shoulder blades down toward your spine.

EXECUTE: Pull your elbows down as you bring your chest and shoulders up to meet the bar. Your chin must reach the bar to count as one repetition. Lower yourself back down until your arms are straight. That's one repetition.

TIPS:

- Don't just let yourself drop after each pull-up. Instead, fight gravity on the way down.
- Don't arch your back to help your chest meet the bar. You want to keep your core tight and your back as flat as possible throughout the move.

PUSH-UPS

SETUP: Place your hands flat on the floor, shoulder-width apart, keeping your arms straight and elbows locked. Straighten your legs behind you and rise up on your toes, so the top of the balls of your feet are touching the floor. Your body should be one straight line from your head to your feet, head facing down at the floor.

EXECUTE: Bend your elbows, slowly lower yourself until your upper arms are parallel to the floor, then push yourself back up. That's one repetition.

TIPS:

- Don't flare your elbows out—this shifts stress onto your shoulder joints. Instead, keep your elbows and upper arms at a 45 degree angle to your torso.
- Keep your back flat—arching it redirects stress onto your lower back. Instead, your spine should stay in line with your legs throughout the move.

PUSH-UP HOLD BOTTOM

For this move, you'll need to place your hands on a pair of equal-height boxes around 9 to 12 inches high. You can use milk crates, aerobic steps, push-up bars—so long as they are sturdy and equal in height.

SETUP: Position both boxes parallel to each other about shoulder-width to start. Kneel between the boxes, place a hand on each box, bend your elbows, and lower yourself all the way down, then straighten your legs behind you. Rise up on your toes so the top of the balls of your feet are touching the floor. Finally, adjust yourself either backward or forward to make sure your elbows are directly over your hands.

EXECUTE: Maintaining this position, hold for the required amount of time.

TIPS:

- Try to pinch your shoulder blades back and down, which will expand the chest and load it in the most extreme position.
- Your body needs to stay in a straight line at all times, so keep your core engaged.
- You may need to experiment with the distance between the objects. You want your elbows to be at a 45-degree angle off your body at the bottom. If your elbows are tucked in close—or flared out to the sides—the exercise won't be as effective.

PUSH-UPS (LOADED)

SETUP (AND EXECUTE): Get yourself in the same position as the Push-Up Hold Bottom. Have a training partner add extra weight to your torso by placing a dumbbell lengthwise over your shoulders, or let them place their hands between your shoulder blades and have them apply gentle and steady pressure.

TIP:

- You can use a weight vest if you'd like, as long as you can remove it fast enough after you're finished with it, so that wearing it doesn't interfere with the pacing of the workout this move is used in.

QUICK-STYLE BICEPS CURLS

SETUP: Grab a barbell with an underhand grip (palms facing up) and your hands shoulder-width apart. Your arms should hang straight down, so that the bar is positioned directly in front of your thighs.

EXECUTE: Keeping your back straight and elbows tucked into your sides, quickly curl the bar up in a semicircular motion until your forearms touch your biceps. Immediately pull the bar back down to the Setup Position, using your triceps (the muscles along the back of the arm). That's one repetition.

TIPS:

- If you don't have access to a barbell, just substitute a pair of dumbbells.
- Speed is everything. Bringing the bar down just as quickly as you've curled it up will prevent gravity from doing the work for you.

REBOUND PUSH-UPS

SETUP: From a kneeling position, place your hands flat on the floor, shoulder-width apart, keeping your arms straight and elbows unlocked. Lift your feet up off the floor.

EXECUTE: Bend your elbows and lower yourself until your upper arms are parallel to the floor, then push yourself back into the Setup Position. At the top, quickly draw your elbows back and pull your hands off the floor. Let your torso fall forward and catch yourself at the bottom by quickly placing your hands flat on the floor midfall. Press yourself back up and repeat.

TIPS:

- For a real challenge, try Beast Mode. Instead of resting on your knees, try straightening your legs behind you and rise up on your toes, so the top of the balls of your feet are touching the floor.
- Don't flare your elbows out—this shifts stress onto your shoulder joints. Instead, keep your elbows and upper arms at a 45 degree angle to your torso.
- Keep your back flat—arching it redirects stress onto your lower back. Instead, your spine should stay in line with your legs throughout the move.

1

2

3

4

ROLLOVER TO HAMSTRING

SETUP: Sit on a mat (or any soft surface that isn't uncomfortable against your spine) with your legs extended in front of you, arms down by your sides.

EXECUTE: Keeping your legs as straight as possible, roll backward—letting the momentum of your legs carry your feet over your head—and try to touch your toes to the floor. Immediately roll forward and reach your hands toward your feet to touch your toes. That's one repetition.

TIPS:

- Let the momentum of the move bring you backward and forward—the exercise should flow like one continuous movement.
- If you can't touch your toes to the floor, can't touch your toes with your hands, or can't do both—that's fine. Just work through the range of motion you're able to do and try to extend that range of motion each time you perform the movement.
- If you need to bend your legs slightly as you roll backward, that's okay (so long as you focus on trying to extend your legs straighter and straighter as you go.)
- It might seem obvious, but make sure to give yourself some room for this movement. As you get going, you may rotate slightly, so have plenty of space before you start.

RUSSIAN LUNGES

SETUP: Stand straight with your feet hip-width apart, arms bent (elbows back, fists forward). Take a large step forward, plant your lead foot on the floor, and sink into a lunge position. Your front leg should be bent at 90 degrees (thigh parallel to the floor; lower leg perpendicular). Your back leg should be as straight as possible behind you with your heel raised off the floor.

EXECUTE: Quickly swing both elbows back, then thrust your arms upward as you simultaneously lift your front knee up (along with the front foot) and your back heel as high as possible. Land in the Setup Position (that's one repetition) and repeat for the required number of repetitions.

TIPS:

- It's important to use your arms to generate enough energy to help raise you off the floor.
- Don't lean forward at the waist as you go. Your torso should remain as upright as possible.
- Your front knee should never buckle inward—it should always be in line with your hip and your ankle. If it does, reduce how high you're hopping until you develop enough coordination and strength in the hips.
- As you jump, you'll notice your back leg will bend. That's normal—just be sure to extend it back into position on the way down.

SCAP HANG

SETUP (AND EXECUTE): Hang from a pull-up bar, palms facing forward with your thumbs around the bar. Keep your head in line with your spine (don't let it fall back or forward) and try not to cross your legs if possible. While you hang, try to imagine spreading your shoulder blades apart.

TIP:

- If you don't have access to a parallel grip pull-up bar that lets your palms face each other, you can do the exercise using a traditional pull-up bar (hands shoulder-width apart, palms facing forward). However, this position can sometimes cause a pinching in the shoulders, so if you have the choice between the two, always go parallel grip.

SCAP HANG (LOADED)

SETUP (AND EXECUTE): Add extra weight to your body by doing any of the following: hanging a weighted chain over your neck and across your shoulders, wearing an exercise weight vest, or strapping on a pair of ankle weights. Then, repeat the same movements as the traditional Scap Hang.

SCAP REBOUNDS

SETUP: Hang from a pull-up bar, palms facing forward, with your thumbs around the bar. Keep your head in line with your spine (don't let it fall back or forward) and try not to cross your legs if possible.

EXECUTE: Without bending your arms, pull down your shoulder blades to raise your chest upward, then (instead of lowering yourself back down), let gravity take over and allow your body to drop. As soon as you finish falling, immediately pull your shoulder blades back down to raise your chest upward. That's one repetition.

TIP:

- This exercise should be done with maximum intensity.

SCAP REPS

SETUP: Hang from a pull-up bar, palms facing forward, with your thumbs around the bar. Keep your head in line with your spine (don't let it fall back or forward) and try not to cross your legs if possible.

EXECUTE: Without bending your arms, pull down your shoulder blades to raise your chest upward, then lower yourself back down. That's one repetition.

TIPS:

- Your elbows should stay locked throughout the movement.
- The movement is very slight—you'll only find yourself rising a few inches.
- If you don't have access to a parallel grip pull-up bar that lets your palms face each other, you can do the exercise using a traditional pull-up bar (hands shoulder-width apart, palms facing forward). However, this position can sometimes cause a pinching in the shoulders, so if you have the choice between the two, always go parallel grip.

SCORPIONS

SETUP: Lie facedown on your stomach with your legs straight and your arms extended out from your sides, palms down.

EXECUTE: Keeping your arms and chest on the floor, squeeze your left glute, lift your left leg as high as you can, then twist your hip and try to touch your left foot to the floor as close to your right hand as possible. Reverse the movement to return to the Setup Position, then repeat with your right leg. That's one repetition.

TIP:

- Your goal is to try to bring your foot up as close to the opposite hand as possible (left foot/right hand; right foot/left hand). However, keep your arms in place and don't slide them down to help your hands get closer to each foot.

SINGLE-ARM BENT-OVER LATERAL RAISES

SETUP: Stand straight with your feet hip-width apart, arms at your sides, holding a weight in your right hand. Keeping your legs straight and knees soft, bend at the hips and lean forward until your torso is as close to parallel as possible. Let your right arm hang straight out toward the floor, palm facing to your left. (Let your left arm relax and rest your left hand along your right thigh.)

EXECUTE: Keeping your right arm straight, sweep it out to your side until your arm is parallel to the floor, then lower it back to the Setup Position. That's one repetition. After performing the required number of reps, repeat the exercise with your left arm.

TIPS:

- The motion should involve only the working arm. You want to minimize any other movement, such as your body turning toward the weight.
- If you can't lower your torso down to parallel, just go as far down as you can, so long as your back remains flat at all times.

SINGLE-LEG CALF RAISES

SETUP: Stand tall on a stable platform 6 to 12 inches high (such as a step or sturdy box) and place the balls of your feet on the edge of the platform so that your heels hang off the edge. Place your right hand against something nearby for support (such as a railing or wall corner), then, bend your right leg behind you so that you're only resting on your left foot. Let your left arm hang down by your side.

EXECUTE: Keeping your left hip and left knee locked, rise up on the toes of your left foot, raising your left heel up as high as you can. Pause, then lower your left heel down as far as possible. That's one repetition. Do the amount of repetitions required, then switch positions to work your right leg.

TIP:

- As you go, stare straight ahead and not at your foot. Your head and neck should be in line with your spine throughout the move.

SINGLE-LEG CALF RAISES (LOADED)

SETUP: Grab a dumbbell in your left hand, then follow the same Setup directions as the Single-Leg Calf Raises.

EXECUTE: Keeping your left hip and left knee locked, rise up on the toes of your left foot, raising your left heel up as high as you can, then hold for the required amount of time. Once you're done, switch positions to work your right leg.

TIP:

- Pick a weight you can manage, but find yourself failing with, before your time is up. When I say failure, I mean having your heel fall below parallel. If your heel never falls below parallel within the required amount of time, then add more weight the next workout (around 2.5 to 5 pounds more).

SPEED RUSSIAN LUNGES

SETUP: Stand straight with your feet hip-width apart. Take a large step forward with your left foot, keeping your heel off the floor, and sink into a lunge position. Your left leg should be bent at 90 degrees (thigh parallel to the floor; lower leg perpendicular). Your right leg should be as straight as possible behind you with your right heel raised off the floor. Finally, bend your arms at 90 degrees, then bring your right arm forward and your left arm behind you.

EXECUTE: Quickly pick up both feet up and switch positions (so that your right leg is forward, left leg back). As you go, simultaneously pump your arms so that your left arm is forward and your right arm is back. Reverse the move by quickly picking up both feet and switching positions once more (so that you're back in the Setup Position). That's one repetition.

TIPS:

- The object isn't to jump as high as possible. Try to stay as low as you can to the floor. You just want to jump sufficiently high enough so that you're able to switch positions.
- Each time you land, you should hear a "stomp" as both feet come in contact with the floor. If you hear your feet scraping across the floor, you're not generating enough force to switch positions.

SQUAT HOLDS

SETUP: Stand straight with your feet hip-width apart and your hands in front of you (elbows bent and fists together). Keeping your chest up and your back flat, sit back into a squat and lower yourself as far down as possible. Your feet should remain flat on the floor throughout the entire move.

EXECUTE: Maintaining this position, hold for the required amount of time.

TIPS:

- Don't stare down—focus straight ahead. Looking down can make it harder to concentrate on staying balanced.
- Your knees should always stay directly above your feet.

SQUAT HOLDS (LOADED)

SETUP: Rest a barbell across the back of your shoulders, then repeat the same movements as the traditional Squat Hold. If you don't have access to a barbell, you can use a pair of dumbbells instead. Grab a dumbbell in each hand, curl the weights up, then rest the ends along the front of your shoulders.

TIP:

- If you have a hard time holding two dumbbells by your shoulders, try the move holding a single heavier dumbbell in front of your chest with both hands, or just let your arms hang straight down.

SQUAT JUMPS

SETUP: Stand straight with your feet hip-width apart and your arms bent, elbows pointing down and your fists in front of your chest.

EXECUTE: Quickly bend your knees and drop down into a squat as you simultaneously swing your arms back behind you. Pushing through your heels, jump up as high as you can as you swing your arms up over your head. As soon as you hit the ground, drop back down into a squat (swinging your arms down and back) and repeat for the required number of repetitions.

TIPS:

- It's important to get your arms in sync with your legs. Pulling them back and swinging them forward will help propel you even higher with every jump.
- The object is to go up and down only—not up and forward—so concentrate on minimizing how far forward or backward you travel as you jump.

STANDING ECCENTRIC HAMSTRING

SETUP (AND EXECUTE): Stand straight with your feet parallel to each other. Your knees should be unlocked, but partially flexed so that your legs never bend during the movement. Fold your arms in front of you. Next, bend at the waist as far as possible, allowing your crossed arms to dangle from your shoulders. Let your head relax so that you're looking back toward your legs. Finally, engage your abdominals and hip flexors to help pull your torso down even further. Hold this position for the required amount of time.

TIP:

- Don't count on gravity doing the work for you. You should be pulling yourself downward, using your abs and hip flexors the entire time.

STANDING LEG CURLS

SETUP: Stand straight with your arms crossed in front of your chest. Raise your right knee up in front of you as high as you can.

EXECUTE: Maintaining your balance on your left leg, quickly straighten your right leg out in front of you, then quickly bend your right knee and curl your right foot in toward you. That's one repetition. As you go, try to keep your toes pulled up as high as possible. Finish the required number of repetitions, then repeat the exercise with your left leg, starting the exercise with your left knee raised up in front of you.

TIPS:

- As you alternate between extending and curling your leg, you need to keep your leg raised as high as you possibly can.
- Do the move as quickly as you can without losing form or your balance.

STANDING STRAIGHT LEG RAISES

SETUP: Stand straight with your feet hip-width apart and your arms crossed in front of your chest.

EXECUTE: Keeping your right leg straight (knee locked) raise it up in front of you as high as you can, then pull the toes of your right foot toward your knee. Contract your abdominal muscles, then hold for the recommended amount of time. Once finished, switch positions to work the left leg.

TIPS:

- Your body should remain straight throughout the move—don't tilt back or roll your hips forward. Your pelvis should remain tucked underneath you at all times.
- You won't be able to hold your leg up at the same angle for the entire duration—that's expected. As your leg begins to lower, don't arch your back. Just keep your leg raised as high as possible, knee locked, even if it's barely off the floor by the time you're done.
- Keep your toes pulled up and your knee locked the entire time. Bending your knee makes it possible to raise your leg higher, which is why some people make this mistake.
- Don't be concerned at first about how high you can lift your leg. (More height will come over time as you practice.)

STATUE OF LIBERTYS

SETUP: Stand straight with your feet hip-width apart and arms down at your sides. Keeping your right arm close to your body, cross it in front of your body so that your right hand is directly in front of your left hip. Rotate your hand so that your thumb faces your hip and your pinkie faces outward.

EXECUTE: Keeping your right arm straight, quickly raise it up and back at an angle straight back as you simultaneously rotate your right palm outward. At the top, your right arm should be extended above you (as close to your head as possible) with your thumb pointing behind you. Pause at the top, then quickly reverse the movement by bringing your right arm back down at an angle, rotating your right palm inward as you go, so that you end up in the Setup Position. That's one repetition.

TIP:

- Move your arm as fast as possible, but always pause both at the top and bottom of the movement.

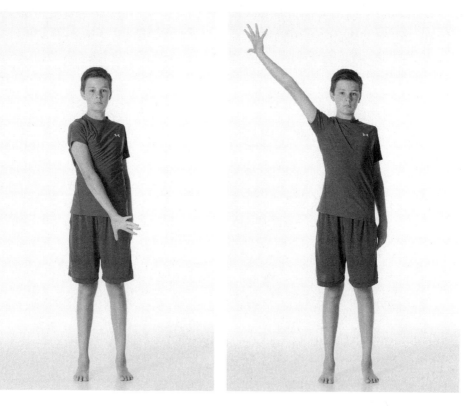

SUPPORTED SQUATS

SETUP (AND EXECUTE): Stand with your feet hip-width apart in front of a sturdy object you can grab around waist level (such as a chain-link fence, a pole, or both sides of a doorknob). Grab the object with both hands, then sit back and sink into a squat position, stopping when your thighs are just below parallel to the floor, knees positioned directly above your ankles. Keeping your chest up and your back flat, hold this position for the required amount of time.

TIPS:

- You shouldn't be struggling to maintain your grip. If you are, you're leaning too far back and relying more on your upper body to support you.
- As your muscles begin to fail, your butt will lower toward the floor. That's entirely fine—just be persistent, take a breath to get back in position, and keep going.

SWINGS

SETUP: Stand straight with your feet wider than shoulder-width apart, arms in front of you, fingers clasped together. Keeping your back flat, squat down as low as possible, letting your arms hang down between your legs.

EXECUTE: Quickly stand up as you simultaneously raise your arms up over your head. Immediately squat down and pull your arms back down into the Setup Position. That's one repetition.

TIPS:

- Your feet should stay flat on the floor at all times.
- At the top of the move, your body should be in full extension. If your hips are pulled back, knees are still bent, or your arms aren't as high as possible, you're limiting the range of motion.
- The move should be done very aggressively—not slowly—but with control at all times.

TOE TOUCHES

SETUP: Stand with your feet hip-width apart and your arms hanging straight down in front of you.

EXECUTE: Keeping your legs straight, slowly bend forward, touch your toes, then rise back up into the Setup Position. That's one repetition.

TIPS:

- If you can't reach your toes, you can touch your ankles, shins, or however far you can bend.
- If touching your toes is easy, touch the floor instead.
- Each time you descend, try to gain a little momentum on the way down so that you're able to reach a little farther each time—if possible.
- Concentrate on contracting your abdominals as you descend. Think about pulling yourself down using your abdominal muscles, instead of just letting gravity do its job.

VERTICAL JUMP TO LUNGE

SETUP: Stand straight with your feet hip-width apart with your arms bent, elbows pointing down, hands in front of your chest.

EXECUTE: Bend your knees as you swing your arms back behind you, then jump straight up as high as you can. As you go, swing your arms forward for momentum and tuck your knees up toward your chest. At the top of the jump, split your legs into a lunge position, placing your left foot forward and your right foot back. When you land, your left leg should be bent at 90 degrees (thigh parallel to the floor; lower leg perpendicular), and your right leg should be as straight as possible—you should be resting on the ball of your foot.

Return to the Setup Position, then repeat the movement, only this time at the top of the movement, split your legs so that your right foot is forward and your left foot is back. That's one repetition.

TIPS:

- Your arms may want to swing out to the sides for balance. Instead, concentrate on keeping your arms in close to your body as they swing back and forth.
- Jump as high as possible each and every time. It's okay to jump up just enough to get into position and glide into a lunge, but only until you begin getting more comfortable with the move.
- Don't let your heels hit the floor upon landing.

Y'S

SETUP: Stand straight with your feet hip-width apart. Bring your arms straight in front of you with your arms turned inward, so that the back of your hands face each other.

EXECUTE: Keeping your arms straight, quickly raise both arms up over your head at an angle so that your body looks like the capital letter Y. As you go, simultaneously rotate your arms outward so that the top of the move, your thumbs are pointing straight back behind you. Immediately pull your arms back down into the Setup Position just as quickly, simultaneously rotating your arms inward as you go. That's one repetition.

TIP:

- Keep your chest up nice and tall—don't let the motion pull your torso forward or cause your shoulders to round at the bottom.

PART IV
Recover

What parents don't understand about training is that every action is a breakdown—it's damage done in a controlled setting with the hope that when they're through, athletes will take the right steps to allow their body to repair, recover, and regenerate. Done right, they will be a different athlete—a better athlete—the next time they walk through the door.

CHAPTER 11

If You're Not Listening to Your Body—You're Losing

The Recover portion of the Tommy John Solution may be the final piece of the puzzle, but it's far from the least important. The fact is, by not taking this last section seriously, then everything your young athlete will have put in up until this point could literally amount to nothing.

I have athletes of all ages come to me that believe recovery is nothing more than using a foam roller, popping an aspirin, lying on a rubber ball to work out the knots, and taking an ice bath now and then. If I'm lucky, some might understand the importance of sleep, but beyond that, the actual concept of recovery is something many athletes never fully grasp.

Part of it has to do with pride, especially when you're dealing with an athlete who is competitive. That desire to be the best often leaves young athletes less likely to admit when they feel pain, fatigue, or anything else that might make them seem like the weakest link on the team.

Others simply feel that recovery is something only to be taken seriously at certain moments, such as immediately after a workout or practice, or taking a day off after a big game or match, or giving their body a chance to recover only after they've injured it.

It's that attitude that's holding back many athletes, especially the young. It's that "whatever doesn't kill me makes me stronger" approach that may eventually prove them wrong if they don't understand what is actually making them stronger in the first place. Yet once you give them not just the right recovery tools but a better sense of what's happening within their body as a result, not only will they find themselves less sore and less fatigued, but they will emerge into a healthier, injury-resistant athlete.

WHAT'S REALLY HAPPENING BEHIND THE SCENES

Here are the facts: Despite the gender or age of your young athlete, or what sport or activity he or she is involved in, there is one thing I am absolutely sure about when it comes to your child—and that's this: *Every minute of the day, your child's body is either in a catabolic state (meaning that it's being broken down) or in an anabolic state (meaning that it's building itself back up).*

They're Always Breaking Down

It's simple science. When you deconstruct any sport to its very essence, each is nothing more than just a culmination of a bunch of simple body movements organized into complex skill sets, done a number of times within a game, period, event, quarter, or inning. And when young athletes train or practice for their sport, all they're really doing is being directed to simplify those complex skill sets into their basic fundamental movements, in a manner where they are performed as reps, sets, timed drills (or however their coach has their practice organized).

Kind of takes a little of the fun out of sports, doesn't it?

Still, that's how a young athletes' body interprets every game, practice, or competition. You see, their body isn't caught up in the moment of possibly going into overtime or relishing that perfect game-winning shot or kick. It's not on the edge of its seat wondering whether it's going to be the MVP or it's going to make it to the state finals.

All it knows is that sport is nothing more than a series of movements that are breaking down its muscles and tissues, leaving its neurotransmitters depleted, and placing stress on ligaments, bones, discs, meniscus, and cartilage from head to toe. That means no matter how long your son or daughter participated that day, and despite how much effort he or she may have put in, the moment he or she steps off the field, court, or out of the gym, your child is leaving it "broken down"—even if he or she isn't the least bit sore or tired whatsoever.

They're Always Building Up

Most young athletes don't realize all the microtraumas and culmination of damage that accrue during training sessions and games. How it takes a certain amount of time, rest, and a storm of other factors to occur for a body to heal itself and return to a state of homeostasis (a fancy word that basically means "back to normal").

It's a perpetual back-and-forth relationship—a negotiation with their body, if you will—in which the body is constantly trying to return to its former self. What young athletes are really doing through training and practice is trying to raise that level of homeostasis—to make their "new normal" something that's much faster, stronger, and more skilled than their "old normal."

When recovery is paid attention to, their body builds itself back up in a way that's a little bit better than it was before they broke it down. But when recovery is ignored (or done with less effort than it deserves), they go into that next game or practice not stronger or faster than they were before—not even at the same level that they were before—but as even less of an athlete than they were before.

They Always Have a Decision to Make

When I have young athletes that are stubborn to do what is required to recover, I make it easy by standing in front of them and telling them straight up:

"Look, right now, at this very second and every moment after that, for as long as you're alive on this planet—your body is either building itself up or breaking itself down. Right now, you are either evolving into a better, stronger, faster athlete or devolving into a weaker, slower, less capable athlete. Not because you aren't doing what's necessary to be the best, but because you're not letting yourself properly recover from the wear and tear your sport is placing on your body. So . . . which side of the fence do you want to be on?"

And then, it all starts to click.

They begin to realize that in my office, I've technically "broken down" their body in a controlled setting. But when they leave my office, it's up to them whether their body builds back up and reaches the next rung of the ladder.

They finally grasp that treating recovery with respect will ultimately decide whether the person that comes back for the next session is even more prepared and developed as a human being than the person I saw the last time. They start to realize that every action they take is a decision that determines how far along they'll go toward reaching their personal goals with performance and being more proficient in their sport.

Finally—They've Got a Big Head Start

Even though this section is designed to speed up the recovery of young athletes, you must understand it's far from the only piece of the recovery puzzle in regard to the Tommy John Solution.

- By having your son or daughter **Rethink** his or her lifestyle, activities, and personal habits, your child's body is already in a better state of healing by just avoiding what has been placing undue stress on it all along.
- By getting your child to **Replenish** his or her body with the right foods—and reduce or eliminate the wrong ones—your young athlete is getting more of the nutrients his or her body needs to repair itself faster and more efficiently.
- By using the exercises and techniques in the **Rebuild** section that correct dysfunction and prevent further damage from occurring, your son or daughter is developing a body that is more injury-resistant—one that can recover from the stress of sport even faster.

These three portions of the Tommy John Solution work in sync with one another, and with all three now in play, your young athlete already has an edge in recovery that no amount of rest could ever mimic.

That's one of the greatest thrills for me working with athletes. It's that moment when they finally realize that all the things that we've done up until that point—all the training, all the nutrition, all the changes to their lifestyle and personal habits—were designed to make an impact on how fast and efficiently their body can recover.

It's that moment of consciousness when they finally recognize that how well athletes recover is ultimately what separates the truly elite from the endlessly injured.

The Recover section is the cherry on top—it is not the immediate solution to a problem. This is the bonus. This is a way to magnify the restorative effect that the other three—Rethink, Replenish, and Rebuild—are already having on your son's or daughter's body. This section is merely what is left over that can't be defined in the other three sections, but is equally important in keeping your child evolving into the athlete he or she was meant to become.

BUT THEY'RE KIDS—THEY BOUNCE BACK, RIGHT?

When we're young, we take youth for granted, but as parents, we can sometimes be equally guilty of doing the same thing. Often, it's easy to assume that because our sons and daughters have more energy than us and always spring back quicker than we do, that recovery isn't something that requires the same level of focus. I'll admit that yes, youth may be on their side, but youth should never be taken for granted.

Can kids bounce back? Compared to adults, they can—to an extent. But comparing the youth of today versus the youth of a generation ago, I wouldn't be so certain. As a parent, you may remember being a child and experiencing a completely different situation for yourself. But keep in mind that you also had a different set of habits in place that your children may not have today.

Now that you've made it through most of this book, you're aware of what's been holding kids back—and how many of those problems were never a part of your world while growing up. That's why I encourage parents that are on the fence about the seriousness of recovery to never assume being young will help a kid's body heal itself. It's that assumption that will leave your child behind, but embracing this section will propel your child so much further.

THE LOSING LINEUP THAT ALWAYS FAILS

Some of the things I'm about to advise you to stop doing with your young athlete will surprise you—actually, I'm counting on that reaction.

The fact of the matter is, a few tried-and-true recovery techniques you've most likely been using with your son or daughter, with good intentions—techniques I have no doubt you've also used on yourself—could be doing more harm than good.

Taking Nonsteroidal Anti-inflammatory Drugs (NSAIDs)

Back in 2007, I had a fourteen-year-old baseball player visit me with pain on the cap of his elbow. At first, I scratched my head, wondering what was going on underneath the surface, since his MRIs came back clear and showed nothing irregular. Yet despite working with me and two others in my office for two months, using all the techniques in this book, his pain never subsided, so he went for a second opinion.

The recommendation by another doctor *was to prematurely fuse the growth plate in his elbow with a screw!*

The boy's father came to me for my opinion, and I told him the truth. How his son's elbow wasn't shattered, that surgery didn't make any sense to me. I asked him to give the process more time to work. He took my advice to heart, and upon further examination, it was found that the boy had a very small stress fracture in his elbow. One that had apparently been there for years and years, but for some unknown reason had never healed.

Everything around that stress fracture was responding appropriately to stimuli. His bones and ligaments were growing normally, and his growth plate was starting to close—everything you would normally see in a kid growing up and training at his age. It remained a mystery why that stress fracture from years past never mended. That is, until it was revealed that the boy had been on a high level of anti-inflammatories for juvenile rheumatoid arthritis—or at least, that was the diagnosis of other doctors at the time.

Because of the level of anti-inflammatories working throughout his system, his body was never allowed the chance to heal itself. The medication was disrupting the recovery process from ever taking place. But once he stopped taking them, the recovery process finally had a chance to finish, and he was able to play without pain. It turned out he never had juvenile rheumatoid arthritis at all—he was just a kid going through the normal growing pains of life.

That boy's father still credits me to this day for saving his son's arm, which always makes me wonder how many other young athletes may be negatively impacted by relying on anti-inflammatories. Advil, Motrin, and Nuprin may be medicine cabinet standbys for pain, but most parents aren't aware that the inflammatory process is actually a healing system for damaged cells. Whether it's present in a ligament, muscle, or just on the surface of the skin, it's a short-term first-step response that begins a massive cascade of events that needs to occur for total cellular regeneration. In other words, inflammation is *supposed* to be there! It's not something you want to eliminate because it's the very first step of the healing process.

That's why from this day forward, when you see the word *anti-inflammatory* on a drug, it should be looked at as antihealing.

When young athletes pop a pill to combat a little soreness after an intense practice or game, it may not seem like that much of a big deal. But essentially, what they are doing is lessening and eliminating certain signals their body needs to hear to start the healing process. New research has shown that nonsteroidal anti-inflammatory drugs (NSAIDs) inhibit bone formation and fracture healing.[1] Even the use of short-term, low-dose NSAIDs inhibits bony healing,[2] and treating postfracture pain with NSAIDs puts patients at the greatest risk of experiencing complications.[3]

But that disruption doesn't stop with their bones. Presently, NSAIDs are also believed[4] to inhibit the healing process of connective tissue, as well as the stimulating effect of exercise on connective tissue protein synthesis, even though they are ironically taken for connective tissue injury and muscle soreness. This means that every time young athletes ease their pain with a pill, essentially they are ensuring their body never adequately recovers from whatever is potentially leaving them sore in the first place.

Another frightening thing about NSAIDs is that they aren't as specific as you may think. When taken, you might assume they act like a heat-seeking missile that hones in on whatever hurts. The reality is, NSAIDs are more akin to a bomb that blasts the entire body, which minimizes or stops the inflammatory process from head to toe, inside and out. So, if your son or daughter has other forms of inflammation that may need to heal—such as liver or small intestine inflammation—the NSAIDs may be slowing or preventing a variety of unknown healing processes from occurring that far outweigh relieving sore muscles.

But that's not the only thing being affected indirectly. Studies are already beginning to show that taking NSAIDs alters[5] the microbiome within the gut, changing the ratio between good versus bad types of bacteria. In addition, researchers from the Perelman School of Medicine at the University of Pennsylvania recently found[6] that the NSAID indomethacin (similar to ibuprofen and naproxen) may reduce prostaglandins in the body (that promote inflammation, pain, and fever), but it simultaneously lowers the prostaglandins that protect stomach lining cells and promote blood clotting.

The final reason I encourage kids to stay away from NSAIDs unless it's absolutely unavoidable (if they suffer from a health condition where chronic inflammation is a symptom, for example) is that they can keep children from hearing what their body may be trying to tell them.

We are supposed to feel pain, and young athletes should be considering what's happening inside their body and noticing what sensations are occurring within it.

What may be most frightening about having kids rely on NSAIDs so frequently is that they start becoming deaf to the feelings that are meant to be felt. The feelings that let them know whether they are performing movements that are safe to do or those they shouldn't be doing.

Pain is their body's way of warning them that there's a problem. It's quite possible that children who use NSAIDs on a regular basis will never hear those warnings until it's much too late.

Icing Every Injury

I cringe whenever I ask athletes whether they did anything to speed up recovery after a game and the answer I hear is, "Oh, yeah—I iced!" If I ask whether they did anything else, the answer is almost always no. But what's even sadder is when I tell them the effort they just spent icing was nothing more than a colossal waste of time.

Today, the market has created a flood of products that allow you to ice any appendage with ease. And when young athletes hurt themselves, no matter what the injury may be, the protocol most parents are told to stick with is still the tried-and-true RICE method (rest, ice, compression, and elevation). Even after physical therapy, many practitioners will typically end a training session by applying ice for ten to fifteen minutes to the area that was just focused on.

The intentions are good, but they got it all wrong.

If you've ever used the RICE method, you have physician Gabe Mirkin to thank for that. Back in the 1970s, it was Mirkin who first noticed that placing severed limbs in ice slowed down their degeneration until they could be reattached. Suddenly, icing became the acceptable way to treat many aches, pains, breaks, and strains. But what many parents don't realize is that Mirkin has since overturned his opinion in the face of new overwhelming evidence.

That's right. The man behind why most of us reach for a resealable plastic bag and some ice whenever our kids feel pain is now telling the world to keep that ice in the freezer.

Over the last few years, it's been widely recognized that applying ice to the body slows down and shuts off blood flow that's critical for bringing in the healing cells of inflammation, particularly insulin-like growth factor (IGF-1)—a hormone that helps muscles and other injured parts to repair and recover.

Even worse, that restriction of blood flow doesn't stop the moment the ice pack comes off. One recent study[7] that examined the magnitude and persistence of vasoconstriction associated with cryotherapy found that blood flow to an injured area remained reduced long after cooling had stopped and the underlying tissues had warmed up to their normal temperature.

Beyond the science, another issue I have with ice is that it also numbs the area, making a person less capable of feeling pain. Before you think I'm a sadist that wants to see young athletes suffer, it's exactly the opposite—I need them to feel that pain to protect them.

You see, chronic icing can give a lot of young athletes a sense of power over their pain. If something aches, it gives them the ability to ice it until it stops hurting, which can cause some athletes to jump back into an activity, exercise, or sport much sooner than they should. And for a period, there might be less swelling and pain, which can buy them a false sense that their injury is getting better as a result—but you can't trick the body for too long.

Eventually, that swelling, blood flow, and every other activity attached with the inflammatory process have to occur to flush out waste and bring in necessary nutrients required to heal that area. But if you put that healing on hold by using ice, your body won't stop trying to treat you, and in some cases, fights back even harder by magnifying the inflammatory process, causing even more swelling and redness to occur. All you're essentially doing with ice is making yourself feel better at the expense of making your body feel worse.

Is there ever a right time to use ice? In my practice, unless something is either broken or dislocated, I always say no to ice, across the board. The only time I'll allow it is if an athlete suffers a sprain, contusion, or bruise from an impact. Then, if you can get ice on that injured area within the first fifteen minutes or so, that would be the only time to apply it, strictly to alleviate the initial pain.

But once that ice bag melts, that's it—you're done. And if you've missed that short window, then I don't want you to bother because, by then, it doesn't matter. After that point, the ice will only be slowing things down, as I mentioned earlier. Instead, it's best to elevate the injured area and get it moving as soon as possible—even if it's a millimeter at a time—to get the wheels of the healing process in motion.

If you have the need to do something because discomfort is too aggravating, applying heat (just to bring some form of relief) is acceptable. But personally, I don't recommend young athletes use heat to the point where they get in the habit of always putting something on their body every time they feel sore. I want them always to be listening to what their body is trying to tell them, instead of constantly turning down the volume.

Stretching Statically

Have you ever seen athletes reach their arm across their body and pull it over with their opposite arm to loosen up their shoulders and upper back? Ever watch them bend their knee, grab their foot from behind and pull their heel toward their butt to stretch their quadriceps, the muscles along the front of the thigh?

These are only a few examples of simple static stretches, which is when you extend a muscle to the end of its range of motion, then hold it in that position for a certain amount of seconds. We've all used these stretches in the past, and maybe you're a parent that still uses them in the present. One thing that I do know is that many young athletes continue to use them to limber up before competition or practice, either because their coaches tell them to, or they assume they work. But let's start with the facts first, shall we?

The entire premise behind static stretches is that by doing them before activity, they are meant to prevent injuries and improve performance by increasing athletes' range of motion. Doing them after activity is also thought to reduce muscle stiffness and delayed onset muscle soreness (DOMS). The problem: There's a lot of science out there that debates their effectiveness.

Research[8] out of McMaster University has shown that static stretching had no effect on reducing the total number of injuries ranging from shin splints, tibial stress reaction, sprains, strains, and lower extremity and limb injuries. Studies have also begun to hint at the fact that static stretching can inhibit an athletes' maximal muscular performance,[9] reduce strength and weaken lower body stability,[10] and even impair their explosive performance up to twenty-four hours.[11]

But if the information out there doesn't convince you, these simple facts seem to work with the athletes I work with:

First things first: no child needs to static stretch—ever.

Children typically don't experience tight muscles—it just doesn't work that way—which is why static stretching is entirely unnecessary, particularly in the young. Even in the state in which many children are coming into my office, no amount of static stretching would ever address their deficiencies, making static stretching not only a waste, but an activity that could increase their risk of injury and bring down their overall output in their sport.

Second, if your young athlete does experience tight muscles, it's actually a neurological issue, not a physiological issue. You see, a muscle's primary job is simply to contract, so it either lengthens, shortens, or holds position isometrically. So, after a grueling practice, if your son or daughter feels a few tight muscles, then guess what? It's not his or her muscles' fault—it's your child's brain that's making them tight.

Why would it do that?

It works like this: Whenever certain tissues of the body become weak, fatigued, or injured, the brain throws other muscles into lockdown mode, making them tight to help protect more important tissue underneath. It's not that something that person did to the muscles to make them tight. It's just the brain using that body's muscles as a defense mechanism.

One example I use with parents is to describe someone under anesthesia. You could take the most inflexible human being on the planet and anesthetize that person, and suddenly, he or she becomes the most flexible person in the world! How is that possible? Because under anesthesia, the brain's normal protective integrated response is shut down. Alcohol serves in that same capacity. If you've ever heard about a car accident where the victim was inebriated but miraculously suffered no injuries whatsoever, it's the same premise.

That said, if the brain is responsible for tightening muscles because certain tissues are weak, fatigued, or injured, then how can static stretching help? The fact remains, static stretching isn't a proven solution for making a muscle stronger, improving a muscle's ability to recover from fatigue, or helping with the healing process. That's why when it comes to making young athletes limber, strengthening their muscles—not stretching them—is the answer, which is exactly what the Tommy John Solution does.

Using Long-Distance Running Improperly

One recovery trick that I used to do when I played pro ball—and that I still see both pro and amateur athletes of every age using as a recovery tool—is distance running after a practice or game.

The thought was—and still is—that a long run helped get blood flowing to flush out lactate (or lactic acid). As their muscles lose strength and energy through exercise and sport, lactate is brought in to counter the depolarization of cells. It's the culprit behind why athletes' muscles feel a burning sensation during exercise. But it's also often blamed for DOMS, pain and soreness that usually occurs a day or two after intense exercise or activity. That's why some coaches still feel a nice long run after practice helps remove lactate, which can prevent or minimize DOMS.

Here's the thing: Even if your son or daughter participated in their sport at a high enough intensity to have a high concentration of lactate build up in his or her muscles, that lactate is cleared naturally from the muscles in about an hour—no matter how intense the workout, practice, or game. Moreover, contrary to popular opinion, lactate does not cause DOMS, which is actually the result of by microdamage done to muscle fibers.

Other coaches wise to that information still may have young athletes run polls or laps after practice because they believe it builds up stamina. But unless the children are running competitively (such as distance running for track), long-distance running doesn't condition the body in the way it's actually being used in most sports.

The majority of activity in most sports is anaerobic in nature, meaning that the activity requires quick bursts of power at a high intensity. Think about what young athletes are doing most of the time on the field, court, or gym. If you look closely, even if they're out there playing for two or three hours, there's a lot of stopping and starting. When they're active, they're active for a few seconds up to a minute—and that's it.

Distance running is purely aerobic in nature: it's a low- to moderate-intensity activity meant to be sustained for an extended period of time. It's also a quadriceps-dominant exercise, relying on a particular set of muscles to move the body in one direction only—forward. Most sports require athletes to be able to go in every direction, which is why using short bursts of activity—such as a circuit of jumps, squats, jumping jacks, sprints, and so forth—would be much more beneficial for them to not only condition their cardiovascular system, but prepare their muscles for the high-intensity, short-burst activity they're typically used for.

I could get into what science already knows about long-distance running and how that can negatively impact an athlete's overall performance. It's a form of high-volume endurance exercise, which has been shown to increase cortisol, which can have a catabolic (degrading) effect on muscle tissue. Training for endurance has also been shown for decades to decrease bone mineral density, as well as lower testosterone[12] and androgen hormones, which are critical in aiding muscle repair.

But my biggest beef with it is this: running is an earned skill set. By using the Tryout Test, you are now aware of the dysfunction that's already taking place in your young athlete—and you're fortunately doing something about it. But so many other young athletes out there aren't privy to what you now know. Without correcting that dysfunction, when they run, their knees and ankles are all over the place, due to poor biomechanics.

That's why, in my opinion, even if they can do it, today's kids haven't earned the ability to run long distances—at least not until they bring their body back into balance.

Skimping on Sleep

There's something about staying up late that makes any kid feel more like a grown-up. Add the fact that nowadays there are so many more distractions that keep kids engaged and entertained 24/7, and you can imagine the difficulty I experience with even the most serious athletes in getting them to respect sleep as the most powerful tool in their recovery toolbox.

Sleep isn't something they have to do—it's something they need to do. It's literally the equivalent of plugging them into a wall, giving the body the uninterrupted time it needs to repair, restore, and rebuild itself. Recent studies[13] have shown that during sleep, the immune system is given a better chance to regroup, releasing T cells (white blood cells that fight viruses and other pathogens) and growth hormones to fight off infection. But even just one late night can disrupt that process, making your son's or daughter's immune system less likely to fight off infection and heal itself.

But from a purely athletic standpoint, the latest research has shown that getting enough sleep goes far beyond the obvious benefits.

New evidence has revealed how getting enough zzz's may better lock in the skills young athletes are being taught. It seems sleep helps improve long-term retention,[14] whereas lack of it handicaps[15] the brain's ability to recalibrate cells responsible for learning and memory—the ones that make it possible to solidify lessons learned and use them once awake. Being sleep deprived has even been shown to negatively impact athletes by increasing their dependence on sugar[16] and eating unnecessary calories,[17] raising their blood pressure,[18] and depressing their immune system,[19] which can lead to missing more practice and events due to illness.

There is even new proof that inadequate sleep may keep your son or daughter from having stronger bones. In a 2017 study,[20] researchers at the Oregon Health & Science University in Portland found that when subjects slept an average of 5.6

hours, within three weeks, all the subjects were significantly lower in a bone formation marker called P1NP. Even more shocking was that the decline was greater in younger subjects, leading researchers to speculate that lack of sleep in our younger years could impact the risk of bone issues in both the immediate future and throughout life.

CHAPTER 12

Don't Just Accelerate the Healing Process—Own It!

E ven though every step of the Tommy John Solution places young athletes' body in a constant state of recovery, there are still a few last-minute things they can do to accelerate the healing process taking place inside them. Whether they choose to incorporate a few or all into their daily routine, these final techniques are guaranteed to enhance what they've accomplished up until now and ensure their body remains as impervious and proficient as possible.

INVEST IN NATURAL ANTI-INFLAMMATORIES

When I tell parents and patients to start taking certain all-natural anti-inflammatory foods, it's always met with complete confusion. After all, it's what I usually share right after I've just told them to stop taking anti-inflammatory drugs (NSAIDs). So, why would I ever suggest someone eat something that naturally reduces inflammation—if inflammation helps the healing process?

It's because, unlike NSAIDs, the foods I'm about to suggest do not turn off or shut down the inflammation process. These foods lessen inflammation by speeding up and helping out the healing process, which causes inflammation to go away faster naturally.

There are many anti-inflammatory foods, and by following the Replenish portion of the Tommy John Solution, your son or daughter is already eating some of those foods without realizing it. Grass-fed and/or organic meats and fish, certain fruits (particularly citrus and berries), cruciferous vegetables, nuts, avocados, and coconut oil are just a few anti-inflammatory foods your son or daughter should now be making a part of their diet. However, there are three major anti-inflammatory foods that I always recommend every young athlete take in certain amounts, particularly during times of increased stress or activity, or during an injury.

1. Cod liver oil: High in the omega-3 fatty acids eicosapentaenoic acid (EPA) and docosahexaenoic acid (DHA), the essential oil extracted from the livers of Atlantic cod boosts the immune system and lowers inflammation by assisting the healing response. It's also been shown to have a helping hand in practically every system of the body, including the digestive, nervous, circulatory, and endocrine system, the collection of glands that secrete hormones that regulate growth and development, sleep, metabolism, and tissue function, among other functions.

If young athletes aren't fond of fatty fish or their schedule prevents them from eating at least two servings of fish weekly, then getting this nutrient-dense food into their diet on a regular basis in the form of an oil supplement is even more important to prevent injury and have them perform at their best.

Why I prefer cod liver oil over fish oil is that, depending on the brand, cod liver oil also has high concentrations of two fat-soluble nutrients that children tend to be majorly deficient in: vitamin A (beneficial for bone and cellular growth, as well as testicular and ovarian function) and vitamin D.

How much to take each day: One teaspoon daily should do it. Personally, I prefer it lemon flavored and in liquid form (over capsules), but stick with whichever version your child prefers. However, before you have your young athlete begin taking any fish oil supplement, always talk with his or her doctor to make sure that a daily boost of omega-3 fatty acids won't interact with any medications your son or daughter may be on (such as anticoagulants).

2. Turmeric: Inside this aromatic bitter spice is curcumin, a chemical revered for its biofunctional properties, especially antioxidant, free radical scavenger, antitumor, antimicrobial, and anti-inflammatory activities—all of which greatly accelerate the healing process.

What's its secret? Some scientists believe[1] that it has to do with how molecules of curcumin implant themselves within cell membranes, making those membranes more stable in a way that boosts their resistance to infection from disease-causing microbes.

How much to take each day: For kids, my recommended dosage is about a tablespoon of ground turmeric daily sprinkled on whatever foods they like. Or they can take it in pill form—most come in 400 mg capsules, so a daily dose of two to four capsules per day should suffice. However, just as with cod liver oil, before you have your son or daughter begin taking turmeric, check with a doctor to make sure it won't interact with any medications.

3. Vitamin C: Essential for the growth and repair of tissues throughout the entire body (including cartilage, bone, teeth, skin, tendons, ligaments, and blood vessels, just to name a few), vitamin C's healing effects on a young athlete's body are simply staggering.

From preventing the damage caused by free radicals and assisting in the production of collagen, the superantioxidant also plays a big part in helping with iron absorption (crucial for helping red blood cells transport oxygen throughout the body).

How much to take each day: This can be tricky because everybody has a different level of how much vitamin C can be tolerated per day. It also can be difficult because a young athlete's need for the vitamin can also differ from day to day.

The good news is that even at high levels, vitamin C is not toxic. It's a water-soluble vitamin, so if young athletes take too large a dose, their body will flush out what it doesn't need. However, taking too much may still leave some kids temporarily feeling flushed or with an upset stomach, so watch your child carefully as you begin increasing his or her daily amount of the vitamin.

I've spoken to many physicians and sports specialists who suggest raising the daily amount of vitamin C far beyond what's recommended to accelerate the healing process. But if exceeding the norm scares you, just know that researchers are currently looking into the many positive effects of megadoses of vitamin C and the many ways it might protect the body from everything from cancer to the common cold.

A recent study[2] out of the Department of Public Health, University of Helsinki, found that subjects given 6 to 8 grams of vitamin C daily actually shortened the length of their colds by 17 and 19 percent, respectively, compared to subjects that were given half that amount (3 to 4 grams). Another recent trial[3] by researchers at the University of Iowa found that infusing brain and lung cancer patients with 800 to 1,000 times the daily recommended amount of vitamin C may make cancer cells more sensitive to radiation and chemotherapy—without having any negative effect on normal cells.

Still, a good place to start for youth (ages 8 to 13) is 500 to 1,000 mg daily. Adolescents aged thirteen years and older can go with a dosage of 1,000 to 2,000 mg per day. If your young athlete is sick or injured, you may benefit from experimenting with taking slightly higher levels, but always be sure to listen to your body.

RELY ON DYNAMIC MOVEMENTS TO WARM UP THE BODY

After working with a young athlete in my office, I'll often have parents ask me what their kids should do as a warm-up before a game or match, especially because I'm not a huge advocate of static stretching. That's when I'll turn to their child, the same kid I've just spent an hour putting through a series of exercises, and ask what he or she thinks would've been a good warm-up to what we just did in my office.

The answer is always on point: "What about a smaller version of what we just did—but for less time and fewer repetitions."

Bingo! See, the only difference between a warm-up and a workout is basically what it does to you. If it depletes you, it's a workout. If it revs up your body just enough to bring blood to your muscles and get your brain firing, then that's a warm up. And unlike static stretching, which keeps the body's muscles and systems in a relatively passive state, dynamic movements stimulate your body's systems and get them prepared for performance.

I'm a big believer that a warm-up should be a mix of the same exact movements you're about to do—whether that's in the gym, or on the field or court—but just do less of them at a lower intensity. That's why what I universally recommend to parents is to look at the movements their young athlete is about to perform, whether in competition or practice, and simply have the child do a certain amount of those movements (20 to 30, on average) at a lower intensity for a certain amount of time (minimum 5 minutes; maximum 10 minutes).

That said, if you're a sports parent with kids in multiple sports, or you just don't want to think that hard, I have a foolproof solution that applies to all sports. Better still, this multimovement warm-up is ideal injury insurance any time a child goes out to play—and it goes like this:

TJ'S ALL-PURPOSE PRE-GAME WARM-UP

I hate to break it to you, but your kid's brain isn't that smart. I take that back—no one's brain is as smart as we think it is.

The reality is, all the movements that human beings master are not sports specific. That's right, all the movements (that when combined in certain patterns create the sophisticated skills that allow your young athlete to pull off sports-specific moves) are simply that—movements.

See, your child's brain doesn't know that it's playing volleyball, baseball, basketball, soccer, football, or any other sport or activity you can throw at it. It's just flexing and extending certain parts of his or her body, whether it's at the ankle, elbow, hip, knee, what have you. It just knows that your son or daughter needs to perform certain actions at certain joints on cue as aggressively as that sport demands.

This six-movement warm-up is designed to get the body ready to move, no matter what sport children are involved in. But here's the catch: You must have them run through all six movements with the same intensity and pace they will most likely perform at in their sport. It's that aggressive pacing that will summon the most from their body. So as they do the following, have them think about what that speed needs to be by asking themselves questions such as:

- How fast do I need to throw or kick?
- How hard do I need to hit or swing?
- How quickly do I need to move?
- How much power do I need when I jump or sprint?

Whatever the answers are to those question, *that* is the pace they need to keep to not only prepare their muscles but tell their brain, "Hey! We're about to do *that* speed—so be ready."

The Routine

1. Calf Jumps for 60 seconds (see page 181)
2. 10 to 30 Prisoner Squats (see page 192): How many they do will depend on their age and ability. The best way to gauge: Do enough so that it feels like a warm-up—and not a workout.

3. 10 Hip Circles in both directions (clockwise and counterclockwise) in all three positions (leg forward, leg to the side, and leg back; see page 168). Start with the left leg extended, then repeat the entire drill with the right leg extended.

4. 10 to 30 Push-ups (see page 194): Again, how many will depend on age and ability. Have them do enough so it's a warm-up and not a workout.

5. 15 to 30 Spine Rotations each way (see page 174)

6. Cross-Crawl Supermans for 2 minutes (see page 183)

All said, doing these six movements should roughly take your young athletes between 7 and 9 minutes. After that, if they want to do something specific to their sport as a warm-up, have them perform one or two actions they count on in their sport that are the most intense thirty times each (10 times at 50% intensity, 10 times at 75% intensity, 10 times at 100% intensity).

- If your child plays baseball or softball, those actions might be mimicking throwing a ball or swinging the bat.
- If your child plays soccer, it could be mimicking a shot on goal.
- For basketball, it might be going from a triple threat to a shot.
- For football, it could be sprinting 5 yards, breaking down and cutting right or left, to a sprint or side shuffle for a few yards, depending on their position.
- If it's volleyball, they could try the power serve and the spike.

TJ'S ADVANCED A-LIST WARM UP!

Although the All-Purpose Pre-Game Warm-Up is incredibly effective, it's also designed to be easy to remember. But when a young athlete comes to me ready to put in even more work (and enjoys the challenge of a more complex warm-up), this advanced version is what I recommend.

continues

TJ'S ADVANCED A-LIST WARM UP! *continued*

The same rules that apply to the All-Purpose Pre-Game Warm-Up pertain here. You'll do all the movements with the same intensity and explosiveness as your sport.

- 15 **Calf Jumps** (see page 181)
- 10 **Squat Jumps** (see page 212)
- 5 **Rebound (or Regular) Push-ups** (see page 198)

Repeat all three movements with no rest in between for three sets total, then rest for 1 to 2 minutes—or just enough to catch your breath.

- 5 **Russian Lunges** each side (see page 200)
- 5 **Groiners** each side (see page 186)
- 5 **Speed Russian Lunges** each side (see page 209)

Repeat all three movements with no rest in between for two sets total, then rest for 1 to 2 minutes—or just enough to catch your breath.

- 10 **Spine Rotations** each way (see page 174)
- 10 **Scorpions** (see page 205)
- 10 **Rollover to Hamstring Stretch** (see page 199)

Repeat all three movements with no rest in between, then rest for 1 to 2 minutes—or just enough to catch your breath.

- 30 **Arm Shakedowns** (see page 178)
- 30 **Statue of Libertys** each arm (see page 216)

Repeat both movements with no rest in between, then rest for 1 to 2 minutes—or just enough to catch your breath.

- End the routine by performing one or two sport-specific actions that are the most intense, 30 times each (10 times at 50% intensity, 10 times at 75% intensity, 10 times at 100% intensity).

PUT YOUR LEGS UP POST-PLAY OR PERFORMANCE

Another effective trick I use with young athletes after any training session, practice, game, or match is having them lie down in front of a wall or fence and place their legs up on it (so that their legs are perpendicular to the ground). Their body should look like a capital L with their legs touching the wall or fence from their heels down to their butt.

I call it a "recovery powwow," because the only thing I ask them to do is just lie there with their feet elevated. I don't want to see a smartphone in their hand. I just want them to lie there, close their eyes if they like, feel what's happening to their muscles as blood begins to circulate the opposite way, and either think about strategy or discuss it with their teammates.

Not only is this simple elevation technique terrific at helping their body recover faster, but what I love is that it covertly gets them to meditate, which will bring them out of fight-or-flight mode and reduce levels of adrenaline and cortisol in their system.

It's hard to get young athletes to consider meditation because to them, the act of not doing something feels like three steps back in their training. That's why to keep them sitting still for that long, I make them think about strategy, along with asking them to reflect on what they can do for the rest of the day that will help move them toward being a better athlete.

As for time, I personally like for them to do it until their feet get tingly and almost on the verge of feeling numb—and then they're done. That feeling generally takes 10 to 15 minutes, which is why I recommend young athletes hold that pose for that amount of time. Any longer is entirely fine, although it's been my experience that getting youngsters to sit still for that long without a smartphone, tablet, or game controller in their hand is nearly impossible—so, good luck!

SWITCH THE ICE FOR A SPICE

I never talk pain rubs or salves for pain because, as I've stressed, I feel athletes—or people in general—need to listen to what pain is telling them. But in those moments where young athletes are already aware of why something aches and just need some form of relief, I prefer an all-natural option of a mix of coconut oil and cayenne powder instead of ice.

continues

SWITCH THE ICE FOR A SPICE   *continued*

What makes cayenne pepper hot in the first place is capsaicin, an ingredient that, when applied topically, temporarily blocks the transmission of pain signals, in addition to increasing circulation to the area. You can purchase all-natural capsaicin-based rubs, but if you're following the Replenish section, odds are that you already have everything you need to make it yourself.

If you're wondering why I insist on an all-natural approach, consider this: Your skin is an organ. When you use a muscle rub, you're absorbing whatever ingredients are inside that rub or cream into your body. And if you're in an injured state, your body often is in a state of heightened absorption to pull in more nutrients to speed healing. That said, doesn't it just makes sense to absorb something that the body recognizes?

My only caveat: Before you try it with your son or daughter, apply it on a small spot to start. Depending on your child's sensitivity, capsaicin may cause temporary burning, itching, or stinging sensations on the skin.

¼ cup coconut oil

1 teaspoon cayenne pepper

⅛ cup grated beeswax

5 to 10 drops of either peppermint or lavender essential oil (optional)

> Fill a medium-size pot with water and place it over low to medium heat.
> Put the coconut oil into a glass jar with a tight-fitting lid, then place the jar in the pot.
> As the oil melts, stir in the cayenne powder and beeswax.
> Once blended, remove from the heat and let cool (adding essential oils if you want the mixture to have a more pleasant smell.)
> Give the mixture a final whisk, seal, and keep in the refrigerator. (It should be good for 1 to 2 weeks.)

LISTEN—AND LEARN—FROM EACH ACHE AND PAIN

Pain is all about perception. Pain is also about negotiation. And when you're dealing with young athletes, if you ask them if anything aches or feel sore, there's always something to point to. It's just a matter of how they handle pain and whether it's something to worry about in the first place.

If something hurts, I'm a big believer in placing a hand on it, recognizing that pain and being present with it, adapting to it (instead of masking it), then watching to see what the body does to remedy it. Mind you, the type of pain I'm talking about isn't anything they would experience due to a fracture, sprain, contusions, or anything that clearly requires medical attention. I'm talking about the good old-fashioned post-sport pain that's usually present in some form or another in most young athletes throughout the year.

Now, without being in front of your son or daughter, I can't assess his or her pain in a precise, professional manner that gets to the heart of the problem. But I have seen enough young athletes over the years to know what most typically experience on a regular basis by participating in sports. The next time they say "ouch," these few guidelines are a good measure of whether you should be concerned:

Soft (generally) means safe: If the pain is originating in a soft area—that is, if the area that hurts is a soft, centered spot, such as the belly of a bicep, or the middle of a thigh, for example—then what's causing it is typically benign.

Hard equals heed: If the pain is in a hard area, such as a joint or bone, but it's just a dull ache, that's usually pain that should be monitored. Still, I tell parents not to freak out about this type of pain (that is, to not change anything regarding how their child trains or how often he or she is involved in his or her sport), but to just keep an eye on it.

Sharp (or burning) is sinister: If any pain feels sharp, burns, or makes your child flinch, that could be a little more severe. But if nothing is broken or sprained, is it necessarily time to throw in all your cards and see a doctor about it? I would still recommend treating it as something to monitor, then watch how the body responds.

After two or three weeks, if the pain has either not lessened or has gotten worse, then seeking guidance from a professional may be advisable. But in the event your young athlete actually has an injury that requires medical attention, that doesn't necessarily mean that the show's over for the season when it comes to his or her sport.

1. Always Train What's Trainable

Too often, if players have an injury that keeps them sidelined—an injury so severe that makes participating in their sport impossible—it's easy to misconstrue what rest really means.

Sure, a doctor will tell them to rest from their activity (and that's entirely okay), but that doesn't necessarily mean they have to rest from all movement, which is the path most athletes typically take—and also why they don't always come back from an injury the same athlete they once were. They let their entire body from head to toe fall behind, even though just a portion of it is injured and requires rest.

If a young athlete comes into my office with the worst possible scenario (a broken bone), but it's been set, the child isn't in any pain, and he or she is capable of moving the rest of his or her body, then it's still go time. This means that if, say, the left arm has been hurt, then the child and I are working everything around that left arm. In fact, I will look at the first joint closer to the body from the affected joint that we can move.

For example, if the problem is at the left wrist, then I'll have the child move the elbow and shoulder of that same arm. If the problem is at the elbow, then I'll have him or her move the shoulder and wrist of that same arm (along with the entire rest of his or her body as well, of course).

Allowing someone's entire body to rest solely because a certain portion of it isn't capable of exercise, prevents some of the natural processes that exercise ignites that can help facilitate healing in the affected area, including improved blood flow and the release of certain anabolic hormones that affect wound healing, such as IGF-1 and testosterone. It's also been shown that exercising helps wounds heal faster by reducing psychological stress.[4] That's why exercising while injured isn't simply about preventing the uninjured portions of that body from falling out of shape for sport, but it's just as important for helping athletes heal and get back to their sport that much faster.

2. Always Move What's Not Trainable

In regard to any injured area, as long as you have a doctor's permission to do so, you should be moving that as well as soon as you can, even if that movement is just a centimeter or two of motion, to get blood flowing into that area. Having the blood flow keeps nutrients rushing in to promote healing and keeps waste moving out. It also reminds your brain how to tell the muscles that support that joint how to move. That's why I've witnessed some athletes come to me with injuries that typically take months to regain their full range of motion, only to watch them accomplish that goal in a matter of a few days.

How to do it: If the problem is with their elbow, wrist, knee, ankle, fingers, or toes, that means begin extending and bending those joints—even if they can only pull off the tiniest of increments. If it's their hips or shoulders, those same rules apply when it comes to moving those areas by rotating them regularly

How often each day they should move what's injured depends on them. A ball-park answer is a minimum of five minutes every four to six hours. As long as they are always moving that area frequently at a level they can tolerate, they will increase their functional capacity much faster, get more nutrients into that area more often, and move through a fuller range of motion in all different planes much sooner.

Final tip: When jumping into this technique, I always recommend that athletes avoid using drugs, over-the-counter relief, tape, or anything else that may prevent them from feeling mild to moderate pain. That way, as they begin to consistently move an injured area, they will hear what their body is telling them and know when they've gone too far. It's honestly their best guide to know if they are within the best range of activity to promote their healing through movement.

KNOW WHEN TO REST—AND WHEN TO CALL IT A DAY

The great news about the Tommy John Solution is that because their body is always kept in a constant state of recovery, the odds of young athletes' pushing themselves too hard are much less than they were before starting the program. When you look at the most common causes of overtraining, it's easy to see why:

- Lack of sleep or proper rest
- Poor nutrition

- Too much psychological or emotional stress
- Too much activity
- Training at a high intensity for a prolonged amount of time

By eating right, getting enough sleep, and adjusting their personal habits and sports schedule, all these situations don't become an issue as often. Even the daily exercise they'll be doing in the Recover section isn't at a high enough intensity that would cause overtraining over time. Still, there could be external factors that could overtax children's central nervous system (the brain and spinal cord) and their muscles, despite bringing their body into a better state of balance.

A gradual or sudden drop in your son's or daughter's performance is one indicator he or she may be pushing too hard, although there are other tried-and-true tells that can also point to overtraining, including:

- Constant fatigue
- A lack of interest in the child's sport of choice
- Irritability or moodiness (more so than usual)
- Anxiety or depression
- Loss of appetite
- Chronic joint pain and/or muscle soreness
- An increase in injuries
- An increase in infections, colds, or aches (due to a weakened immune system)
- Depression or increased feelings of anxiety
- Difficulty sleeping or restlessness

If you suspect your child may be overdoing it, and you're certain he or she is doing everything by the book (meaning—this book), then take a closer look at what might be the outside source:

- **Are your child's practices balanced?** Recovery days should be built into your child's training program by his or her coaches so that an intense practice is always followed by a recovery practice to give your young athlete's body enough time to heal.
- **Are your child's games spaced out far enough?** When possible, it's always best to avoid multiple competitions or practices on the same day. If that's

impossible at certain times, then make sure the following day is left as a rest day.

- **Is your child bothered by something else entirely?** Just checking in with your son or daughter to see where he or she is at, both emotionally and physically, may help you spot something that's causing a new source of stress in your child's life that may be impacting him or her negatively (such as an impending test, a situation with a friend, puberty issues, and so forth).

Read Their Mind by Reading Their Body

Let's face it: Whether it's pride or puberty, kids aren't always as forthcoming about feeling as if they are being pushed too hard. Fortunately, there are a few ways for parents to instantly tell if their young athlete might be avoiding the overtraining question (or not showing the obvious symptoms):

1. Check your child's neck: One thing I instinctively look for before any session with young athletes is whether their shoulders seem to be a little closer to their ears. Or I might touch them along their neck to see whether those muscles are relaxed or like ropes. Many athletes tend to have this defensive posture response to overtraining, almost as if their body is trying to protect itself.

2. An inhale is insightful: Another helpful method I use is having athletes take a long, deep breath. I don't give them time to think about it, and I don't tell them how to do it. I surprise them by simply saying, "Hey, take a deep breath for me before we start."

Most of the time, a lot of kids tend to breathe through their mouth and elevate their shoulders because they are sympathetically dominant. Their breathing almost makes them seem terrified and hypersensitive. But if your children are following the Tommy John Solution, that response should have already begun to change. They should now instinctively be breathing through their nose into their belly, so if you see them revert to old habits, it could be a sign of overtraining.

3. Have their hands help you: There's a big difference between neurological fatigue and physical fatigue. Athletes can be physically exhausted and have sore muscles, but it's still possible to perform like an A-list player. But neurological fatigue is an entirely different matter altogether. Even if they come in feeling fully prepared for battle, if things aren't firing properly in their brain, it not only can affect their performance, but place them at a higher risk of injury.

The central nervous system (CNS) tells your muscle fibers to contract, among its many other responsibilities. It's the network that lets your brain communicate more efficiently with your body. But when your CNS is exhausted, it dulls the signals sent back and forth through nerve cells—the ones that allow the brain to tell your body how to respond in every situation. It also leaves you inherently weaker, since the neural network responsible for getting your muscle fibers to contract is fatigued.

Neurological fatigue in your young athletes can be measured several different ways. You can try these two.

Use a dynamometer: This handheld device measures grip strength. All you need to do is have them hold it and squeeze daily (at around the same time of day) for one to two weeks. That will give you a baseline number to go by regarding how strong their grip is. After that, when in doubt, test them daily. If their grip strength falls below 20 percent or more of their average, they are most likely experiencing neurological fatigue and should take a day or so off to rest.

Try the Tap Technique: If you don't feel like spending money on a dynamometer (which can range from economical to pricey), another way to test neurological fatigue doesn't cost anything.

For right-handers, have them place their left hand on their thigh or out in front of them, then have them touch the pads of the fingers on their right hand on top of the back of their left hand. (If you have a lefty, just switch positions, so their left hand is on top.) Once in place, have them tap their fingers for ten seconds as fast as they possibly can and count the number of taps.

Don't try to count by watching them because it should be so fast that you won't be able to see how quickly their fingers are moving. Instead, keep count by listening, or record it on your phone so you can feel comfortable that you got an accurate number.

Record their efforts three times—in the morning, afternoon, and evening—and you'll see fluctuations between the three. (That's normal, by the way, since the body operates in different states at various times of the day.) Have them do the test every day for five to seven days, then take the average for each time of day—you now have your neurological baselines.

The next time they seem "off," or if you just want to check their central nervous system for the sake of checking it before a practice or game, have them retake the test. Typically, if a young athlete is 20 percent or more off his or her average, it's a clear sign of being neurologically fatigued.

If your young athletes' CNS is fried during a practice day, you may want to have them skip it and make it a free play day. Or, if possible, make it a day where they practice mostly movements and not necessarily skill work. By the way, it's not important to know these numbers if it's just a day when they're going to have a catch with Dad, play a pickup game, or do anything related to the sport that's leisure.

If it's fried on game day, odds are, your young athletes wouldn't want to sit out on the sidelines—and that's fine. However, at least you'll be aware of a possible issue with their performance once they get out there.

TJ'S MVP LIST—RECOVER (IN A NUTSHELL)!

1. **Avoid:**

   - Taking nonsteroidal anti-inflammatory drugs (NSAIDs)
   - Icing every injury (Only apply ice on an injured area within the first 15 minutes strictly to alleviate the initial pain.)
   - Stretching statically
   - Long-distance running
   - Skimping on sleep

2. **Invest in natural anti-inflammatories:**

   - **Cod liver oil** (1 teaspoon daily with doctor's approval)
   - **Turmeric** (1 tablespoon daily, or two to four 400 mg capsules, with doctor's approval)
   - **Vitamin C** (8 to 13 years old: 1,000–2,000 mg daily; 13 years and older: 3,000–5,000 mg daily); when sick or injured (8 to 13 years old: 4,000 to 6,000 mg daily; 13 years and older: 8,000 to 10,000 mg daily)

continues

TJ'S MVP LIST—RECOVER (IN A NUTSHELL)! *continued*

3. **Rely on dynamic movements to warm up the body, using either:**

   - TJ's All-Purpose Pre-Game Warm-Up
   - TJ's Advanced A-List Warm-Up

4. **Put your legs up post-play or performance.**

5. **Listen—and learn—from each ache and pain.**

   - Soft (generally) means safe.
   - Hard equals heed.
   - Sharp (or burning) is sinister.

6. **Always train what's trainable when injured.**

7. **Always move what's not trainable when injured.**

8. **Know when to rest—and when to call it a day.**
   Take a day off if you experience more than two of the following:

   - Constant fatigue
   - A lack of interest in a sport
   - Irritability or moodiness (more so than usual)
   - Anxiety or depression
   - Loss of appetite
   - Chronic joint pain and/or muscle soreness
   - An increase in injuries
   - An increase in infections, colds, or aches (due to a weakened immune system)
   - Depression or increased feelings of anxiety
   - Difficulty sleeping or restlessness

Epilogue

I've worked with so many families over the years, but eventually, there comes a time to say good-bye. When young athletes are so dialed into what they need to do to be the most functional human being they can be—when their parents are entirely on-board with supporting them in a way that prevents their children from ever falling backward and helps them safely soar forward—that the need to see me often is no longer necessary. Instead, all that family needs to do from that point forward is simply stay the course.

But I'll be honest. That moment is always bittersweet for me.

It means that even though I won't get to enjoy working with those young athletes on a regular basis anymore, it also means I don't have to worry about their being negatively affected by health, developmental, and dietary issues. It means instead of hearing about what hurts, I get to hear about all their achievements—both athletically and academically—when I bump into them outside my practice. It means instead of trying to piece together what they're doing wrong, I feel good knowing they're now doing everything right.

When I know a family will continue to put in the effort, I not only get to watch their children become better athletes, but I get to see them be a part of changing what's taking place in youth sports today. One by one, they are turning the tide by preventing themselves from becoming a statistic. It's an incredibly gratifying feeling that's hard to shake, but it sadly goes away—as soon as the next young athlete in need steps through my office door.

That's when I realize the gravity of the situation—that the fight is far from over. But now, I have a new ally. Because now, you've become part of the solution.

With this book, you have everything you need at your fingertips to stop the de-evolution of your son or daughter. You have the means to protect your child from injury and watch him or her evolve into the exceptional athlete they were destined to be.

That said, I'm going to share with you exactly what I tell every parent and young athlete that moves on after successfully using and infusing my techniques. Because as I remind them, following the traditional methods and techniques in this book won't always be easy, especially when you're eventually challenged by certain people along the way. Plus, it's also possible to fall off the path between seasons, to think that phoning it in will yield the same results, and to find yourself losing sight of why you sought out this approach in the first place.

So, this is what I tell them—and I want you (and your son or daughter) to return to this section as often as possible to keep your young athlete moving forward. Especially if you're ever in doubt, or feel you may need a reminder why to stay the course.

1. Stay strong. Along the way, you may run into certain naysayers that might dismiss a few of the things in this book. When that happens, it pays to remember where those comments are coming from.

- Are they coming from a parent that may be comparing your child with theirs and could be looking at yours in a competitive way?
- Is it someone with any justifiable background regarding how the human body operates, or simply someone that believes he or she understands what works best?
- Is it someone that may feel threatened or challenged (such as a coach or youth sports organizer) by what you're suggesting because it's not in line with what he or she teaches?

All I ask is that you consider the source, look for a possible reason for that person's skepticism, and ask him or her to present data to disprove you. Throughout this entire book, I've armed you with plenty of facts that help justify why this program works and why it is so desperately needed. Odds are, the person challenging you won't be able to defend his or her position, which should speak volumes.

2. Stay informed. Yes, your kid is removing barriers that once prevented that young athlete from experiencing his or her unlimited potential. Yes, your child is less likely to suffer from the unnecessary injuries associated with youth sports. But I want you to watch the headlines, and even go so far as to set up search alerts that flag the latest news in youth sports regarding "Tommy John surgery," "ACL tears," "sports specialization," "injuries in sport," and anything else that may refresh your memory about the growing epidemic still taking place in youth sports today.

It's not over. In fact, far from it. You're going to be witness to things getting much worse in youth sports over the years. But sometimes when a parent is on the winning side, which is exactly where you are by sticking with the Tommy John Solution, it's easy to get shortsighted. So, stay up-to-date, for both your sakes. And who knows? You may find yourself passing this book onto others when you start seeing those numbers rise even further. At least that's my hope—to make you a part of the solution that ends the problem.

3. Stay balanced. Even though the Tommy John Solution is a four-step plan, the whole is so much greater than the sum of its parts. Each of the four parts significantly builds upon and improves the other three. For example, if you stick to the Replenish section to the letter, it will significantly improve how well your son or daughter performs in the Rebuild section, how fast he or she heals in the Recover section, and can even give your child more focus with following the rules in the Rethink section. That is, if you try to do half of it, you won't get half of the results. You'll get less than half—guaranteed.

As I said earlier in the book, the Tommy John Solution is an all-or-none effort. Dialing it back only does a disservice to your child, and we both know that their future is so worth the effort.

4. Finally, stay open to the possibilities. Even though you bought this book initially to help your son or daughter, remember that almost everything inside it can have the same impact on your life. Ultimately, this book is about restoring what was once natural in all human beings—and not just your children. And that means you, too.

Even though this book is a culmination of what I use with young athletes, the Tommy John Solution is something I use with athletes ranging from college age to pro. It's a tailored prescription I do with adults of all ages to help them maintain and sustain, even if they never participated in a single sport in their life. It's a human performance program that I live by and will continue to live by for the rest of my life. Because it's a program that you can use for the rest of your life.

So, do me this favor.

As you watch your young athlete change for the better—and he or she will—remind yourself that you're also capable of doing the same. Then, consider taking the program for a test spin yourself. Who knows? It may help your son or daughter stick with the program, just having you right there by his or her side. But what I'm certain it will do is allow you to be the best version of yourself. A happier, healthier version that never misses a moment of your child's life.

Notes

Chapter One

1. http://www.statisticbrain.com/youth-sports-statistics/.

2. Geneviève Piché, Caroline Fitzpatrick, and Linda S. Pagani, "Associations Between Extracurricular Activity and Self-Regulation: A Longitudinal Study from 5 to 10 Years of Age," *American Journal of Health Promotion* (2015).

3. Anna M. Adachi-Mejia, Jennifer J. Gibson Chambers, Zhigang Li, and James D. Sargent, "The Relative Roles of Types of Extracurricular Activity on Smoking and Drinking Initiation Among Tweens," *Academic Pediatrics* 14, no. 3 (2014): 271, doi: 10.1016/j.acap.2014.02.002.

4. Piché, Fitzpatrick, and Pagani, "Associations Between Extracurricular Activity and Self-Regulation."

5. K. M. Kniffin, B. Wansink, and M. Shimizu, "Sports at Work: Anticipated and Persistent Correlates of Participation in High School Athletics," *Journal of Leadership & Organizational Studies* (2014), doi: 10.1177/1548051814538099.

6. Geoffrey A. Power, Fábio C. Minozzo, Sally Spendiff, Marie-Eve Filion, Yana Konokhova, Maddy F. Purves-Smith, Charlotte Pion, Mylène Aubertin-Leheudre, José A. Morais, Walter Herzog, Russell T. Hepple, Tanja Taivassalo, and Dilson E. Rassier, "Reduction in Single Muscle Fiber Rate of Force Development with Aging Is Not Attenuated in World Class Older Masters Athletes," *American Journal of Physiology—Cell Physiology* 310, no. 4 (2016).

7. https://www.safekids.org/sites/default/files/documents/skw_sports_fact_sheet_feb_2015.pdf.

8. http://www.nationwidechildrens.org/kids-sports-injuries-numbers-are-impressive.

9. B. J. Erickson, B. U. Nwachukwu, S. Rosas, W. W. Schairer, F. M. McCormick, B. R. Bach Jr., C. A. Bush-Joseph, and A. A. Romeo, "Trends in Medial Ulnar Collateral Ligament Reconstruction in the United States: A Retrospective Review of a Large Private-Payer Database from 2007 to 2011," *American Journal of Sports Medicine* 43, no. 7 (July 2015): 1770–74, doi: 10.1177/0363546515580304.

10. N. A. Smith, T. Chounthirath, and H. Xiang, "Soccer-Related Injuries Treated in Emergency Departments: 1990–2014," *Pediatrics* 138, no. 4 (October 2016).

11. N. A. Beck, J. T. Lawrence, J. D. Nordin, T. A. DeFor, and M. Tompkins, "ACL Tears in School-Aged Children and Adolescents Over 20 Years," *Pediatrics* 139, no. 3 (March 2017), pii: e20161877, doi: 10.1542/peds.2016-1877.

Chapter Two

1. http://www.aspenprojectplay.org/sites/default/files/StateofPlay_2016_FINAL.pdf.

2. J. J. Lang, M. S. Tremblay, L. Léger, T. Olds, and G. R. Tomkinson, "International Variability in 20 m Shuttle Run Performance in Children and Youth: Who Are the Fittest from a 50-Country Comparison? A Systematic Literature Review with Pooling of Aggregate Results," *British Journal of Sports Medicine* (September 20, 2016), pii: bjsports-2016-096224.

Chapter Four

1. Michael Garrison, Richard Westrick, Michael R. Johnson, and Jonathan Benenson, "Association Between the Functional Movement Screen and Injury Development in College Athletes," *International Journal of Sports Physical Therapy* 10, no. 1 (February 2015): 21–28.

Chapter Five

1. Loyola University Health System, "Intense, Specialized Training in Young Athletes Linked to Serious Overuse Injuries," ScienceDaily, April 19, 2013.

2. D. R. Bell, E. G. Post, S. M. Trigsted, S. Hetzel, T. A. McGuine, and M. A. Brooks, "Prevalence of Sport Specialization in High School Athletics: A 1-Year Observational Study," *American Journal of Sports Medicine* 44, no. 6 (June 2016): 1469–74.

3. Jacqueline Pasulka, Neeru Jayanthi, Ashley McCann, Lara R. Dugas, and Cynthia LaBella, "Specialization Patterns Across Various Youth Sports and Relationship to Injury Risk," *Physician and Sportsmedicine* 45, no. 3 (June 2017): 344–52.

4. Neeru Jayanthi, Courtny Pinkham, Lara Dugas, Brittany Patrick, and Cynthia LaBella, "Sports Specialization in Young Athletes—Evidence-Based Recommendations," *Sports Health* 5, no. 3 (May 2013): 251–57.

5. American Academy of Orthopaedic Surgeons, "Nearly Half of Today's High School Athletes Specialize in One Sport: Only 22 Percent of Professional Athletes Want Their Own Children to Focus on a Single Sport," ScienceDaily, March 14, 2017.

6. American Medical Society for Sports Medicine, "Effectiveness of Early Sport Specialization Limited in Most Sports, Sport Diversification May Be Better Approach at Young Ages," ScienceDaily, April 23, 2013.

7. Ibid.

8. American Orthopaedic Society for Sports Medicine, "Fatigue Contributing Factor in Kid's Pitching Injuries," ScienceDaily, March 5, 2016.

9. Loyola University Health System, "Young Athletes from Higher Income Families More Likely to Suffer Serious Overuse Injuries," ScienceDaily, April 11, 2014.

10. http://www.ncaa.org/about/resources/research/estimated-probability-competing-college-athletics.

11. http://www.ncaa.org/about/resources/research/estimated-probability-competing-professional-athletics.

12. Daniel J. Madigan, Joachim Stoeber, and Louis Passfield, "Perfectionism and Attitudes Towards Doping in Junior Athletes," *Journal of Sports Sciences* 34, no. 8 (2015): 700.

13. University of Haifa, "75 Percent of Athletes' Parents Let Their Child Skip Exams for a Game," ScienceDaily, August 26, 2008.

Chapter Six

1. https://www.commonsensemedia.org/sites/default/files/uploads/pdfs/census_factsheet_mediauseprofiles.pdf.

2. Neeru Jayanthi, Courtney Pinkham, Lara Dugas, Brittany Patrick, and Cynthia LaBella, "Sports Specialization in Young Athletes—Evidence-Based Recommendations," *Sports Health* 5, no. 4 (May 2013): 251–57.

Chapter Seven

1. www.fitness.gov/resource-center/facts-and-statistics/#footnote-2.

2. Desiree Leek, Jordan A. Carlson, Kelli L. Cain, Sara Henrichon, Dori Rosenberg, Kevin Patrick, and James F. Sallis, "Physical Activity During Youth Sports Practices," *Archives of Pediatric and Adolescent Medicine* 165, no. 4 (2011): 294–99.

3. J. Reedy and S. M. Krebs-Smith, "Dietary Sources of Energy, Solid Fats, and Added Sugars Among Children and Adolescents in the United States," *Journal of the American Dietetic Association* 110, no. 10 (October 2010): 1477–84.

4. L. Setaro, P. R. Santos-Silva, E. Y. Nakano, C. H. Sales, N. Nunes, J. M. Greve, and C. Colli, "Magnesium Status and the Physical Performance of Volleyball Players: Effects of Magnesium Supplementation," *Journal of Sports Science* 32, no. 5 (2014): 438–45.

5. https://www.cdc.gov/salt/pdfs/children_sodium.pdf.

6. Erica M. Schulte, Nicole M. Avena, and Ashley N. Gearhardt, "Which Foods May Be Addictive? The Roles of Processing, Fat Content, and Glycemic Load," *PLoS One* 10, no. 2 (February 18, 2015).

7. K. Northstone, C. Joinson, P. Emmett, A. Ness, and T. Paus, "Are Dietary Patterns in Childhood Associated with IQ at 8 Years of Age? A Population-Based Cohort Study," *Journal of Epidemiology & Community Health* 66, no. 7 (July 2012): 624–28.

8. Renee Dufault, Walter J. Lukiw, Raquel Crider, Roseanne Schnoll, David Wallinga, and Richard Deth, "A Macroepigenetic Approach to Identify Factors Responsible for the Autism Epidemic in the United States," *Clinical Epigenetics* 4, no. 1 (April 2012): 6.

9. L. Eugene Arnold, Nicholas Lofthouse, and Elizabeth Hurt, "Artificial Food Colors and Attention-Deficit/Hyperactivity Symptoms: Conclusions to Dye For," *Neurotherapeutics* 9, no. 3 (July 2012): 599–609.

10. D. McCann, A. Barrett, A. Cooper, D. Crumpler, L. Dalen, K. Grimshaw, E. Kitchin, K. Lok, L. Porteous, E. Prince, E. Sonuga-Barke, J. O. Warner, and J. Stevenson, "Food Additives and Hyperactive Behaviour in 3-Year-Old and 8/9-Year-Old Children in the Community: A Randomised, Double-Blinded, Placebo-Controlled Trial," *Lancet* 370, no. 9598 (November 3, 2007): 1542.

11. www.hsph.harvard.edu/news/press-releases/study-finds-inadequate-hydration-among-u-s-children/.

12. Barry M. Popkin, Kristen E. D'Anci, and Irwin H. Rosenberg, "Water, Hydration and Health," *Nutrition Reviews* 68, no. 8 (August 2010): 439–58.

13. Mitchell H. Rosner, "Preventing Deaths Due to Exercise-Associated Hyponatremia," *Clinical Journal of Sport Medicine* 25, no. 4 (2015): 301.

14. D. Leek, J. A. Carlson, K. L. Cain, S. Henrichon, D. Rosenberg, K, Patrick, and J. F. Sallis, "Physical Activity During Youth Sports Practices," *Archives of Pediatric and Adolescent Medicine* 164, no. 4 (April 2011): 294–99.

15. Ian Needleman, Paul Ashley, Lyndon Meehan, Aviva Petrie, Richard Weiler, Steve McNally, Chris Ayer, Rob Hanna, Ian Hunt, Steven Kell, Paul Ridgewell, and Russell Taylor, "Poor Oral Health Including Active Caries in 187 UK Professional

Male Football Players: Clinical Dental Examination Performed by Dentists," *British Journal of Sports Medicine* 50, no. 1 (2016): 41.

16. A. E. Field, K. R. Sonneville, J. Falbe, A. Flint, J. Haines, B. Rosner, and C. A. Camargo, "Association of Sports Drinks with Weight Gain Among Adolescents and Young Adults," *Obesity* 22 (2014): 2238–43.

17. Academy of General Dentistry, "Sports and Energy Drinks Responsible for Irreversible Damage to Teeth," ScienceDaily, May 1, 2012.

18. Leslie A. Ehlen, Teresa A. Marshall, Fang Qian, James S. Wefel, and John J. Warren, "Acidic Beverages Increase the Risk of In Vitro Tooth Erosion," *Nutritional Research* 28, no. 5 (2008): 299–303.

19. Fernando E. Garcia-Arroyo, Magdalena Cristóbal, Abraham Said Arellano-Buendía, Horacio Osorio, Edilia Tapia, Virgilia Soto, Magdalena Madero, Miguel A. Lanaspa, Carlos A. Roncal-Jimenez, Lise Bankir, Richard J. Johnson, and Laura-Gabriela Sanchez-Lozada, "Rehydration with Soft Drink–like Beverages Exacerbates Dehydration and Worsens Dehydration-Associated Renal Injury," *American Journal of Physiology—Regulatory, Integrative and Comparative Physiology* (2016): ajpregu.00354 .2015, doi: 10.1152/ajpregu.00354.2015.

20. www.mayoclinic.org/healthy-lifestyle/nutrition-and-healthy-eating/expert-answers /juicing/faq-20058020.

21. https://health.gov/dietaryguidelines/2015/guidelines/appendix-7/.

22. Sibylle Kranz, Mary Brauchla, Joanne L. Slavin, and Kevin B. Miller, "What Do We Know About Dietary Fiber Intake in Children and Health? The Effects of Fiber Intake on Constipation, Obesity, and Diabetes in Children," *Advances in Nutrition* 3 (January 2012): 47–53.

23. M. D. DeBoer, H. E. Agard, and R. J. Scharf, "Milk Intake, Height and Body Mass Index in Preschool Children," *Archives of Disease in Childhood* 100 (2015): 460–65.

24. D. Feskanich, H. A. Bischoff-Ferrari, A. L. Frazier, and W. C. Willett, "Milk Consumption During Teenage Years and Risk of Hip Fractures in Older Adults," *JAMA Pediatrics* 168, no. 1 (January 2014): 54–60.

Chapter Eight

1. C. Y. Chang, D. S. Ke, and J. Y. Chen, "Essential Fatty Acids and Human Brain," *Acta Neurologica Taiwan* 18, no. 4 (December 2009): 231–41.

2. F. Gomez-Pinilla and A. G. Gomez, "The Influence of Dietary Factors in Central Nervous System Plasticity and Injury Recovery," *PM & R: The Journal of Injury, Function, and Rehabilitation* 3, no. 601 (2011): S111–S116, doi:10.1016/j.pmrj.2011 .03.001.

3. T. R. Dhiman, G. R. Anand, L. D. Satter, and M. W. Pariza, "Conjugated Linoleic Acid Content of Milk from Cows Fed Different Diets," *Journal of Dairy Science* 82, no. 10 (October 1999): 2146–56.

4. J. F. Guzmán, H. Esteve, C. Pablos, A. Pablos, C. Blasco, and J. A. Villegas, "DHA- Rich Fish Oil Improves Complex Reaction Time in Female Elite Soccer Players," *Journal of Sports Science and Medicine* 10, no. 2 (June 1, 2011): 301–5.

5. T. D. Mickleborough, "Omega-3 Polyunsaturated Fatty Acids in Physical Performance Optimization," *International Journal of Sport Nutrition and Exercise Metabolism* 23, no. 1 (February 2013): 83–96.

6. B. Tartibian, B. H. Maleki, and A. Abbasi, "The Effects of Ingestion of Omega-3 Fatty Acids on Perceived Pain and External Symptoms of Delayed Onset Muscle Soreness in Untrained Men," *Clinical Journal of Sport Medicine* 19, no. 2 (March 2009): 115–19.

7. G. I. Smith, P. Atherton, D. N. Reeds, B. S. Mohammed, D. Rankin, M. J. Rennie, and B. Mittendorfer, "Omega-3 Polyunsaturated Fatty Acids Augment the Muscle Protein Anabolic Response to Hyperinsulinaemia-Hyperaminoacidaemia in Healthy Young and Middle-aged Men and Women," *Clinical Science* (London) 121, no. 6 (September 2011): 267–78.

8. R. H. Eckel, A. S. Hanson, A. Y. Chen, J. N. Berman, T. J. Yost, and E. P. Brass, "Dietary Substitution of Medium-Chain Triglycerides Improves Insulin-Mediated Glucose Metabolism in NIDDM Subjects," *Diabetes* 41, no. 5 (May 1992): 641–47.

9. V. Van Wymelbeke, A. Himaya, J, Louis-Sylvestre, and M. Fantino, "Influence of Medium-Chain and Long-Chain Triacylglycerols on the Control of Food Intake in Men," *American Journal of Clinical Nutrition* 68, no. 2 (August 1998): 226–34.

10. T. C. Wallace and V. L. Fulgoni III, "Assessment of Total Choline Intakes in the United States," *Journal of the American College of Nutrition* 35, no. 2 (2016): 108–12.

11. D. Aune, N. Keum, E. Giovannucci, L. T. Fadnes, P. Boffetta, D. C. Greenwood, S. Tonstad, L. T. Vatten, E. Riboli, and T. Norat, "Nut Consumption and Risk of Cardiovascular Disease, Total Cancer, All-Cause and Cause-Specific Mortality: A Systematic Review and Dose-Response Meta-analysis of Prospective Studies," *BMC Medicine* 14, no. 1 (December 5, 2016): 207.

12. J. Tabeshpour, B. M. Razavi, and H. Hosseinzadeh, "Effects of Avocado (*Persea americana*) on Metabolic Syndrome: A Comprehensive Systematic Review," *Phytotherapy Research* (2017), doi: 10.1002/ptr.5805.

13. Dominika Średnicka-Tober, Marcin Barański, Chris Seal, Roy Sanderson, Charles Benbrook, Håvard Steinshamn, Joanna Gromadzka-Ostrowska, Ewa Rembiałkowska, Krystyna Skwarło-Sońta, Mick Eyre, Giulio Cozzi, Mette Krogh Larsen,

Teresa Jordon, Urs Niggli, Tomasz Sakowski, Philip C. Calder, Graham C. Burdge, Smaragda Sotiraki, Alexandros Stefanakis, Halil Yolcu, Sokratis Stergiadis, Eleni Chatzidimitriou, Gillian Butler, Gavin Stewart, and Carlo Leifert, "Composition Differences Between Organic and Conventional Meat: A Systematic Literature Review and Meta-analysis," *British Journal of Nutrition* 115 (2016): 994–1011.

14. Stefan De Smet, Ruud Van Thienen, Louise Deldicque, Ruth James, Craig Sale, David J. Bishop, and Peter Hespel, "Nitrate Intake Promotes Shift in Muscle Fiber Type Composition During Sprint Interval Trainńńing in Hypoxia," *Frontiers in Physiology* 7 (2016).

15. Andrew R. Coggan, Joshua L. Leibowitz, Catherine Anderson Spearie, Ana Kadkhodayan, Deepak P. Thomas, Sujata Ramamurthy, Kiran Mahmood, Soo Park, Suzanne Waller, Marsha Farmer, and Linda R. Peterson, "Acute Dietary Nitrate Intake Improves Muscle Contractile Function in Patients with Heart Failure—Clinical Perspective," *Circulation: Heart Failure* 8, no. 5 (2015): 914.

16. Luis Condezo-Hoyos, Indira P. Mohanty, and Giuliana D. Noratto, "Assessing Non-digestible Compounds in Apple Cultivars and Their Potential as Modulators of Obese Faecal Microbiota in Vitro," *Food Chemistry* 161 (2014): 208.

17. University of Illinois, Urbana-Champaign, "Dark Honey Has More Illness -Fighting Agents Than Light Honey," ScienceDaily, www.sciencedaily.com/releases /1998/07/980708085352.htm, accessed April 15, 2017.

Chapter Nine

1. https://www.wsj.com/articles/why-children-need-chores-1426262655.

Chapter Ten

1. Pedro A. Latorre-Román, Felipe García-Pinillos, Víctor M. Soto-Hermoso, and Marcos Muñoz-Jiménez, "Effects of 12 Weeks of Barefoot Running on Foot Strike Patterns, Inversion-Eversion and Foot Rotation in Long-Distance Runners," *Journal of Sport and Health Science* (October 2016).

Chapter Eleven

1. A. Nagano, M. Arioka, F. Takahashi-Yanaga, E. Matsuzaki, and T. Sasaguri, "Celecoxib Inhibits Osteoblast Maturation by Suppressing the Expression of Wnt Target Genes," *Journal of Pharmacological Sciences* 133, no. 1 (January 2017): 18–24.

2. M. R. Chen and J. L. Dragoo, "The Effect of Nonsteroidal Anti-inflammatory Drugs on Tissue Healing," *Knee Surgery, Sports Traumatology, Arthroscopy* 21, no. 3 (March 2013): 540–49.

3. B. A. Foulke, A. R. Kendal, D. W. Murray, and H. Pandit, "Fracture Healing in the Elderly: A Review," *Maturitas* 92 (October 2016): 49–55, doi: 10.1016/j.maturitas .2016.07.014, Epub July 21, 2016.

4. K. Dideriksen, "Muscle and Tendon Connective Tissue Adaptation to Unloading, Exercise and NSAID," *Connective Tissue Research* 55, no. 2 (April 2014): 61–70.

5. M. A. Rogers and T. M. Aronoff, "The Influence of Non-steroidal Anti-inflammatory Drugs on the Gut Microbiome," *Clinical Microbiology and Infection* 22, no. 2 (February 2016): 178.e1–9.

6. Xue Liang, Kyle Bittinger, Xuanwen Li, Darrell R. Abernethy, Frederic D. Bushman, and Garret A. FitzGerald, "Bidirectional Interactions Between Indomethacin and the Murine Intestinal Microbiota," *eLife* 4 (2015).

7. S. Khoshnevis, N. K. Craik, and K. R. Diller, "Cold-Induced Vasoconstriction May Persist Long After Cooling Ends: An Evaluation of Multiple Cryotherapy Units," *Knee Surgery, Sports Traumatolology, Arthroscopy* 23, no. 9 (September 2015): 2475–83.

8. L. Hart, "Effect of Stretching on Sport Injury Risk: A Review," *Clinical Journal of Sport Medicine* 15, no. 2 (March 2005): 113.

9. L. Simic, N. Sarabon, G. Markovic, "Does Pre-exercise Static Stretching Inhibit Maximal Muscular Performance? A Meta-analytical Review," *Scandinavian Journal of Medicine and Science in Sports* 23, no. 2 (March 2013): 131–48.

10. J. C. Gergley, "Acute Effect of Passive Static Stretching on Lower-Body Strength in Moderately Trained Men," *Journal of Strength & Conditioning Research* 27, no. 4 (April 2013): 973–77.

11. Monoem Haddad, Amir Dridi, Moktar Chtara, Anis Chaouachi, Del Wong, David Behm, and Karim Chamari, "Static Stretching Can Impair Explosive Performance for at Least 24 Hours," *Journal of Strength & Conditioning Research* 28, no. 1 (January 2014): 140–46.

12. K. J. MacKelvie, J. E. Taunton, H. A. McKay, and K. M. Khan, "Bone Mineral Density and Serum Testosterone in Chronically Trained, High Mileage 40–55 Year Old Male Runners," *British Journal of Sports Medicine* 34, no. 4 (August 2000): 273–78.

13. Luciana Besedovsky, Stoyan Dimitrov, Jan Born, and Tanja Lange, "Nocturnal Sleep Uniformly Reduces Numbers of Different T-cell Subsets in the Blood of Healthy Men," *American Journal of Physiology—Regulatory, Integrative and Comparative Physiology* 311, no. 4 (2016): R637.

14. S. Mazza, E. Gerbier, M. P. Gustin, Z. Kasikci, O. Koenig, T. C. Toppino, and M. Magnin, "Relearn Faster and Retain Longer," *Psychological Science* 27, no. 10 (October 2016): 1321–30.

15. Graham H. Diering, Raja S. Nirujogi, Richard H. Roth, Paul F. Worley, Akhilesh Pandey, Richard L. Huganir, "Homer1a Drives Homeostatic Scaling-Down of Excitatory Synapses During Sleep," *Science* 355, no. 6324 (February 2, 2017): 511–15.

16. Aric A. Prather, Cindy W. Leung, Nancy E. Adler, Lorrene Ritchie, Barbara Laraia, and Elissa S. Epel, "Short and Sweet: Associations Between Self-Reported Sleep Duration and Sugar-Sweetened Beverage Consumption Among Adults in the United States," *Sleep Health* (December 2016): 272–76.

17. H. K. al Khatib, S. V. Harding, J. Darzi, and G. K. Pot, "The Effects of Partial Sleep Deprivation on Energy Balance: A Systematic Review and Meta-analysis," *European Journal of Clinical Nutrition* May 2016): 614–24.

18. Radiological Society of North America, "Short-term sleep Deprivation Affects Heart Function," ScienceDaily, December 2, 2016.

19. S. A. Gharib et al., "Transcriptional Signatures of Sleep Duration Discordance in Monozygotic Twins," *Sleep* 40, no. 1 (January 2017).

20. The Endocrine Society, "Prolonged Sleep Disturbance Can Lead to Lower Bone Formation," ScienceDaily, April 2, 2017.

Chapter Twelve

1. J. Barry, M. Fritz, J. R. Brender, P. E. Smith, D. K. Lee, and A. Ramamoorthy, "Determining the Effects of Lipophilic Drugs on Membrane Structure by Solid-State NMR Spectroscopy: The Case of the Antioxidant Curcumin," *Journal of the American Chemical Society* 131, no. 12 (April 1, 2009): 4490–98.

2. Harri Hemilä, "Vitamin C and Infections," *Nutrients* 9, no. 4 (2017): 339.

3. J. D. Schoenfeld, Z. A. Sibenaller, K. A. Mapuskar, B. A. Wagner, K. L. Cramer-Morales, M. Furqan, S. Sandhu, T. L. Carlisle, M. C. Smith, T. Abu Hejleh, D. J. Berg, J. Zhang, J. Keech, K. R. Parekh, S. Bhatia, V. Monga, K. L. Bodeker, L. Ahmann, S. Vollstedt, H. Brown, E. P. Shanahan Kauffman, M. E. Schall, R. J. Hohl, G. H. Clamon, J. D. Greenlee, M. A. Howard, M. K. Shultz, B. J. Smith, D. P. Riley, F. E. Domann, J. J. Cullen, G. R. Buettner, J. M. Buatti, D. R. Spitz, and B. G. Allen, "O2–and H2O2-Mediated Disruption of Fe Metabolism Causes the Differential Susceptibility of NSCLC and GBM Cancer Cells to Pharmacological Ascorbate," *Cancer Cell* 31, no. 4 (April 10, 2017): 487–500.e8.

4. J.-P. Gouin and J. K. Kiecolt-Glaser, "The Impact of Psychological Stress on Wound Healing: Methods and Mechanisms," *Immunology and Allergy Clinics of North America* 31, no. 1 (2011): 81–93, doi:10.1016/j.iac.2010.09.010.

Acknowledgments

Where do you start when you begin to thank the people responsible when your entire life's work is put onto paper?

When it comes to the healing, performance, and function of the human body, no single person can take credit. It's an inside job, flowing from the potential and power we all have contained within our hundreds of trillions of cells that make the impossible possible and miracles occur every day. And because I'm always one to give credit outside of myself . . . let's keep that ball rolling.

I'd first like to thank my family, especially my parents for raising me in an environment that allowed me the safety and opportunities to explore my youth athletic abilities in any sport I desired. I always had a full refrigerator to nourish my growing and developing body, a warm bed to rest and repair, as well as your unyielding support. From the day I hit my first (and second) home run over the fence in sixth grade (in the same game!) to the defining moment when I struck out the first sixteen times, I came to the plate facing varsity caliber pitching as a freshman in high school. You guys are the reason I was given this life—and I love you.

My brother, Travis, who selflessly and tirelessly agreed to always be my worthy opponent when challenged whether it'd be ruthless battles of Wiffle ball, ball tag, or Butt's Up. Thanks for putting up with me all those years, brother.

"Thank you" doesn't even begin to cover what my sister, Tamara, and her family, Patrick and Tyler, have done in my life. Their undying love and support over the years while I discovered my passion remains immeasurable, and I am truly grateful for all of you.

I'd like to thank Vladimir Curguz, owner of Vlad's Gym in Lake Bluff, Illinois, who has been a colleague and one of my good friends for over a decade. He is the sole reason I explored expanding my education into training, nutrition, and rehab. His wealth of knowledge of the human body always amazed me and he challenged me to be better than just a typical American "make 'em sweat; make 'em tired; cut carbs, fat, and sugar" trainer. I've never seen someone have so much passion for the art of human performance.

With that said, his vast knowledge and level of exercise programming experience is why I teamed up with him to develop the "Re-evolution Routines" presented as part of the Tommy John Solution. I cannot thank him enough for his time, guidance, and tutelage, he selflessly offered up to help us present the most comprehensive long-term athletic development training plan for athletes of all ages, gender, and developmental levels that will ultimately challenge the mind, body and spirit of every human athlete who participates.

John McNulty, owner of Neuro Strength Lab in Lake Forest, Downers Grove, and Chicago, Illinois. John hired me as a sports performance coach and rehab specialist two days after I decided to finally retire from professional baseball, another defining moment in my life. Over the course of twelve years John, Vladi, and I collaborated on thousands of cases, worked with the highest performing athletes in all sports, and in some cases, saw twelve-year-olds evolve into full scholarship athletes under our collective guidance.

A special thank-you to Peter Fawcett, who not only was one of my favorite, most compliant patients (and now a truly amazing friend), but also pushed me into actually considering writing a book. I can't recall how many mornings he would come to my office with pillow-head to get his spine checked, adjusted, and train stating "Hey, TJ . . . I'm serious . . . you need to write a book." Pete ignored my polite and frustrating brush-offs and pulled some strings and set up a call with Heather Jackson, of Heather Jackson Literary Agency, who is now my agent, and was the person responsible for this project's even coming to life. "Hey, Pete . . . I've written a book."

Heather Jackson, "Mama Bear." An amazing mother, agent, and friend in a world I'm navigating for the first time as a newbie author. I cannot think of anyone better to be my pilot and copilot at times than you. You're one of a kind. I love what we've done so far and what we will do in the future together. Boom!

Myatt Murphy, without a doubt the only person who could've pulled this off at the level it deserves. Your professionalism, work ethic, and intuition are truly what I needed to make sure this was shaped into exactly how I envisioned it long ago.

There aren't many people on the planet who could engage in forty hours of phone conversations with me without going crazy, but your resilience and passion gave this project its wings. Thank you and let's keep going, brother.

Jay Schroeder, owner of EVO Ultrafit. Jay was a coach who was instrumental in teaching me to question everything I thought I once knew about training and performance. Read everything. Question everything. And set no limit on yourself.

The Weston A. Price Foundation and its vast information and research on nutrition. Other notables are George Hackenshmidt, Thomas Kurz, Herbert M. Shelton, and Nikolai Amosov whose collective research drove me to trust the raw power of the five essentials to life—body movement, sunshine, rest, breathing, and nourishment—and the effect they have on the performance and healing of human athletes. I'd also like to thank Pavel Tsatsouline, Gray Cook, Mark Rippetoe, Jon Barron, Dr. Joe Dispenza, and Bruce Lipton for not only enlightening me in regards to breakthroughs and philosophies in training, movement, the power of the mind and the effect our beliefs have on the performance and healing of our bodies, but offering up their knowledge and experience to all those in the healing arts so we can all get back to putting the power of healing and function back where it belongs . . . inside of us all.

I also want to thank at Da Capo for helping to bring this book to so many, especially Dan Ambrosio, Amber Morris, Miriam Riad, Michael Giarratano, Renee Sedliar, Matthew Weston, and Kevin Hanover.

A special thanks to everyone that made the imagery in this book as spectacular as it is. When you work with the best (Mitch Mandel, Troy Schnyder, Staci Foley, and Cynthia Rush), you get the best. Thank you for your patience, professionalism, and hitting the ball out of the park on literally a moment's notice.

A heartfelt thank-you to not only two of the best models an author could hope for, but two exceptionally gifted young athletes: Jack Rush and Katie Rush. The endurance, kindness, and generosity you exhibited during the shoot are the traits I hope this book will infuse in every athlete who applies its principles. Thank you both for representing what it stands for.

And finally, to the thousands of clients/athletes whom for seventeen years I've experimented on, challenged, and pushed to the limit of your potential. A lot of tears, laughs, and a lot of growing and learning together. I believe that no meeting, conversation, or engagement is random. Everything and everybody are playing their part in the tapestry of events that culminate into what we call life. Thank you for being a part of mine.

Index